Kreissle von Hellborn

The Life of Franz Schubert
Volume II

AF281530

Salzwasser

Kreissle von Hellborn

The Life of Franz Schubert
Volume II

1. Auflage | ISBN: 978-3-84605-080-4

Erscheinungsort: Frankfurt, Deutschland

Erscheinungsjahr: 2020

Salzwasser Verlag GmbH

Reprint of the original, first published in 1869.

FRANZ SCHUBERT.

VOL. II.

THE LIFE

OF

FRANZ SCHUBERT.

TRANSLATED FROM THE GERMAN

OF

KREISSLE VON HELLBORN

BY

ARTHUR DUKE COLERIDGE, M.A.

LATE FELLOW OF KING'S COLLEGE,
CAMBRIDGE.

WITH AN APPENDIX

BY

GEORGE GROVE, ESQ.

IN TWO VOLUMES.—VOL. II.

1869.

CONTENTS

OF

THE SECOND VOLUME.

CHAPTER XII.

(1824.)

CHAPTER XIII.

(1825.)

CHAPTER XIV.

(1826.)

CHAPTER XV.

(1827.)

CHAPTER XVI.

(1828.)

CHAPTER XVII.

CHARACTERISTICS OF SCHUBERT.

CHAPTER XVIII.

GENERAL SURVEY.

CHAPTER XIX.

CHAPTER XX.

LIFE OF SCHUBERT.

——+——

CHAPTER XII.

(1824.)

AFTER the death of Professor Leopold Kupelwieser, in the year 1863, a letter of Franz Schubert's was discovered amongst his papers, dated March 31, 1824, the contents of which afford a painful and surprising insight into the melancholy thoughts which then fettered the mind of the composer.

The failure of so many hopes—more particularly in respect of the performance of his operas in the theatre —narrow circumstances, constant bodily ailments, the protracted absence of several of his most intimate friends from Vienna,[1] and finally, it may be assumed, some unhappy love affair—all these causes tended to make Schubert serious and depressed, a state of

---

[1] Kupelwieser was in Italy, Schober in Prussia.

mind which about this time gave way to a phase of deep dejection, bordering at times on absolute despair. To the bright, happy period of existence which had been allotted him there succeeded—certainly only for a short passing time—a condition of physical prostration and moral depression, such as we never meet with but once during the whole of Schubert's career.

Leopold Kupelwieser,[1] urged by an intense longing to see Rome, and there pursue his studies in the art of painting, had, as a young man of twenty-seven years of age, at the beginning of this year, with a Russian nobleman of the name of Alexis Beresin, travelled to Italy, and resided for some time in that city.[2] The following lines addressed to him (at the time we speak of) are here given:—

'Dear Kupelwieser,—I have been anxious some time past to write to you, but I didn't know how to manage it. An opportunity, however, is now offered me through Smirsch,[3] and at last I can once more pour out my

[1] L. Kupelwieser, born at Pisting, in Lower Austria, in the year 1796, was Professor and Imperial Rath at the Kunstakademie in Vienna, and died there on November 17, 1862.

[2] After the two travellers had crossed over to Sicily, they were both attacked with nervous fever. Beresin died, but Kupelwieser recovered, and remained in Italy up to the year 1825.

[3] The letter is addressed, 'Al Signor Leopoldo Kupelwieser, pittore tedesco, recapito al Caffè greco a Roma.' The Kupelwieser family very kindly allowed me to examine the letter. Smirsch, at that time Cassier at the Kaiserlichen Hof, and a clever flower-painter, took care of Kupelwieser's business matters during his residence in Italy. S. still lives on a pension at Vienna.

heart to somebody. You are so good, so honest and true, you will surely forgive me much which others would take great offence at. In one word, I feel myself the most unhappy, the most miserable man on earth.

'Picture to yourself a man whose health can never be re-established, who from sheer despair makes matters worse instead of better; picture to yourself, I say, a man whose most brilliant hopes have come to nothing, to whom the happiness of proffered love and friendship is but anguish, whose enthusiasm for the beautiful (an inspired feeling at least) threatens to vanish altogether, and then ask yourself if such a condition does not represent a miserable and unhappy man?

'Meine Ruh' ist hin, mein Herz ist schwer,
Ich finde sie nimmer und nimmermehr.

'I can repeat these lines now every day; for every night, when I go to sleep, I hope never again to awake, and every morning renews afresh the wounds of yesterday. Friendlessly, joyously, should I drag on the days of my existence, were it not that sometimes my brain reels, and a gleam of the sweet days that are gone shoots across my vision. Our society (a reading society [1]), as you will have known by this time, came to an end, from the reinforcement of the coarse crew,

[1] These social evenings, for reading and study, were passed at Schober's and Bruchmann's. The classics were cultivated, and even

addicted to beer-drinking and sausage-eating; its dis-
solution followed in two days, although I gave up attending immediately after your departure. Leidesdorf,[1]
with whom I am intimately acquainted, is a thoroughly
sound good man, but so deeply depressed and melancholy, that I fear I have gained from him more than
is good for me in this respect. Then, both his and my
affairs are not prosperous, consequently we never have
money.

'Your brother's opera[2] (I don't admire his conduct
in absenting himself from the theatre) was declared
impracticable, and no demand of any sort was made for
my music. Castelli's Opera, 'Die Verschwornen,' has
been received with applause at Berlin. The music is
by a resident composer there.[3]

'Thus I have composed two operas to no purpose
whatever. I have done very little new in the way of
songs;[4] but, to make amends, I have made several
attempts in instrumental things, for I have composed
two quartetts for violins, viola, and violoncello, besides an octett, and I intend to write an additional

Homer was a subject. Schubert used to attend these 'æsthetic teas.'
Franz v. Schober and Bruchmann usually were the readers.

[1] Leidesdorf, picture and music seller in Vienna, established himself
afterwards in Florence. One part of Schubert's compositions was published by him.

[2] Josef Kupelwieser, compiler of the text for the Opera 'Fierrabras.'

[3] I have not been able to ascertain what Berlin composer set 'Die
Verschwornen' to music.

[4] The catalogue only shows six.

quartett;[1] thus I hope to pave the way for a grand symphony.

'The latest news in Vienna is that Beethoven intends giving a concert, when we are to have his new symphony, three numbers out of the new Mass, and a new overture.[2] God willing, I intend also to give a similar concert next year.[3] Now I conclude, not wishing to use too much letter-paper, and greet you a thousand times. If you were to write all about your artistic and intellectual state just at present, and your life generally, nothing would give greater pleasure to your true friend, FRANZ SCHUBERT.

'My address would be, "An die Kunsthandlung Sauer & Leidesdorf," because at the beginning of March[4] I go with Esterhazy to Hungary.'

In close connection with this gloomy letter are the following extracts from his diary, showing as they do his frame of mind at the time they were penned:—

'Grief sharpens the understanding and strengthens the soul, whereas joy seldom troubles itself about the former, and makes the latter either effeminate or frivolous.'

---

[1] These stringed quartetts are the well-known in A minor, in E-flat, and E major.

[2] The Ninth Symphony, the D Mass, and Overture (Op. 124). The concert came off on May 7.

[3] This plan was not realised until the year 1828.

[4] He must have meant May.

'From the very depths of my heart do I hate the narrow one-sided view of things which makes so many wretched people believe that what they pursue, and that alone, is the best, and that everything above or beyond it is worth nothing. One beauty should accompany a man throughout his whole life—that is true—and yet the flash of this enthusiasm should illuminate all else besides.'

'*March* 27.—No one fathoms another's grief, no one another's joy. People think they are ever going to one another, and they only go near one another. Oh, the misery of him who knows this by experience!'

'My productions in music are the product of the understanding, and spring from my sorrow; those only which are the product of pain seem to please the great world most.'

'The loftiest inspiration is but a step removed from the absolutely ludicrous, just as the deepest wisdom is so near akin to crass stupidity.'

'With faith man steps forth into the world. Faith is far ahead of understanding and knowledge; for to understand anything, I must first of all believe something. It is the higher basis on which the weak understanding rears its first columns of proof: reason is nothing but faith analysed.'

'*March* 29.—O Fancy! thou unsearchable fountain, from which artists and philosophers quench their thirst! Oh, stay with us, although known and honoured but by few, stay with us, if only to guard us against that so-called enlightenment, that skeleton without flesh and blood.'

That the darkness, as of night, which lowered over Schubert's soul had in no way paralysed his creative powers, his compositions which first appeared at this time are ample proof. The most considerable of these is the octett (cited in his letter to Kupelwieser) for stringed and wind instruments, a work which, if not conspicuous for depth of thought, is at all events full of beauty, and bears the genuine Schubert stamp.[1]

This work (according to a statement of Herr Doppler) was written by Schubert under the orders of Count Ferdinand Troyer,[2] Obersthofmeister of the Cardinal Archduke Rudolf of Austria, in the year 1824, and performed under Schuppanzigh's lead as first violin,[3]

---

[1] This is written for two violins, viola, clarionet, bassoon, French horn, cello, and contrabass. On reading the original score (in Spina's possession), we find it was begun in February, and finished March 1. The octett was published in parts by Spina as Op. 166. Dr. L. v. Sonnleithner has made a pianoforte arrangement of the work.

[2] Count Troyer, a pupil of Josef Friedlowsky, Professor at the Conservatorium at Vienna, was a distinguished clarionet-player. A gentleman of the name of Melzer played the double-bass, and Radecki took the horn part.

[3] Ignaz Schuppanzigh, born at Vienna, in the year 1776, was the founder of the well-known and illustrious Quartett Association, and at that time leader of the Thursday morning concerts, which were given at the Augarten. When Prince Rasumoffsky (Russian ambassador at Vienna) wished to get together a select stringed quartett, Schuppanzigh, and, at his suggestion, Franz Weiss (born in 1788, in Silesia, died at

with the Count as clarionettist, for the first time at
Vienna, at the Spielmanns' on the Graben, where
Troyer lived. Weiss and Linke, two of the famous
Rasumoffsky party, were two of the other performers.
In the year 1827, it was successfully given at the series
of subscription-concerts of Herr Schuppanzigh, and
subsequently in two towns in Germany. After a lapse
of thirty-four years, Herr Josef Hellmesberger revived
the octett at a quartett concert given at the end of the
year 1861, at Vienna, and presented it in an abbreviated
form as a novelty. It was admirably received.[1]

Of a like kind and meaning with the octett are the
stringed quartetts in A minor, E-flat, and E major,
which may be cited as the first and freshest offerings
made by Schubert in the way of chamber music. The

Vienna in 1830) as tenor, and Josef Linke (born 1783, at Trachenberg,
in Prussian Silesia, died at Vienna in 1837) as violoncellist, all entered
the Prince's service, and formed, with the Prince himself, who took the
part of second violin, the world-renowned Beethoven Quartett Party.
When the Prince's private band was broken up, Schuppanzigh travelled
for several years through the north of Europe, and returned afterwards
to Vienna, where he became a member of the Court orchestra in the
year 1824, and from the year 1828 (under Count Gallenberg) he became
director of music at the Court Theatre. He died at Vienna in March 1830.

[1] The octett is in six movements, and consists of an Adagio F
major $\frac{4}{4}$, followed by an Allegro (in the same key and time); an Andante
(B-flat major $\frac{4}{4}$); an Allegro vivace (D minor $\frac{3}{4}$), with trio; an Andante
(C major $\frac{2}{4}$), with seven variations; a minuett (Allegretto F major $\frac{3}{4}$),
with trio and coda, and a short subject, Andante molto (A-flat $\frac{4}{4}$);
and the finale (Allegro F major $\frac{2}{4}$), also with a short middle movement (Andante molto), winding up with the introductory theme (Allegro
molto).

introduction and variations for pianoforte and flute (Op. 160), and an unpublished sonata for pianoforte and harp in A minor, belong to this period; also the well-known ' Salve Regina' (published as Op. 149) and the ' Contributions' to the much-applauded collection of six-and-thirty original ' Allemandes' for the pianoforte, published by M. F. Leidesdorf, at Vienna.[1]

The duett for pianoforte and flute (Op. 160) may very likely have been a work commissioned by and adapted to the powers of some particular person. I am inclined to think that it was written for the accomplished flute-player Ferdinand Bogner,[2] Honorary Professor of the Conservatorium at Vienna, who, from his relationship with the family of Fröhlich, knew and was kind to Schubert, or for that ' admirable flute-player' mentioned by the Court actress Sofie Müller in her diary for the year 1825 (which we shall have to allude to again), who, although his name is not recorded, probably was the same gentleman here alluded to. The composition consists of an introduction and the theme ' Trockene Blumen,' from the ' Müllerlieder,'

---

[1] Czerny, Horzalka, Pixis, Preisinger, Schoberlechner, and Worzischek likewise contributed each their mite to the publication.

[2] Ferd. Bogner, born at Vienna in the year 1786, pupil of the flutist Florian Heinemann, was of great repute as a flute-player. He was officially connected with the Imperial Hofkammer, since the year 1821 a Professor at the Conservatorium in Vienna, and repeatedly performed in public. B. married Barbara Fröhlich, a singer and teacher of singing at Vienna, and died June 24, 1846.

set to seven variations. All that Schubert probably
intended was to give to the flute and pianoforte-player
an opportunity for a trial of their skill as executants
on their respective instruments. Both parts are filled
with roulades, and the composition is only enjoyable
on the supposition that it be performed with equal
rapidity, purity, crispness, and ensemble on the part of
both performers.[1]

Of vocal compositions, we may cite ' Der Gondelfahrer,' and the quartett of the same name (for men's
voices), both in different styles. The quartett ranks
amongst the most successful of Schubert's compositions
in this style, and after its first performance in private
society at Vienna, was often sung and always welcomed.
In the family residence of Madame Lascny (née Buchwieser, and of great repute as a vocalist) Schubert had
the happiness of hearing in the second bass part Luigi
Lablache, whom he delighted to honour.

In the May of 1824, Franz followed the family of
the Count Carl Esterhazy to Zelész. This excursion,
and a lengthy stay at that country seat, where he could
shake off the dust and turmoil of city life and pass
his days in peace in an atmosphere irradiated by his
genius, proved the most efficacious cure against that fit

---

[1] It never seems to have been given in public during Schubert's lifetime ; at Vienna lately (in March 1862), it was given at a private subscription soirée at the Hall of the Musikverein, by Herren Doppler and
Dachs.

of despair which had shortly before overwhelmed him. In the quiet of his rural seclusion, he wrote several important compositions,[1] and a letter of the 18th of July, written to his brother Ferdinand in Vienna, shows that in the interim his mind had given way to serious but still calmer and more complacent views of existence. The letter runs thus :—

'I am surprised to hear of your quartett association, and particularly that you have been able to get Ignaz up to the point of joining. But it will be better that you should stick to other quartetts rather than mine, for there is nothing in them excepting the fact that they probably please you, who like everything of mine. What I value most of all is your recollection of me. Was it merely sorrow at my absence that drew tears from you, which you could not trust yourself to write about? Or, on thinking about me, oppressed as I am by indefinable longings, did you feel yourself enveloped round with a gloomy veil of sorrow? Or did all the tears which you have already seen me shed come to your remembrance? For, come what may, I feel more plainly than ever at this moment that you and none else are my own precious friend, interwoven with every fibre of my soul! In order that these lines may not perchance

---

[1] The duett for piano (Op. 140), composed in June, marches, dance music (composed in October), 'Gebet vor der Schlacht,' 'Abendroth,' and some pianoforte exercises were written at this time in Zelész.

mislead you to a belief that I am unwell or out of
spirits, I hasten to assure you of the contrary. Certainly that happy joyous time is gone when every
object seemed encircled with a halo of youthful glory,
and that which has followed is the experience of a
miserable reality, which I endeavour as far as possible
to embellish by the gifts of my fancy (for which I
thank God). People are wont to think that happiness
depends on the place which witnessed our former
joys, whilst in reality it only depends on ourselves;
and thus I learned a sad delusion, and saw a renewal
of those of my experiences which I had already
made at Steyr, and yet I am now much more than
formerly in the way of finding peace and happiness
in myself. As a proof of this, I shall show you a
grand sonata and variations upon an original theme,
both for four hands, which I have already composed.
The variations have met with very hearty applause.
With regard to the Lieder I have handed over to ——,
I comfort myself, as only a few of them are to my
liking, the "Wanderers Nachtlied" and "Der entsühnte," not the "entführte Orest,"—a mistake which
I cannot help having a good laugh at. Try and get
these as soon as you possibly can. I am delighted to
hear you are so well, the more so as I hope by next
winter to enjoy the same good health myself. Greet
for me parents, brothers, sisters, and friends. I kiss

you a thousand times. Write as soon as possible, and farewell, farewell most heartily. Your ever loving brother,

'FRANZ.'

Our tone-poet seems to have kept up an active correspondence with Franz von Schober, who was in Prussia in the years 1824 and 1825, with the intention of choosing some new path of life in that country. This is hinted at in a letter of Schober's to Schubert (dated Breslau, December 2, 1824), and from that letter, which breathes throughout a vein of sadness, I borrow the following extract:—

' Beloved Schubert,—You will have ascertained from my letter to Zelész, that it was written under the worst circumstances possible. You, my true, ever dear friend, have loved me for my own sake, and my love has never seemed valueless to you. Schwind too, and Kupelwieser, will remain true to me also. And are we not those very people who found our very life and being in art whilst others merely trifled with it? are not we those who understood the voice within us in a way that only a German can understand it? I feel that I was too much given up to a multitude of men and things, and squandered my powers and time; it was necessary that I should tear myself away, that the whole atmosphere around me should be purified, and that I should become once more zealous and active; now that one of

these events has happened, and the other is in process
of being, I can see, on the whole, a better and more
advanced state of things, and should everything fail,
I shall return heart whole and lovingly to your arms,
which are the only ones I care about. I have a distant
hope still to get a glimpse of you this winter—this
would be a fair but fantastic dream. The Baron B., who
is fond of odd adventures and unusual things, wishes,
for the sake of a rendezvous, which he had arranged
this summer at Carlsbad, to post off one evening for a
subscription ball in Vienna, pass a night there, and
return by the mail next day. Should this come to
anything, he has invited me to drive with him : just
after leaving Carlsbad he was full of this scheme. Now,
however, he seems absorbed in all sorts of projects,
and his enthusiasm has simmered down. But should
the plan be realised, I would tell you the place where
you might expect me, and we might pass a glorious
night together.'

We find that Schubert made occasional efforts as a
poet, from the libretto he set to the trio composed in
honour of his father's birthday fête, as well as the
'contributions' to Salieri's jubilee festival in shape
of the Lied 'In das Stammbuch eines scheidenden
Freundes,' and the passage in Schober's letter of the
year 1824, in which he thanks Schubert for 'his poem,
so true, so full of feeling.'

Here must be quoted the two poems [1] (the first dated September 1820, the second with the title 'Mein Gebet,' dated May 8, 1823), which although betraying, as Schumann says, an unpractised hand, still show a poetical aptitude and bias which people conversant with Schubert knew him to be possessed of.

'Lasst sie nur in ihrem Wahn,'
Spricht der Geist der Welt,
'Er ist's, der im schwanken Kahn
Sie mir erhält.'

Lasst sie rennen; jagen nur
Hin nach einem fernen Ziel,
Glauben viel, beweisen viel
Auf der dunkeln Spur.

Nichts ist wahr von alledem,
Doch ist's kein Verlust,
Menschlich ist ihr Weltsystem,
Göttlich bin ich's mir bewusst.

MEIN GEBET.

Tiefer Sehnsucht heil'ges Bangen
Will in schön're Welten langen;
Möchte füllen dunklen Raum
Mit allmächt'gem Liebestraum.

Grosser Vater! reich' dem Sohne,
Tiefer Schmerzen nun zum Lohne,
Endlich als Erlösungsmahl
Deiner Liebe ew'gen Strahl.

---

[1] These, as well as the narrative 'My Dream,' were in Ferdinand Schubert's possession, and in the year 1838 were published by him in the 'Leipziger Musikzeitung.'

Sieh, vernichtet liegt im Staube,
Unerhörtem Gram zum Raube,
  Meines Lebens Martergang
  Nahend ew'gem Untergang.

Tödt' es und mich selber tödte,
Stürz' nur Alles in die Lethe,
  Und ein reines kräft'ges Sein
  Lass', o Grosser! dann gedeih'n.

Lastly, we have his narrative of 'a dream,' the interpretation of which is fairly enough left to the reader.

MY DREAM.

July 3, 1822.

'I was one brother amongst a number of brothers
and sisters. Our father, our mother, were worthy people. I was deeply and fondly attached to the whole
circle. My father took us out one day on a party of
pleasure to a favourite spot. My brothers were in a
state of great glee, but I was wretched. Well, my
father came up to me, and bade me enjoy the delicacies
before me; but I could not. Whereupon my father,
in a rage, banished me from his presence. I turned
away my steps, and with a heart full of boundless love
for those who despised it, I wandered into the distant
country. For long years I felt myself preyed on alternately by the greatest pain and most fervent love.
Then the news of my mother's death was brought to me.
I hastened away to see her, and my father, softened by
affliction, did not stop my going then. Then I gazed

on the dead body of my mother. My eyes filled with tears. Like the good old past days, to which my departed mother thought we should carry back our memories, as she did in her lifetime, she was lying dead before me. And we followed her poor body with mourning and woe, and the coffin sank into the earth. My father once more took me into his favourite garden; he asked me if I liked it. But the garden was distasteful to me, and I dared not trust myself to say anything. My father, kindling, a second time asked me if I liked the garden. I trembled, and said "No." Then my father struck me, and I fled. And a second time I turned my steps away, and, with a heart full of boundless love for those who scorned it, I once more went forth a wanderer in the world. For many, many long years I sang my Lieder. If I would fain sing of love, it turned to pain; if I would sing of pain, it turned to love. Thus I was divided between love and sorrow. And once I was told of a pious maiden who had just died. And a crowd gathered round her tomb, and in the midst of that crowd many youths and old men wandered for ever, as though in bliss. They spoke gently, as though dreading to awake the maiden. Heavenly thoughts seemed, like light sparks, to be for ever darting on the youths from the maiden's grave, and a gentle rustling noise was heard. I felt bashful, and ashamed to walk there. "It is by a miracle only," said the people, "that you are conducted to this circle." But I advanced to the grave with slow steps, full of devotion and firm faith, my eyes fixed on the grave, and before I could have thought it possible I found myself in a circle from which there arose spontaneously a wonderful strain of music, and I felt the bliss of eternity concentrated, as it were, into one moment. I saw, too, my father, reconciled and loving towards me. He clasped me to his arms and wept. But I wept more sorely than he.'

CHAPTER XIII.

(1825.)

SCHUBERT AND VOGL'S TOURS THROUGH THE SALZKAMMERGUT—A
LETTER FROM ANNA MILDER TO SCHUBERT—A LETTER FROM
SCHUBERT'S FATHER—A LETTER OF SCHUBERT'S TO SPAUN—A LETTER
FROM M. SCHWIND TO SCHUBERT—FRANZ DESCRIBES HIS TOURS IN
A LETTER TO HIS PARENTS—A BUSINESS LETTER FROM HÜTHER TO
SCHUBERT—FRANZ DESCRIBES HIS TOURS TO HIS BROTHER FERDINAND
—A LETTER OF BAUERNFELD TO SCHUBERT, AND THE ANSWER—
SCHUBERT'S RETURN TO VIENNA—HIS MUSICAL ENERGY THIS YEAR
—SCHUBERT AGAIN JOINS SCHOBER.

OUR tone-poet having, during his earlier residence
in Styria, tasted by anticipation the sweets and enjoyed the beauty of country life, yearned once more
for the mountains and blue lakes of Upper Austria.
Even before the summer-time set in he was off on
an excursion which this time was to extend itself to
Salzburg, Gastein, and the mountains of the Tyrol.

In Upper Austria he met, according to agreement,
his friend Vogl, who had, on March 31, hurried on
before Schubert to Steyr.[1] The singer was housed, as

---

[1] We find from a diary published by Mailath, in the year 1832, of the
famous actress Sofie Müller (who in 1824 came from Mannheim to
Vienna, and died at Hietzing in the year 1830), that Jenger, Vogl, and
Schubert, for the first months of the year 1825, were frequent visitors
and guests at her house, and that she herself would delight in singing
the most recently composed songs of Schubert, or listen, in a state of

usual, at the Paumgartners'; Schubert took up his quarters alternately at Koller's and Scheumann's.[1]

rapture, to Vogl's performance. Amongst the new songs may be cited ' Die junge Nonne,' that out of the ' Pirat,' ' Das Fragment aus Aeschilus,' 'Ihr Grab,' 'Der Einsame,' and 'Drang in die Ferne.' The ' old ' Lange (actor, pianist, painter, and opera composer, died at Vienna in the year 1827) was occasionally present at these performances. On the 30th of March, the day before Vogl's departure, the whole party assembled for the last time at her house. Schubert's departure is alluded to again in the diary for the months of April and December. He played with Jenger the overture 'to his opera,' and produced the Lieder from ' The Lady of the Lake.' Müller spent the summer in Gratz, where she had become acquainted with the Pachlers, a family we shall meet with again in the year 1827. Jenger (Johann Baptist), born at Breisgau, was an intimate friend of Schubert's, and accompanied his songs on the piano exquisitely. Jenger died at Vienna in 1855.

[1] A few days before Schubert left, the younger Schellmann wrote the following note and poem. Scheumann was at the time detained at Vienna, and submitting to his last examinations. The contents of this letter, which is in my possession, are shortly these:—

' Dear Schubert,—To say how do you do? to fetch my gloves, which I left at your house, and the book I lent you, such are the reasons for my being here—and all, even to the book, of which I found one half, are wrecked and come to nothing. Farewell! Greet for me all my Steyrian friends, Vogl, the Pepi, and particularly my pet treasure, which you detected so easily. Take this note with you; it will remind you of a promise.   V. S.

DAS STERNCHEN.

(Written in pencil.)

1.

Ein Sternchen möcht' ich sein
Mit hellem, goldnem Schein,
Und säh' sie Nachts aus ihrem Haus
Zum schmalen Fensterchen heraus,
Wollt' ich so freundlich strahlen,
Ich müsste ihr gefallen.

When summer began, the two artists, like wandering minstrels, started forth on their beautiful country expedition, bent on making at one time a stately convent, at another a city or town, ring with their already famous lays. They made considerable halts at Linz and Gmunden, and again at the proper starting-point of their wanderings—Vogl's birthplace.[1] Everywhere they fell in with friends and acquaintances who received them with open arms.[2] The still living witnesses of these days of Schubert's wanderings talk with delight

---

2.

Und was mein Mund nicht laut
Zu sagen sich getraut
Von meiner Liebe heissem Schmerz,
Das wollt' ich strahlen in ihr Herz,
Das Sternchen sollt' ihr's sagen,
Sie müsste mich beklagen.

This poem was probably set to music by Schubert.

[1] Schubert came to Steyr on May 29, and remained there up to the beginning of June. He was again at Steyr from July 28 to the middle of August, and a third time from the 12th to the 21st September. He spent a fortnight in Linz, and at Steyeregg a little over a week at the country-house of Count Weissenwolf. The journey to Gastein was made between the second and third visit to Steyr. On these excursions Schubert's almost inseparable companion was Vogl.

[2] At Gmunden, Hofrath Schiller, who was at that time Oberamtmann of the Salzkammergut, gave them a welcome; so did Klodi, now in his eighty-fifth year, but still intellectual and vigorous; he owned the castle and property adjoining Ebenzweyer. At Linz they fell in with the Spauns, one of whom, Anton Spaun, became famous in the literary world. At Steyeregg they were entertained very hospitably by the family of Count Weissenwolf, not to mention other friends in Steyr, St. Florian, &c.

of the happy hours they passed in the society of the unassuming and at that time happy and cheerful Schubert. Music, of course, they had to their hearts' content, and the staple of such enjoyments consisted of Schubert's newest songs, given by Vogl, or Schubert's pianoforte compositions; and that the manifold distractions of these days never quenched the restless genius of the tone-poet is proved by the quantity of compositions which were written whilst he was touring and away from home. Some letters, written at that time by Schubert, partly to his family, partly to his friends and acquaintances, or the answers received by him,[1] may here be quoted, arranged in chronological order, as they give us some insight into his thoughts, and throw a considerable light on his life and actions.

On June 2, Anna Milder-Hauptmann, the public singer, wrote to the Lieder-composer, for whom she entertained sentiments of great veneration, the following somewhat careless and inartistic lines. The letter came from Berlin, where she had lived since the year 1816 :—

' Most honoured Herr Schubert,—I cannot forbear giving you an account of a musical evening's entertainment I was present at on the 9th of this month. I sang "Suleika" in public, and you will understand

---

[1] The originals of the collected letters received by Schubert from the years 1825 to 1828 inclusively, were, with few exceptions, procured for me by Herr J. Herbeck.

that this was by particular request. The "Erlkönig" and "Suleika" pleased immensely, and I am delighted to send you this newspaper; I trust it will give you real pleasure. People here hope soon to see "Suleika" in print, and I suppose she will soon put in an appearance. Trautwein is the most honest music-publisher at Berlin. Should you wish to publish "Suleika" here, I advise you to employ him.

'How about "Die Empfindungen an einem Platz," by Göthe?[1] Have you thought at all about it? I leave here on the 30th, and probably before I start shall hear nothing of you, which I shall regret extremely. I go to Ems in August for the sake of my health; if you could find an opportunity of sending me there, or to Paris, where I shall be during September and October, some of your compositions, I should be greatly pleased. How is Vogl? Well, I hope. Greet him for me a thousand times. I regret that when I was in Vienna I was not fortunate enough to meet him. Have the goodness to tell him that I intend journeying to Paris, and shall most certainly not sing there, although of course the public knows much better than I do. Farewell, and when you compose don't forget

'Yours most devotedly,

'ANNA MILDER.'

---

[1] 'Verschiedene Empfindungen an einem Platz,' a rather long poem, descriptive of the feelings of a maiden and her lover, a languishing adorer, and a hunter. Schubert never set it to music.

The letter had been delivered to Schubert's father in Vienna, and he forwarded it to Franz on June 8, with the following note from himself:—

'Dear Son,—Madame Milder's father gave me this letter for you, and bade me read from the Berlin newspapers a glowing account of an evening's entertainment given by his daughter during the present month, on which occasion your compositions were very highly spoken of.

'I as well as all your belongings are surprised at your not letting us hear anything of you. Numberless are the greetings and good wishes which I am charged on all sides to convey to you. Your last co-tenant[1] sent his servant here to make some enquiries after you. I and all my circle are, thank God, well, and in the hope of a cheering answer from you, with every wish for your true and lasting happiness,

'I am your affectionate father,

'F. SCHUBERT.[2]

'My hearty respects to your esteemed patron and friend, Herr v. Vogl.'

The first of Schubert's letters before me is one to Josef Spaun, his former comrade and attached friend

---

[1] Schubert lived at that time at an oil-merchant's, near the Carls-kirche.

[2] Whether Schubert replied to Milder's friendly letter I have never ascertained; in the answer to his father's letter (of July 25, 1825) there is a passage which has reference to Milder's letter.

at the Convict, and, at the time this letter was written,
' Bankal-Assessor.'   Schubert wished to pay him a visit
at Linz, but Spaun shortly before his friend's arrival,
had been transferred in an official capacity to Galicia.
The letter is as follows:—

'Linz: July 21, 1825.

' Dear Spaun,—You may well imagine my uncommon
vexation in being obliged in Linz to write a letter to
you in Lemberg.   Deuce take that abominable duty
which separates friends from one another, when they
had scarce sipped the cup of friendship!   Here I am
sitting still in Linz, half dead with the melting heat
and perspiration.   I have a whole number of new
songs, and you are not here.   Are you not ashamed?
Linz without you is a body without a soul, a rider without a head, broth without salt.   If I didn't get good
beer at Jägermaier's and decent wine at the Schloss-
berg, I should go and hang myself on the parade out of
grief for the soul of the Linzers which has taken wing
and flown away.   You see I am utterly out of sorts
with the general lot of Linz folk, whereas in your
mother's house, surrounded by your sisters, besides
Ottenwalt and Max, I am thoroughly happy; a faint
shadow of their spirit seems to radiate from the material form of an occasional Linzer.   Only I fear this
light will become beautifully less by degrees, and then
I shall fall to pieces in sheer despair.   After all, it
is downright misery to see everything ossified into

"fade" prose (*zur faden Prosa verknöchert*), whilst the majority of humdrum people jog on in perfect self-complacency, as long as they can comfortably slide over the quagmire into the abyss below. It certainly is much harder work as one mounts upwards in the scale, and yet it would be an easy matter to get rid of the common elements if the upper classes lent a helping hand.

'For the rest, don't let your hair grow gray with misery at being so far away from us. Brave the simple fate; let your gentle spirit expand like a flower-garden, that you may diffuse the warmth of life in the cold North, and show your divine origin wherever you go.

'Contemptible is the grief which stealthily creeps upon a noble heart; cast it away from you, and tear to pieces the vulture which is gnawing at your soul.

'I hear from Schober that he intends returning to Vienna. Now tell me, what does he mean by that? Don't mistake me; I delight in him, and hope that by his good sense and cheerfulness he will restore and enliven a society which has certainly become very much reduced and deteriorated.

'Since May 20 I have been in Upper Austria, and was very sorry to learn that you had left Linz two days before. I should have been so glad to see you once more before you had handed yourself over to the Polish devil.

'I only stayed in Steyr for four days, after which we (Vogl and I) went to Gmunden, where we spent six weeks very pleasantly. We lodged at Traweger's:[1] he has a splendid grand piano, and is, as you know, a great worshipper of my littleness. I lived very happily there, and did exactly as I liked. We had a great deal of music at Hofrath v. Schiller's, and some of my new songs out of W. Scott's "Lady of the Lake" were given; the hymn was particularly well received.

'I am very glad you have come across the young Mozart. Greet him for me.

'Now farewell, my dear Spaun; think often of your sincere friend,

'FRANZ SCHUBERT.

'Write still to me at Steyr.'

Of all his Viennese friends, the genial Moriz Schwind seems to have kept up the liveliest correspondence with Schubert, for it is plain that one or more letters preceded that we are about to quote. The first of his letters is of a somewhat mysterious kind, and will only be perfectly understood by those who have realised the connection existing between the somewhat visionary and

---

[1] Traweger was a merchant at Gmunden. Carl Schubert seems already to have paid him a visit in 1818, or at all events to have made his acquaintance, for he writes to Franz:—'Traweger, who was exceedingly kind and good to me, as being your brother, begs to be kindly remembered to you, and says you ought to think of him, if you have any songs for four or eight men's voices.'

extravagant painter and the more realistic musician. The letter, however, shall be given unabridged, for it gives important testimony to the fact of a solid and characteristic friendship existing between the two friends, and Schubert's letter to Bauernfeld (of September 19) refers to both of Schwind's letters.

'My dear Schubert,—I am almost inclined to think that my last letter contained something which was unpleasant to you. I will be candid, and confess to you something which still harasses and annoys me. You of course remember the fact of your not having come on the last occasion to H——. I must of course be completely blind if I were to let such a thing annoy me; nay, more, were it anything but agreeable to me, that you should do just as you please, and only trouble yourself about that which I, perhaps, have a right to ask you for. But had you ever given yourself a thought of the great love I have for you, you certainly would have come. However little this may hinder me from being to you, and doing for you, all that I have done so gladly hitherto, yet I fear I shall not have the pleasure of feeling that kindness reciprocated, as I see that in a course of many years I have failed to make any real way over your mistrust and fear to find yourself loved and appreciated. This may give rise to some bitter jests, which, painful as the utterance has been, I have not been able to suppress

That confounded irony and bitterness certainly originate in matters like these. Why should I not say so? Ever since I knew you and Schober, I have been accustomed to find myself understood in all things. But others of the cynical and sneaking sort come with their disjointed schemes, intrigues, and associations, and at first we let them pass, then we join them, and as man is no flawless diamond, he loses himself irredeemably for the paltry boon of a companionship which he is obliged to tolerate. If that be too bitter a saying, I was unfortunately often too good-natured. Pray let me have an answer to this; however outspoken and rough I may be, anything is better than these harassing thoughts, which I cannot rid myself of. I hear that you are expecting me soon; but, alas! it cannot be. I must at once devote myself, heart and soul, to painting, and a whole summer is the least period I can possibly allow for the chances of acquiring any real certainty and facility. I must also be on the lookout for Schober, and therefore cannot run away immediately; he will fret quite sufficiently at your not being here. Then I go with all energy to Grinzing, where more than one hard week's toil has to be forgotten. I have wished to write on other matters, but I hear you mocking, as usual, although you know just as well and better than I do how delightful that intercourse is in which a man and his friend mutually understand one another. The lady forwards you the enclosed newspaper. You will observe how she has tried to annihilate your friendship with Tieze, whom in her presence you have so constantly complimented. All here desire their kindest remembrances to you, and people here never tire of talking and thinking of the days when you were amongst us.

'I don't know if I wrote to you that I have been with Grillparzer. He expressed himself greatly pleased with my "Hochzeit," and assured me that were ten years to pass, he will remember every figure in the picture.[1]

' Failing the patronage and pay of a Grand Duke of Weimar, we could ask for nothing but the intellectual criticism of men of mark, so you may imagine how pleased I was as I went home. For the rest, he showed himself extremely friendly, and talked a good deal,

---

[1] Schwind had painted a picture representing the marriage of Figaro. Helmina Chezy mentions (in her 'Denkwürdigkeiten') this picture in the following way :—'My eldest son Wilhelm got together a number of poetical and distinguished friends, of whom he would tell me stories daily. He was intimate with Bauernfeld, Ernst v. Feuchtersleben, Andreas Schumacher, Christian Huber, and other very promising poets, whose gifts were ripening. Moriz Schwind, likewise, the genial artist, was always at home amidst this circle of friends. That summer Schwind was at work on his valuable painting "Die Hochzeit des Figaro." What power, what depth of thought, what a fund of irresistible humour, what cheerfulness! Who is to be the possessor of this valuable artistic work? Only in the best works of the Florentine school have I found so close an alliance and blending of romance with the spirit of the antique.' Wilhelm Chezy also mentions this picture in his ' Erinnerungen.' The picture made a great sensation at the time

chiefly about the defective and artificial tendency of
certain artists and savants whom we know. That he
takes just the same view of "Die Hochzeit des Figaro "
as I do, was no small triumph for me. Nothing has
come of his opera, for it is not his own property,
and he cannot do exactly as he likes with it.[1] He
hopes, therefore, to get a commission from Berlin for
you, in the shape of an opera for the Königstadt
Theatre. The director is on the look-out for an opera,
and Grillparzer knows him. He often said it was to
him a matter of real interest. Bauernfeld is working
hard, and begs to be remembered. Many kind remembrances to Herr v. Vogl ; he must certainly not
forget, at some opportune and critical moment, to coax
the fairest Frl. Amalia out of those two drawings.[2] I
have not got them, and as I must paint them soon,
let me have them, for I cannot get on without them.
Fr. v. Lascny and I don't hit it off. When you come
to Ebenzweyer, mind and hunt up all the pretty
things.

'Write to me soon, and say how you are getting on,
what you are doing, and if you find what I told you
corroborated. Say everything that is polite for me to

---

[1] Probably 'Melusine,' which Beethoven was to have written, and
which, subsequently, Kreutzer set to music, and produced at the Josefstadt Theatre.

[2] This must refer to Amalie, the daughter of Hofrath Schiller, in
Gmunden.

Hofrath Schiller. When I think of last year, I consider my most abject devotion as all too clumsy. Do
you know anything of Fritzi Dornfeld, of Linz and
Florian? When I have finished here I shall go and
roam about from curiosity. Farewell!

'Yours,

'SCHWIND.'

The letter addressed on July 25 to Gmunden was in
the interval sent off to Schubert, who had gone to
Steyr. On the same day Schubert sent the following
letter to his parents :—

'My dearest Parents,—I admit the justice of your
rebuke at my long silence; but, as I am averse to
writing mere empty words, and the present time with
me offers but little of interest, you will forgive me
if I have kept all news of myself from you until after
the receipt of your affectionate letter. I was delighted
to hear of the good health and state of all my family,
and to this clean bill of health I am enabled, thank
the Almighty for it, to add another in my own case.
I am now once more in Steyr, having spent six weeks
in Gmunden. The environs are perfectly lovely—I am
enchanted with the country; and the dwellers there,
especially the excellent Traweger, have made me deeply
sensible and grateful for all the good they have done
me. At Traweger's I was just as at home—not the
slightest constraint or ceremony. After the arrival of

Herr Hofrath Schiller, who is monarch of the entire Salzkammergut, we—that is, Vogl and I—dined daily at his house, and had heaps of music there, as well as at Traweger's. My new songs out of Walter Scott's "Lady of the Lake" were very warmly approved of. My audience expressed great delight at the solemnity of my hymn to the Blessed Virgin; it seems to have infected the minds of listeners with a spirit of piety and devotion. I believe I have attained this result by never forcing on myself religious ecstasy, and never setting myself to compose such hymns or prayers except when I am involuntarily overcome by the feeling and spirit of devotion; in that case, devotion is usually of the right and genuine kind. From Gmunden we travelled to Puschberg, where we fell in with some friends, and spent a few days; from thence to Linz, where we stayed eight days, passed alternately at Linz and Steyreck. At Linz I lodged at Spaun's house; Spaun's migration (of which you have heard) to Lemberg is a subject of great regret to his family. I read some letters from him, which he had written from Lemberg. They were in a very melancholy vein, and showed an intense longing for home. I wrote to him at Lemberg, chiding him for his weak, womanish behaviour, although probably in his place I should have been still more lugubrious. At Steyreck we put up at the Countess of Weissenwolf's, a great worshipper of my poor gifts; she has all my songs, many of which

she sings beautifully. The songs from Walter Scott
made so favourable an impression upon her that she
let slip an observation that the dedication of these
Lieder to her would be a real pleasure. [They were
dedicated to the Countess.] I intend to have some
other arrangement with the publication of these songs,
the present one inviting so little attention; they must
have the illustrious name of Scott on the preface, and
thus make people more curious; with the addition of the
English text, they might help to make me better known
in England, if only once I could but make some fair
terms with art purveyors; but in that matter the wise
and beneficent management of the Government has
taken care that the artist shall remain for ever the
slave of every miserable huckster.

'With regard to Milder's letter, I am very glad to
hear of the favourable reception given to "Zuleika,"
although I should like to have examined the review for
myself, to see if there was anything to be learned from
it; for, however favourable the criticism may be, the
whole thing may be simply ridiculous, if the reviewer,
as is often the case, has not the proper understanding
and capacity for reviewing.

'I find my compositions everywhere all over Upper
Austria, especially in the Florian and Kremsmünster
convents, where, with the help of an admirable pianoforte-player, I produced, with signal success, my four-
handed variations and marches. The variations from

my new sonatas for two performers (Op. 42) pleased particularly. These I played alone, and not without success, for some assured me that the keys, under my hands, sounded like singing voices, which, if it be true, is a delightful compliment, as I cannot endure that execrable hacking (*vermaledeite Hacken*) peculiar to even distinguished pianoforte-players—it neither tickles the ear nor moves the feelings.

'I am at present in Steyr, and should you wish to favour me with a line, your letter will be sure to find me here, as we stay only for ten days or a fortnight, and then go on to Gastein, to one of the famous water-ing-places, about five days distant from Steyr. I always enjoy this excursion immensely, as, on passing through the most beautiful line of country, I get to know it thoroughly; and on my way back shall visit Salzburg, so famous for its beautiful situation and surroundings. As we shall not have returned from our tour until the middle of September, and have then promised to go to Gmunden, Linz, Steyreck, and Florian, I can hardly be in Vienna before the end of October. Still I must ask you to hire me lodgings near the Carlskirche, and be good enough to pay down 28 florins for me in advance. I will on my arrival repay you, and very gratefully, as I have already promised that the money shall be forth-coming. It is possible I may arrive sooner than I now meditate. For the whole of June and half of July the weather was very unsettled; for fourteen days it was

very hot—I became thoroughly weak from mere heat—
and now it remains for nearly four days incessantly
without a break. Give my kindest love to Ferdinand
and his wife and children. He knuckles down, I suppose, still to the landlord of the " Kreuz," [1] and can't
get rid of Dornbach; that man certainly must have
been ill seventy-seven times, and nine times thought
himself at death's door—that is if death be the worst
thing that can befall us poor mortals. Could he only
see these divine mountains and lakes, the look of which
threatens to crush or to swallow us, he would not be so
enamoured of the petty life of men as not to esteem
it a great happiness to be restored anew to life and
strength and energy.

'What of Carl? [Schubert's brother, a landscape-
painter]. Will he travel or stay at home? He has
now a great deal to do, for a married artist is bound to
publish pieces from nature as well as copies ; and if both
kinds succeed, he is doubly to be praised, for that is
no light matter to attain unto. I renounce it on that
account. Ignaz is, I suppose, just now probably at
Hollpein's; for being there morning, noon, and night,
he can't very well be at home. I still marvel at his
perseverance, only one doesn't know for certain whether that be real merit or not, whether heaven or the

---

[1] The Weigert public-house, now Wittmann's, where Schubert's family
used to assemble. Franz never liked going there, for the host adul-
terated the wine, and it always gave him a headache.

other place be what such conduct deserves. Schneider [Schubert's brother-in-law] and his wife are on the look-out for the little Schneider or Schneiderin that is to be; they must mind that the Schneiders be as the sand on the seashore for multitude, and that no swaggerer (*Aufschneider*) or clipper of reputation (*Zuschneider*), no cut-purses or bravos (*Gurgelab-schneider*), get the upperhand.

'And now I really must finish this gossip : I thought I must needs compensate for my long silence by an equally long epistle. Kiss Marie and Pepi and the tiny Probstl Andre for me a thousand times. Pray greet everything and everybody that ought to be greeted. In the hope of a speedy answer, I remain, with all love, your most dutiful son,

'FRANZ.'

A business kind of letter, we here insert, is from Herr Hüther, written from Vienna, in the name of the firm of Pennauer, of Vienna, to Schubert. It bears date July 27, 1825.[1]

'Most honoured Friend,—I learned, on my return from Leipsic, that you had already started on your journey to Upper Austria. But no one here could give me any reliable address, so that until to-day I was obliged to forego the pleasure of enquiring after your welfare,

[1] It is addressed 'To Herr Michael v. Vogl, Associate of the Hofcapelle and Chamber-singer, for Herr Franz Schubert, in Steyr.'

and of entering into any negotiations respecting your
new compositions. Only to-day for the first time I learn,
through Herr v. Pinterics, of your staying with Herr
v. Vogl, and avail myself of the present moment to
send you a letter forthwith. Knowing what company
you are in, I can only make a guess at your present
welfare, so I pass at once to business, and make so
free as to ask you what you have lately composed,
and would feel disposed to publish. Further, I desire
to ask you how many songs from W. Scott's works
you have set; if the German translation is in the
metre of the English original, and whether it would
admit of the text in both languages being set to your
music. Pray let me know the lowest price you would
at first offer, and be assured that I shall do my very
best to arrange a good edition and large sale for your
compositions. I have published "Die junge Nonne," and
a second volume of Lieder follows next month, but the
Sonata (in A minor, Op. 42), which is already engraved
and for which I daily expect the Archduke Rudolf's
written permission to be allowed to dedicate the work
to him, will appear in the month of September. Pray
let me know how I can send you copies of the songs.
I hope you will be pleased with the edition, for although some insignificant errors were found on three
proof-sheets in the two songs, these were immediately
set right, and only the first twenty copies, which were
not delivered collectively at once, have remained un-

corrected. I will send you, by a private source, a copy of the sonata directed to the address of Herr v. Vogl; and be good enough to examine it accurately, for I am exceedingly anxious to publish the work free from all errors. Will you please let me know how long you intend to absent yourself from Vienna. It would give me great pleasure to hear that you had written a work for four hands; and let me entreat you to turn your mind to the composition of a really brilliant work of no inordinate length—for instance, a grand Polonaise or Rondeau with an introduction, or a Fantasia. Once more, let me ask you to propose the most reasonable terms you can in respect to the Lieder from W. Scott, and pray be good enough to send your letter only to us, addressed, "A. Pennauer, Publisher, Vienna." I hope you will have really fine and favourable weather, so that during your stay you may not be prevented from making excursions into the enchanting country about you. Please remember us most kindly to Herr v. Vogl, and think sometimes of us poor and quite deserted Viennese. Receive the assurance of my highest esteem and consideration, with which I remain your most devoted servant,

'FR. HÜTHER.

'P.S.—It will probably interest you to hear something of our theatres. I can tell you with certainty

that Barbaja has taken for ten years the management of
the Opera, and that all the members of the chorus are
already re-engaged by Duport. But with the German
opera! . . . it's all over; I hear they have only ballet
and Italian opera. Count Palffy must certainly get
hold of a partner with plenty of money. The wish is
a good one, but it must be a very difficult one to
realise. People are yet uncertain respecting the fate
of this theatre; meantime Herr Carl,[1] of the Bavarian
Theatre, has hired the theatre for a trial of three
months, and begins to act there on August 15.'

Schubert had answered, probably in his dry humorous fashion, M. Schwind's letter already mentioned.
On August 1, Schwind writes to him again :—

'Dearest Schubert,—I must have written fine nonsense to you, as I gather from that pretty song, "Dia-
mant und Fragment;" but what connection of the
faintest kind these things have with one another,
passes my comprehension. Come what may, however,
I have learned something which I should never have
dreamed of—that some one has been abusing you to
H——. I won't believe N—— was guilty, nor, I hope,

---

[1] As already stated, Barbaja's lease, and with it the joint administration
of the theatre at Vienna, ended on March 13, 1825. Carl (of Bernbrunn),
known in after times as the director of the Isarthor Theatre, at Munich,
starred there as an actor from August 1825 to March 1826, and in the
August of that year entered into contract for a lease with the Count
Palffy. In the year 1835 he disposed of the theatre by auction.

will you, and it would very much surprise me if the others were implicated. If you had only said that matters would necessarily turn out differently, or if I could have thought for a moment that you would go there!—for you too will understand very well that I had no great desire for such company. Meantime, devil take me if I don't sweep about the house, to see if there be anything which looks like a public recantation of any charge against you. I can, however, assure you by all the saints, that I have no idea of such a thing.

'The 6th, Evening.

'I have, in a roundabout way, put the question to N——, but still as pointedly as I could; and the idea has been so completely absent from her mind, that, I'll answer for it, she has not behaved in an odd way at all, much less equivocally. I hope, when you return, you will think no more of the matter.

'Schober is here. He greets you a thousand times. He is still the same old fellow, only more animated and fresh. To-day a letter of Kupelwieser's has come from Padua; he will certainly be here in three weeks. "Die junge Nonne" has appeared. I have a great deal to do; I don't know when I can get away, but certainly hope to see you. Farewell, and write to us soon. Bauernfeld goes on examining and writing moral essays, and we get on very cheerily together,—so far as we can be without you. If you see Resi Clodi, greet her for me; I should be very glad indeed to see her again. Remember me to Herr Vogl, and remind him of the two drawings which Mali has. Pinterics, Doblhoff, and everyone salute you.   Yours,

'SCHWIND.

'I had nearly forgotten the most important part of my letter. Schober has spoken with Tieck, who has become Theater-Hofrath in Dresden, about your opera "Alfonso." You must write immediately, and say if it is still in Dresden, or if not, where it is, for Tieck is expecting news of it. I have no more time. Farewell a thousand times!'

On August 14, Schwind writes again :—

'Dear Schubert,—I don't know where you are, but this letter will of course be forwarded to you. You will have ascertained by my last letter, if you received it, that Schober is here. Kupelwieser, too, has been here for the last eight days. According to the last letters, we could only expect him after three weeks had elapsed. He looks in excellent condition, and has a capital head of hair, which, owing to a nervous fever, he was obliged for a long while to go without. They both greet you a thousand times. You must come here once without fail. Schober and Kupelwieser lodge together.

'Your landlord must know for certain if you have really determined to take your old lodgings this winter. Write definitely on this point, and I will let him know. If certain business matters turn out as I hope they will, I have fixed to stay here, but shall probably lodge "auf der Wieden." Rieder is appointed professor at the "Ingenieurs-Akademie," at a salary of 600 florins. Suspicions are afloat that he will marry. If you are really seriously competing for the post of Court organist, you can certainly succeed. All that you will have to do is to live moderately, as—assuming an opposite case to your own, that your whole body of friends become conspicuous for impecuniosity—you certainly will be obliged to satisfy the bodily and spiritual longings for roast pheasants and punch at your solitary hermitage, which will in no point be inferior to life on a desert island, or the condition of our friend Robinson Crusoe. There doesn't seem to be any more talk about the theatre—at all events about operas; and as in winter we get no harmony at Wasser-burger, we must whistle a bit to ourselves. How I delight in thinking on that first Schubertiade! We can entertain great expectations of your Symphony. Old Hönig is made dean of the juridical faculty, and in this capacity will give a soirée. This is an excellent opportunity, and people count upon a performance.

'September 1.

'I have been, since I wrote, a little out of sorts, but am now fresh and light again. As long as one keeps up one's courage and determination to be sincere, everything else settles itself. I cannot come, for I have too much to do. In order, however, you should not think I am detained by certain people, know that I go first to Weikenstein, afterwards to Atzenbruck, where Schober now is, in order to enjoy a little country air. Although I do not have it direct from you that you are quite recovered, still I flatter myself that I and Bauernfeld not being able to come might have been the reason for your not turning up earlier. Kupelwieser is extremely industrious, and Schober seems to be making vigorous preparations; but, successful as everyone may be in this fashion, our association without you lacks vitality and cheerfulness. Depend on it, you will find, when you come back to us, the sphere of life and activity enlarged since you left. N——, the only one you doubt about, shows a boundless attachment to you, and in many ways and so naturally displays an interest in your affairs, that if I am to be relied on at all, I can answer for it that you won't make music before anyone who has a greater esteem for you, or takes a warmer interest and deeper delight in your welfare.

'Worschizek[1] is on his last legs, and there will be a

---

[1] Johann Hugo Worschizek, born at Wamberg, in Bohemia, died at Vienna on November 19, 1825. Within two months after the above

serious agitation on the question of the Court organ-
istship. As far as I can learn, the successful man will
be he who can best acquit himself as an extemporary
performer on a given subject.

'At Gmunden you will have an organ at your service
to practise upon. Lastly, let me beg of you to entreat
Herr Vogl with all possible earnestness, day and night,
to get hold of, at all costs, the two drawings I have
mentioned, and bring them with him. I hope that I
and my art will be more to him than the lady in question, let her be as amiable as she pleases. I wish him
all success in winning her favour and friendship; nay,
in emergency, I will back him with every disinterested
effort. I should very much like to paint these things,
and don't know whom to take for my friend—who is
against me or who is on my side.

'I remain yours as long as I am true to myself, and,
on my own behalf and all whom you love, I hope
to get information very soon, or an answer from you.

'Yours,

'SCHWIND.

'Everything that is agreeable from Pinterics, Doblhoff, Randhartinger; and believe me, on my honour,
I am charged with the heartiest messages from the

letter had been written, Worschizek composed a great number of pianoforte and vocal pieces, a cantata, a symphony, and church music, some
of them esteemed as works of merit. He was Imperial Court Organist,
and Simon Sechter succeeded him.

little person. I get letters from home wherever I may be.'

Schubert meanwhile undertook a short mountain excursion, and sent from Gmunden, on September 12, the following detailed account of his journey to his brother Ferdinand :—

'Dear Brother,—In accordance with your wishes, I should be very glad to give you a detailed account of our journey to Salzburg and Gastein; but you know how little fitted I am for descriptive writing. On my return to Vienna, however, I shall be called on for a detailed account of every accident that has befallen me, so that I had rather venture now to commit my history to paper than tell it by word of mouth, and try to sketch a weak picture of all those extraordinary beauties; believing, as I do, that I am a better hand at writing than talking.

'About the middle of August we set off from Steyr and drove by way of Kremsmünster, which I have frequently seen, but do not like passing by, it is so beautifully situated. One looks over a lovely valley, broken by small undulating hills. On the right side rises a good-sized mountain, through the peaks of which one can see from the carriage-road the huge monastery. The post-road at this point crosses a stream, and one has a fine view of the tower of the observatory. Here we felt at home, from old associations, especially Herr v. Vogl, who has studied at the place. We were received in a very friendly manner, but we continued our journey without halting, and nothing out of the way happened to us, but we got on as far as Vöklabruck, where we arrived at evening—a miserable place. Next day we passed on by way of Strasswalchen and Frankenmarkt to Neumarkt, where we dined. These places, in the Salzburg district, are distinguished by the peculiar fashion in which their houses are built. Nearly everything is of wood. The wooden cooking apparatus stands on wooden ranges, which are fastened to the outside of the houses, and around the houses are wooden galleries. On all sides hang targets riddled to pieces; these are preserved as war trophies from very ancient times, for one frequently finds on them the dates of the years 1600 and 1500. Here we first fell in with Bavarian money. From Neumarkt, which is the last stage before Salzburg, one gets the first glimpse of the snow-covered tops of mountains emerging from the Salzburg valley. About an hour from Neumarkt the country is exceedingly beautiful. The Waller-See, which pours forth its clear bluish-greenish water, lights up this fair scene in an enchanting way. The situation is very lofty, and from that point one goes by a constant descent as far as Salzburg. The mountains appear higher and higher; the Untersberg, with its ghosts and legends, particularly peers above the rest like magic. The villages show signs of the wealth of former days. In the commonest peasants' houses one finds

on all sides marble window-ledges and doors, sometimes even staircases of red marble. The sun darkens
and the gloomy clouds lower over the black mountains
like children of the mist; but they touch not the peak of
the Untersberg—they glide past him, as though afraid
of its dreadful inmates. The far-off valley, which is
studded with isolated castles, churches, and peasants'
huts, becomes plainer and plainer to the enchanted
eye. Towers and palaces gradually appear; at last one
drives by the Kapuzinerberg, where the mighty rampart
of rock rises perpendicularly from the roadside, and
looks grimly down upon the wayfarer. The Untersberg, with its attendant mountains, becomes gigantic;
its majesty seems almost to crush us. And now our
road lies through some beautiful avenues to the town
itself. Fortification works, formed of massive square
stones, surround this famous seat of the ancient Electoral Princes. The gates of the town announce by the
inscriptions over them the departed power of the Papacy.
Nothing but houses of four or five stories fill the rather
wide streets, and passing the wonderfully decorated house
of Theophrastus Paracelsus, one goes over the bridge
of the Salzach, which roars along in dark and sullen
majesty. The town itself made a somewhat gloomy
impression upon me, for the miserable weather dark-
ened the old buildings still more; and, besides this,
the fortress, standing on the highest point of the Mönchberg, nods with ghostly greeting to all the streets of

the town. As the rain (a very constant occurrence here) came on immediately after our arrival, we could see little else besides the numerous palaces and beautiful churches which we got a sight of as we drove by. By Herr Pauernfeind, a merchant well known to Herr v. Vogl, we were introduced to Count v. Platz, President of the Landrechte, by whose family, our names being already known to them, we were most hospitably received. Vogl sang some of my songs, whereupon we were invited for the following evening, and asked to produce our seven pet Lieder before a select circle. All these, under the wing of the " Ave Maria," mentioned in my first letter, were well received by the whole party. The way Vogl sings these things, and I accompany him—so that whilst the performance lasts we seem to be one—is quite an unheard-of novelty amongst these people. Next morning, after we had ascended the Mönchberg, from which one overlooks a great part of the town, I was astonished at the number of beautiful buildings, palaces, and churches. There are but few inhabitants; many of the buildings are empty, many are inhabited by one, at most from two to three families. Grass grows on the squares and in the public places, of which there are many very fine ones, and also between the pavement-stones, so little are they trod upon.

'The cathedral is an exquisite building, built on the pattern of St. Peter's Church in Rome—of course in a miniature form. The body of the church is cross-shaped; it is surrounded by four immense courts, out of which each single one forms a separate square. Before the entrance stand stone figures of the Apostles, in gigantic size. The interior of the church is supported by a number of marble pillars, and adorned with the statues of the Electors; and everything throughout the entire building is exquisitely finished. The light which falls through the cupola illumines every corner. The rare brightness thus produced heightens the devotional effect, and ought to be recommended to all church architects. On the four public squares which surround the church are some vast fountains, adorned with handsome and boldly conceived figures. From the cathedral we went to the monastery of St. Peter, where Michael Haydn resided. The church here also is wonderfully beautiful. Here, as you know, is the monument of M. Haydn. It is very fine, but is badly placed in an obscure out-of-the-way corner. The inscriptions, all about in different directions, have something childish about them; Haydn's head is contained in an urn. I thought to myself, May thy pure and peaceful spirit hover around me, dear Haydn! and if I can never become like thee, peaceful and guileless, at all events, none on earth has such deep reverence for thee as I have. (Sad tears fell from my eyes, and we went on.) That day we dined at Herr Pauernfeind's; and as the weather in the afternoon allowed us to make out-door excursions, we ascended the Nonnenberg, with its not very lofty but very beautiful prospect. From the summit one overlooks the whole Salzburg valley. It is almost impossible to describe to you the loveliness of this valley. Imagine to yourself a garden several miles in extent, in which one can see through the trees numberless castles and country-houses; imagine a river creeping along like a serpent in twining folds; think of meadows and plains covered, like so many carpets, with the loveliest colours, and then the grand massive rocks which encircle them like bands; and lastly, miles of huge trees ranged in rows—all this girt about by a range of the loftiest mountains, as though they were sentinels watching over this exquisite valley. Imagine all this, and you have some faint conception of its unspeakable beauty. What I have yet to say of the lions of Salzburg, which only opened out to my view on my journey homewards, I leave until the proper time, for it is my wish to continue my description in a proper chronological order.

'Steyr: September 21.

'You see from this date that several days have elapsed between this and my last letter, and that from Gmunden we have, alas! settled down again at Steyr. To continue, then, the diary of my journey (which I already repent of—it takes me tco long). The following day was the loveliest day in the world, and of the world. The Untersberg, or more properly the Oberste, shone and glistened amidst his squadron and attendant crowd of other mountains in, or, strictly speaking, near the sun. We drove through the above-described valley and fancied ourselves in Elysium ; with this advantage over the Paradise of old, that we sat in a charming carriage—a luxury desiderated by Adam and Eve. Instead of wild beasts, all sorts of pretty girls met us on our way. It really is very wrong that in so lovely a country I should make such gloomy jokes, but to-day I can't be serious for a single moment. Thus we steered on, absorbed in our dreams of beauty, through the fair day and the still fairer scenes, and nothing came to our view but a trumpery building which they call "Monat-Schlösschen," because an Elector had it built in one month for his mistress. Everyone here knows the story ; but no one takes the smallest offence—a spirit of toleration quite delightful. This small building lends its charms towards the varied beauty of the valley. After some hours we arrived at Hallein, a remarkable town, but uncommonly dirty and dismal. All the inhabitants look like ghosts, pale, hollow-eyed, and thin enough to make tapers of, or lucifer-matches. The horrible contrast suggested by a comparison of the Ratzenstadtl with the other valley made a very fatal impression on my mind. It is as though one fell straight from heaven upon a dungheap, or listened to something öf the immortal A. after a piece of

Mozart's. Vogl was not to be induced to look on Salzburg with all the salt-works; his great soul, impelled by gout, was aspiring to Gastein, just as the wanderer in a dark night gropes about for some lighted halting-place. Accordingly we drove along past Gölling, where already the first inaccessible mountain-tops began to show themselves, and through whose awful ravines the wanderer travels on towards the Pass Lueg. After painfully and slowly crawling over a tall mountain, huge mountains before us and on either side of us, so that one would think the world in these parts had been nailed up with boards, one looks down, after having scaled the highest point of the mountain, into a fearful ravine, and then for the first time one feels a palpitation of the heart. Recovering a little from the first shock, one sees the mighty ramparts of rock, which, in the distance, seem to shut up like a blind alley, and then one puzzles one's head in vain thinking where there possibly can be any outlet or passage. Amidst these awful scenes of nature man has sought to perpetuate the memory of his still more dreadful inhuman actions. For here it was where, the Bavarians on one side of the Salzach, and the Tyrolese on the other, the river roaring deep between them, inflicted that dreadful murderous slaughter, whilst the Tyrolese, secreted in the holes of the rocks, uttering their hellish cries, fired on the Bavarians, who were striving to win the Pass, and fell wounded into the abyss, without seeing whence the shots proceeded. This shameful action, which was continued for several days and weeks, they tried to mark by building a chapel on the Bavarian side of the pass, and erecting a red cross in the rock on the Tyrolese side. These emblems were partly intended as memorials, and partly to appease the wrath of Heaven by such sacred mementos. O glorious Christ, how many wicked deeds must Thy sacred image appear to sanction! Thou Thyself, the cruellest memorial of human guilt, men set up Thy image, as though they would say, Lo! with insolent feet we have trampled upon the most perfect creation of the great God; should we feel disturbed, compunction of heart, in annihilating that noxious insect called man? But we turn our eyes from such despairing considerations, and regain our cheerfulness as we emerge from the gloomy pass. After descending for a considerable time, the two walls of rock seem to close in nearer with each other, and the road, at a point where the river is two fathoms broad, begins to get narrower, when, at a time one least expects it, the path opens out to the view of the agreeably surprised traveller, under a high over-hanging rock close to the angry chafing Salzach. The road from this point, although still overhung by lofty rocks, becomes wider. At noon we came to Werffen. A market-place with a considerable fortress, erected by the Electoral Prince of Salzburg, is being now re-stored by the Emperor. On our return we ascended this fortress; it is very high, and we got a fine view over the valley, which is bordered on one side by the immense Werffner mountains, which one can trace as far as Gastein. Gracious heaven! it's an awful business having to describe one's travels. I can't say more. As I intend to come to Vienna in the early part of October, I will present you with my diary in *propriâ personâ*, and where I have omitted anything, you shall have it from my own lips.'

On September 13, Bauernfeld wrote the following lines to his 'fat' friend, who at that time was again with Vogl at Steyr:—

'Dear Schubert,—I hardly know if you can identify the writing of your correspondent; or if, to right yourself completely, it will not be necessary for you at once to have recourse to the signature at the end. Know, then, that I am Bauernfeld. I salute you in all hearty affection; but to the point at once, for you must get this letter as soon as possible, and I must have it posted in a quarter of an hour.

'First of all, then, I write to know if you will keep your room, for your landlord keeps on asking about this.

'Secondly. Moriz Schwind and I propose to you to join us in sharing a common lodging-house for all three, if you are content. Do say yes; we should so like to join forces.

'Thirdly. The aforesaid plan cannot be carried out

at once—not before October or November. Up to that period I shall live at Schober's; you can do as you please. Please let me have a clear and unhesitating answer to all this scheme.

'How fares it with thee, fattest of friends? I declare I believe your stomach is a size larger. Heaven keep it and bless it! Schober is in Atzenbruck; Schwind went there yesterday. I shall probably soon follow him, but only for a few days. Write to me immediately, and let me know your address. Delivered at the lithographical establishment of Herr Trenschenski, at Zwettelhof. Farewell, farewell, farewell!

'If you only write me a respectable letter, I will, perhaps, answer with a good long and sensible ditto. Your friend,

'BAUERNFELD.'

A few days afterwards (September 18–19), Schubert sent the following reply from Steyr:—

'Dear Friend,—Your letter to me certainly passed out of my memory; time, which destroys everything, and your rapid and coarse handwriting, brought matters to this pass. I fancy I am a match for you in that last speciality. With regard to my lodgings at the Frühwirth's, I intend to retain them, and have tried to let him know as much through my own family. In case it has been forgotten, or that he is anxious and punctilious, please let one or all be so good as to give him for me twenty-five florins, and assure him that I shall come at the end of October. As regards our joint occupation, I should like the thing very much; but knowing as I well do what comes of such mutual student associations, I should not like to be left at last to tumble between two stools. Meanwhile, should we hit upon some really feasible plan, I can always separate with good grace from my landlord. The aforesaid twenty-five florins ought to be delivered to him for October, and I will pay them back punctually on my arrival. I am longing very much for Schober and Kupelwieser: in the one case to see how a man appears after all his plans have been frustrated, in the other how a man looks who comes from Naples and Rome. Schwindl is a regular Sphinx; for of the two letters he wrote to me one is worse confused than the other. Such a farrago of sense and nonsense I never saw. If by this time he has not done some very fine things, his brainless talk ought never to be forgiven. Greet those three for me, also Rieder and Dietrich, should you see them. Congratulate Rieder for me on his professorship. Steiger and Louis Hönig visited me in Gmunden, much to my satisfaction. If you had added but a single fraction to your already huge understanding, you would have honoured me with your presence. That, however, is not to be expected from such young men as you, in love with fire and sword. How often will you have been thoroughly miserable, and drowned your sighs and woes in beer and punch! Ha! ha! I had wellnigh forgotten to tell you that I have been at Salzburg and Gastein, the environs of which surpass in beauty the boldest flights that fancy ever took. Farewell! Yours,

' SCHUBERT.

' Greet all friends for me. Write me something, only let it be sensible,—peradventure a musical poem.

' N.B.—Vogl has just told me that possibly, at the end of this month or the beginning of October, he may be going with Haugwitz to Italy; in that case I shall come earlier—say the beginning of October.'

Vogl did actually go to Italy, in search of remedies for the gout, and he remained there till the spring of 1826, when he celebrated his marriage. Schubert —who, for various reasons, had associated himself with Vogl—had no further occasion for staying.[1] He with-

---

[1] In the following letter to Steiger, Schubert laments that because of Vogl's departure he cannot accompany him and his friends on their way to visit Clodi, the overseer, in Ebenzweier:—

'Dear Steiger,—I am extremely sorry that I cannot accompany you to Clodi's, as we go to-day to the Atter-See, and this expedition cannot be put off, as Vogl has determined to leave Gmunden "to-morrow." I only learned this early to-day, therefore you will excuse me. Do not be angry; I am very sorry. Of an evening I hope to see you in your hospitable home. With regard to the salt-works, all you have to do is to make enquiries at the Kuffen firm for H. Kinnsberger, to whom I spoke yesterday. ' Yours,

' SCHUBERT.'

The original of this letter is in the Imperial Library at Berlin.

drew to Linz, where he found his friend Gahy. They
hired together a one-horse chaise, which, three days
after they started, landed both wanderers happily at
the Frühwirth's. The good temper and cheerfulness
which had accompanied Schubert during his entire
stay in Upper Austria did not forsake him on his
homebound journey. This journey, however, was wisely
timed; for Herr Gahy tells me that, on his arrival
in Vienna, his pecuniary resources were in a very depressed state.

Thus ended, apparently, one of the happiest years of
the artist's life. Alas! he was not destined, much as
he wished it, to revisit once more those fair and rural
scenes which had become so dear to him.

With regard to Schubert's musical activity during
this year, we may point to the following weighty results
in the way of composition: the songs from W. Scott's
' Lady of the Lake,' which he brought finished to Upper
Austria, and the pianoforte Sonata in A minor (Op. 42,
dedicated to the Archduke Rudolf). Both the songs
and the sonata are stated to have been completed at
Gastein.[1] We must supplement the list of songs
by a series of songs equally well known and successful

---

[1] The songs were dedicated as Op. 52 to the Countess Sofie v.
Weissenwolf, née v. Breuner, at whose castle in Upper Austria Schubert
and Vogl passed some of their time. This lady, born in 1794, was
married in 1815 to Count Johann Nep. Weissenwolf. The Countess was
musical, and had a contralto voice. She died in 1847.

at the time,[1] and there is scarcely any doubt that two of these, 'Heimweh' and 'Die Allmacht,' were written at Gastein, as Franz met at this place Ladislaus Pyrker, who had from the outset of Schubert's career taken a vivid interest in his tone-poems. The 'Trauermarsch' and 'Marche héroïque' (Op. 66), the first written on the death of the Emperor Alexander, the latter on the coronation of the Emperor Nicholas of Russia, as a pianoforte piece for two performers, must also be ascribed to this period.[2]

The vocal quartett 'Der Tanz,' by Schnitzer, with pianoforte accompaniment, is not published, and has remained, therefore, almost entirely unknown. It was an occasional composition ordered for the Kiesewetter family; the libretto was intended as a sort of sermon pointed at the daughter of the house, Irene (afterwards Madame Prokesch v. Osten), a young lady passionately addicted to dancing, on the possible results of her Terpsichorean mania.[3]

---

[1] 'Der blinde Knabe,' 'Sängers Habe,' 'Im Wald,' 'Auf der Brücke,' &c. Less known are the two grand airs from the play 'Lacrimas.'

[2] Schubert wrote both these marches out of pure love for composing, no one having ordered the pieces in question. Herr Lickl told me that the composer tried at the time in vain to dispose of them at Steiner's or anywhere, whilst other quite inferior works found willing customers.

[3] The poem contains the two following strophes:—

> Es redet und träumet die Jugend so viel
> Von Tänzen, Galoppen, Gelagen,
> Auf einmal erreicht sie ein trügliches Ziel,
> Da hört man sie seufzen und klagen.

Schubert's music (Allegro giusto C major $\frac{4}{8}$), in light tripping measure, with the soprano part embroidered with elaborate roulades, admirably expresses the sense of the poem, and was frequently performed at the time in private circles.

A sonata very recently engraved as a 'relic,' the 'last' sonata for pianoforte in C, deserves, although an unfinished work, to be mentioned, as the first movement is grandly designed, and bears the stamp of a really valuable artistic work.[1]

Lastly, we must mention a pianoforte accompaniment by Schubert for a melodrama, concluding with a finale, half declamatory, half musical. The dramatic poem for which this music was adapted was entitled 'Der Falke.'[2]

In the year we are now reviewing Schubert had the honour, probably unsolicited by him personally, of being elected as 'Ersatzmann' in the representative

---

Bald schmerzet der Hals und bald schmerzet die Brust,
Verschwunden ist alle die himmlische Lust ;
Nur diesmal noch kehr' mir Gesundheit zurück,
So flehet vom Himmel der hoffende Blick.

[1] It was published by Whistling, in Leipsic, and is dated April 1825. The four movements are, Moderato C major $\frac{4}{4}$, Andante A minor $\frac{6}{8}$, Minuetto A major $\frac{3}{4}$, with Trio $\frac{3}{4}$, and a Rondo-fragment Allegro C major $\frac{2}{4}$.

[2] The composer of the poem is Freiherr Adolf v. Pratobevera. Kuno speaks the concluding words before his death. Schubert wrote by request the pianoforte accompaniment, in which form the verses were recited at the scenic representation of the poem.

body of the Musikverein. Nothing is known of what his actual labours were in this capacity.

Late in the summer of 1825, some time before Schubert's return from Upper Austria, Franz Schober, after two years' absence in Prussia, had returned once more to Vienna.

The Schubert alliance, the foundations of which were widely disturbed by his own and Kupelwieser's wandering life, was once more consolidated, and at the end of the following year the composer once more took up his quarters at Schober's.

CHAPTER XIV.

(1826.)

FRANZ IS A CANDIDATE FOR THE POST OF VICE-HOFCAPELLMEISTER—
WEIGL SUCCEEDS—A SCENE IN THE COURT OPERA-HOUSE—SCHUBERT
AND SCHECHNER—ANTON SCHINDLER, FRANZ ZIERER AND JOSEF
HÜTTENBRENNER—LETTERS FROM THE PUBLISHERS PROBST, BREIT-
KOPF, AND HÄRTEL TO SCHUBERT—COMPOSITIONS: 'DIE WINTER-
REISE,' 'DIE NACHTHELLE,' THE STRINGED QUARTETTS IN D MINOR
AND G MAJOR—THE RONDEAU BRILLANT—LETTER OF THANKS FROM
THE COMMITTEE OF THE MUSICAL SOCIETY.

SCHUBERT, since the year 1816, in which he was an un-
successful candidate for the post of musical instructor
in Laibach, took no further steps for securing for himself an independent position by the profits arising from
the sale of his compositions. Josef Hüttenbrenner
affirms that he let the opportunity slip of obtaining the
post of Court organist. It was not before the year
1826 that he felt himself compelled (probably acting on
the advice of well-intentioned friends) to become a candidate for the office of Vicecapellmeister in the Imperial
Hofcapelle at Vienna.

The Emperor Francis, by a resolution of January 8,
1826, and in accordance with a suggestion made on
January 24, 1825, by Count Moriz Dietrichstein, had

nominated the Metropolitan Capellmeister Johann Wittasek, of Prague,[1] to the Vicecapellmeistership at the Imperial Court, although Umlauff[2] had been previously suggested as a candidate. 'He is' (so run the words of the resolution) 'known to me personally as an excellent composer of church music, and also as a good music-master. This is very desirable here just now, especially as Körner, the Court tenor, is beginning to fail.'

As Wittasek did not accept the post, a second scrutiny followed. On December 29, 1826, Count Harrach, at that time Hofmusikgraf, sent the following announcement to Obersthofmeister Prince Trautmannsdorf:—

'After Salieri's death, on May 7, 1825, Eibler became Hofcapellmeister, and the deputyship vacant by Eibler's promotion has not yet been filled up. Count Moriz Dietrichstein, on July 24, 1825, proposed Umlauff, but nothing was decided, and consequently a new scheme is allowed.

[1] Wittasek (Johann Nepomuk August), born 1770, at Horin, in Bohemia, wrote dance-music, Lieder, sonatas, concertos, symphonies, cantatas, and classical music, which were popular even in the years 1805–1810. Failing health and advanced old age made him determined to refuse the proffered dignity. He died at Prague in 1839, as President of the Society for the Improvement of Church Music.

[2] Umlauff (Michael), born at Vienna in 1781, an admirable musician, became Weigl's colleague in the Opera House. Beethoven had a great opinion of him, and he and Shuppanzigh were the chief leaders of the Akademien, founded by Beethoven in the year 1824, when the D Mass and D minor Symphony were first brought before the public.

'The competitors are :—1. Seyfried,[1] Capellmeister in Vienna ; 2. Girowetz,[2] Capellmeister at the Theatre Royal; 3. Franz Schubert, composer ; 4. Conradin Kreutzer;[3] 5. Joachim Hoffmann, artist; 6. Anselm Hüttenbrenner, director of the Styrian Musikverein ; 7.

[1] Seyfried (Ignaz Ritter von), born 1776, at Vienna, a pupil of Mozart's and Kozeluch's on the piano, and of Haydn's in thorough-bass, gave himself up, in the year 1795, entirely to the art of music, in which he developed remarkable energy. His works in dramatic music were written very mainly for the theatre in Vienna, where, from 1797 to 1827, he officiated as Capellmeister and opera director. He made several successful efforts in melodramas. When the actor Carl undertook the management of the theatre, he withdrew, and wrote church and chamber music. He was not in high favour with Beethoven. Seyfried died at Vienna in 1841, and rests in the Währing churchyard.

[2] Girowetz (Adalbert), born 1763, at Budweis, in Bohemia, originally a law student, became subsequently a secretary in the service of the Count Fünfkirchen, at whose castle, in Chlumetz, he wrote his first symphonies and chamber music, which enjoyed great popularity. He travelled in Italy, remained two years in Naples, and afterwards proceeded to Paris and London, where he remained three years, constantly employed as a composer, and very well received. In the year 1804, he became Operncapellmeister at Vienna, and after giving up his lease, retired on a pension. He wrote a great number of works of every sort and kind. Of his operas, those which most pleased were 'Agnes Sorel' and 'Der Augenarzt.' Girowetz died at Vienna in 1850.

[3] Kreutzer, born 1782, at Mösskirch, in the province of Baden, came to Vienna in the year 1804, where he remained up to the year 1811. From 1812 to 1816, he lived at Stuttgart; about the year 1821 he came to Vienna, where (under Barbaja's management) he was elected Hof-theater-Capellmeister, a post he occupied up to 1833. In this year he undertook the post of Capellmeister at the Josefstadt Theatre; in 1840 he left Vienna, went to Cologne, and afterwards as music director to Riga, where he died in 1849. Kreutzer's fertility of musical resource is well known.

Wenzel Würfel;[1] 8. Franz Gläser,[2] Capellmeister at the Josefstädt Theatre.

'These candidates are men of merit, and each and all have more or less claims well worthy considera- tion.'

In detailing these merits in each candidate, it is said in respect of Schubert :—'Schubert appeals to his ser- vices as Court singer, confirmed by a testimonial of Salieri, who taught him composition, and vouches for the fact of his having composed five Masses, which have been given in several churches.'[3]

---

[1] Würfel, born 1791, at Planim, in Bohemia, wrote several pianoforte pieces, and the Operas 'Rübezahl' and 'Der Rothmantel.' He was professor of music at Warsaw about the year 1815. In the year 1824 he came to Vienna, and in 1826 was elected Capellmeister of the Court Theatre.

[2] Gläser, Franz (born 1792), composer of the Operas 'Die Brautschau,' 'Der Bernsteinring,' and 'Des Adlers Horst,' as well as several romances and marches, was elected Capellmeister at the Leopoldstadt Theatre in the year 1826, afterwards went to Berlin, and from thence (1842) to Copenhagen, where he died, as Hofcapellmeister, in 1861.

[3] Up to this period no Mass of Schubert's had been given in the Chapel Royal. Dr. Hauer told me the following story :—'Some time in the year 1827, I was sitting, after an evening's music, with Schubert at the coffee- house "Zum Rebhuhn," sipping confidentially a cheerful glass of "Schwarzen," when my friend said to me : "Not long since I brought Hofcapellmeister Eibler a Mass to be performed by the Imperial choir. On hearing my name, Eibler declared he had never heard a composition of mine of any kind. I certainly am not an over-conceited man, but should have thought that the Hofcapellmeister of Vienna must have already heard something of mine. A few weeks afterwards I came again to enquire after the fate of my bantling, when Eibler said the Mass was

The matter of filling up the appointment was a rapid business. Weigl and Umlauff were the only two proposed. By a resolution of January 22, 1827, the Emperor nominated the Capellmeister of the Hoftheater, Josef Weigl,[1] to whom he is said some time before to have made certain promises respecting the appointment, to the place of Vicehofcapellmeister, at a salary of a thousand gulden, with two hundred in addition for maintenance-money. Thus were Schubert's hopes of laying the foundations of a settled existence and of living in a sphere of congenial activity, without immoderate claims being made on his time and attention, shattered at one blow. On hearing the news, Schubert is reported by Spaun to have said: 'I should have

good, but not composed in the style the Emperor liked. So I took my leave, thinking to myself, ' I am not fortunate enough, then, to be able to write in the Imperial style.'"' That Eibler refused Schubert's Mass (probably that in A-flat) will excite no surprise, as what the Emperor Francis took special delight in was the style of the Reutter Masses ('which contained short and easily performed fugues'). See the letter of Count Moriz Dietrichstein to Count Lichnowsky, of February 23, 1823, on the composition of a Mass of Beethoven's for the Imperial choir, in Schindler's 'Life of Beethoven,' vol. ii. p. 30.

[1] Weigl (Josef), son of Josef Weigl, who had migrated from Bavaria to Vienna (first violoncello of the Italian Opera, and member of the Imperial band), was born in 1766, at Eisenstadt, in Hungary. He wrote a great number of operas, operettas, cantatas, oratorios, sacred music for the church, ballet music, Landwehrlieder, &c. Of his operas, 'Das Waisenhaus' and 'Die Schweizerfamilie' are the best known. The last of these was given in March 1809, for the first time, in Vienna. In 1790 or 1791 Weigl had succeeded Salieri as Hoftheater-Capellme:ster He died at Vienna in February 1846.

much liked to receive that appointment, but I must feel satisfied in its having been bestowed upon so worthy a man as Weigl.'

These words will prove that Schubert had either changed his opinion respecting Weigl, whom in the year 1819 (rightly or wrongly we cannot here stop to examine) he had suspected of intriguing against him, or, assuming his reasons for this suspicion to have been well grounded, had, in his good-natured way, determined to forget the whole matter.

A. Schindler gives the following account of another opportunity which was given to Schubert of obtaining a fixed appointment at the Court Opera-House in Vienna :—

' Schubert had the chance, in the year 1826, of extricating himself from embarrassed circumstances by obtaining a very respectable appointment. Owing to the departure of Capellmeister Krebs to Hamburg, the conductorship at the Kärnthnerthor Theatre became vacant, and Schubert's friends (Vogl being in the very front rank) took all possible pains to get Schubert elected. The young composer succeeded also in attracting the attention of Duport, the official manager; his actual appointment, however, was to be made dependent on a trial of his qualifications in setting to music some operatic scenes put together and composed for the purpose. This task he accomplished, and the chief part was intended for Schechner.[1] Whilst attending to pianoforte rehearsals, the lady called Schubert's attention to the impracticable nature of the chief air for the soprano, and begged him, by curtailments and simplifying the accompaniments, to make some alteration in his music—a request pointedly refused by Schubert. At the first orchestral rehearsal it became evident that the singer could not get through the air already mentioned, and Schubert was entreated by his friends and acquaintance to make some alterations. To no purpose. He adhered to his first refusal. Then came the general rehearsal, and all went very prosperously until the air, the chief feature of which was an outburst of passion. It turned out as people expected. The singer, in a continual struggle with the orchestra, especially with the wind instruments, was absolutely overpowered by the mass of sound crashing down on her colossal voice.

---

[1] Schechner (Nanette), born at Munich in the year 1806, was one of the finest singers in Germany. As a pupil of Weber, the actor, she became a member of the chorus of the Italian Opera at Munich, and there found an opportunity in Cimarosa's Opera 'Orazj e Curiazj,' of taking the part of Curiazio, in place of the famous Grassini. Her success was brilliant, and her reputation was founded on this performance. For some time she sang in Italian opera, but afterwards took to singing in German, and, in 1825, came to Vienna, where she was a great favourite. In 1827 she went to Berlin, where she triumphed in the close company of such a singer as Sonntag. Repeated attacks on the chest induced her, in the year 1835, to leave the stage. Since the year 1832, when she became the wife of the gallery-inspector and painter Waagen, at Munich, she passed the rest of her days at that city in retirement, and died on April 30, 1860.

She sank exhausted on a chair standing at the side of the proscenium. There was a deep silence throughout the house, and consternation on every face. Whilst this was going on, Duport, the manager, was seen advancing now to one group, now to another, as they came on the stage, or talking mysteriously to the prima donna or the Capellmeisters who were present. As for Schubert, he sat, during a scene painful to every one who witnessed it, like a marble figure, fixed to his chair, with his eyes riveted upon the pages of the score lying open before him. At last, after a long pause, Duport stepped in front of the orchestra, and said, in a very polite tone : " Herr Schubert, we should like to put off the performance for some days; and I must ask you to make the necessary alterations in the scena, at all events, and to make it an easier matter for Fräulein Schechner." Several of the players in the orchestra now exhorted Schubert to give way. Schubert's wrath, after he had listened to Duport's speech, only grew more intense, and calling out at the top of his voice, " I alter nothing !" he shut up the score with a bang, put it under his arm, and walked off as fast as he could home. There was an end to all hope of his appointment.'

This is Anton Schindler's account ; but the credibility of his testimony on many other points has frequently been shaken, and here we have him with a solitary episode out of Schubert's life, which it is difficult to harmonise with the honest good-tempered manner of our composer. It must also be remarked, in common truth and justice, that an eye-witness of that rehearsal at the theatre, Franz Zierer (Professor at the Conservatorium at Vienna, and at that time a member of the Court Opera band), allows that Schubert's scena, owing to the abruptness of the intervals, was a matter of great difficulty for Schechner's already failing powers ; and this witness, so far from remembering any such furious and passionate scene as that described by Schindler, asserts, on the contrary, that Schubert, during the rehearsal, behaved in his usual quiet and self-contained manner. Josef Hüttenbrenner, on the other hand, goes so far as to say that the singer expressed herself delighted 'with the wonderfully beautiful air by Schubert,' and that his succeeding to the appointment was wrecked not on the rock of his own obstinacy, but simply that of theatrical intrigue. I have never ascertained whether this scena is still in existence, nor do I know what its peculiar characteristics were. According to Zierer, it was a grand independent vocal scena, with an orchestral accompaniment. But neither the air by Schubert, nor that from Kreutzer's 'Cordelia,' which Schechner substituted for it, have ever been sung in public since that time.

We cannot help thinking that, had Schubert succeeded in obtaining the post, he would not have kept it for any length of time, as he lacked nearly all the requisite qualifications for such a duty; and his restless creative spirit would have rather hindered than helped him in the fitting discharge of the duties incidental to his office.[1] If one would think of Schubert as connected with any settled habits of official life, it can only be in his capacity of Court organist, a post for which he was perfectly fitted, and which, sooner or later, would have paved the way for him to a Deputy Court-Capell-meistership, which duty he might also have discharged with ease and comfort to himself. The longing for perfect independence (according to Josef Hüttenbren-ner) led him to reject the chance that was held out to him; and when at last the wish awoke within him, of procuring a certain means of livelihood by the accept-ance of office, so as not exclusively to depend on the somewhat precarious sale of his compositions, then cir-cumstances had changed to his prejudice, and he was, this time against his will, restored to his former liberty.

As regards the precarious sale of his compositions just mentioned, the business letters of several music publishers of the years 1826, 1827, and 1828 (which are published here in chronological order) show that Schubert at that time opened communications with

---

[1] There has been something said of Schubert's having performed the office of 'Correpetitor' for two days at the Court Opera-House. This office he was absolutely unsuited for. Zierer is further of opinion that Schu-bert never at any time stood for the office of Capellmeister or that of 'Correpetitor.' Even Dr. Leopold Sonnleithner, with all his familiarity with Schubert's history, can give us no information on this point.

foreign publishers, and that Schott in Mayence and
Probst in Leipsic were amongst the foremost firms to
interest themselves in his works. But throughout almost the entire correspondence of the composer with
the publishers that I have met with there is interwoven
a chain of petitions to Schubert, importuning him more
or less urgently to write pieces offering no inordinate
difficulties to the performer, and not to tax in an
overstrained way the musical capacities of his hearers.

The following letter of the music-publisher Probst
(dated Leipsic, August 26, 1826) is in this respect
highly characteristic. It runs thus:—

' I thought myself much honoured, and fortunate also,
in becoming acquainted with you through your esteemed
favour of the 12th inst., and in thanking you heartily
for your confidence, I most cheerfully offer my best
services towards helping on, as best I can, the spread of
your artistic reputation. Only I must candidly confess
to you, that your often genial, but at the same time
occasionally eccentric efforts, are not as yet sufficiently
and universally understood by our public. In the
selection, therefore, and delivery of your manuscript
works, pray be good enough to take great care. Some
carefully selected Lieder, some pianoforte works for two
and four hands, not too difficult, and written in an un-
derstandable fashion, would, I think, answer your purpose
and my wishes. When once the ice is broken, all will

go well and easily; at the outset we must, to some extent, humour the public. Please send your manuscripts to be forwarded to me by Herr Lähne, book-keeper for Artaria & Company. Receive the assurance of my distinguished consideration.

'Your obedient servant,

'H. A. PROBST.'

The following letter from Breitkopf & Härtel, dated Leipsic, September 7, 1826, is characterised by a studied reserve and cautious language:—

'For your kindly expressed wish that we should undertake the publication of some of your compositions, we feel most grateful, and assure you it would be very agreeable to us to establish cordial and mutual relations with you as between author and publisher. But not being as yet acquainted with the marketable success of your compositions, and unable, in consequence, to make any definite pecuniary offer to yourself (a matter only to be settled or approved of by a publisher after a success has been established), we must leave it to you whether, in order possibly to found a lasting connection between us, you will facilitate matters, and for the first work or the first works you purpose sending us you will be content to receive in return a certain number of copies after they have been struck off. We do not doubt of your consent to this arrangement, as you, like ourselves, will attach more value to the introduction of a permanent connection than the publication of any particular work. Assuming we have judged correctly, we propose that you should first of all send us one or two pieces for the pianoforte, either solo pieces or for four hands. Should our hopes of success be realised, so that we should be able for your following works to offer a regular money payment, it will give us great pleasure to form a connection so acceptable to both parties concerned.

' Your most obedient servants,

' BREITKOPF & HÄRTEL.'

A number of chamber compositions and vocal pieces, solo and concerted, which were written at this time, speak eloquently for Schubert's unceasing energy. Of his well-known vocal compositions referable to this period, including also the following Lieder, ' Ueber Wildemann,' ' Ständchen,' ' Trinklied ' [1] (out of Shakspeare's ' Antony and Cleopatra '), we must point to the first part of the ' Winterreise,' and of concerted vocal

[1] ' Ständchen ' and ' Trinklied ' are thus marked in Schubert's handwriting:—' Composed at Währing, July 1826.' Herr Franz Doppler (of the musical firm of Spina) told me the following story in connection with the 'Ständchen:'—' One Sunday, during the summer of 1826, Schubert, with several friends (Doppler amongst the number), was returning from Pötzleinsdorf to the city, and, on strolling along through Währing, he saw his friend Tieze sitting at a table in the garden of the " Zum Biersack." The whole party determined on a halt in their journey. Tieze had a book lying open before him, and Schubert soon began to

music to ' Nachthelle,'[1] and the quartett for male voices,
' Grab und Mond ' (in the collection entitled ' Die

turn over the leaves. Suddenly he stopped, and pointing to a poem,
exclaimed, "Such a delicious melody has just come into my head, if I
but had a sheet of music-paper with me!" Herr Doppler drew a
few music-lines on the back of a bill-of-fare, and in the midst of a
genuine Sunday hubbub, with fiddlers, skittle-players, and waiters
running about in different directions with orders, Schubert wrote that
lovely song.'

[1] One of Schubert's most picturesque and poetical works was given at
one of the Thursday concerts of the Musikverein, on January 25, 1827.
By way of invitation to this performance, Schubert received from his
friend Ferdinand Walcher (at that time Archducal Hofrath in Vienna)
the following letter, in my possession :—

'Cre - do   in   u - num   De - um.

'You don't believe me, I know, but you will, nevertheless, when I tell
you that Tieze, this very evening, will sing your "Nachthelle," * to which
N. Fröhlich invites you with the three enclosed tickets, which I have the
honour of transmitting to you, because of the deep snow which lies on
the road to the jolly "Plunzen."   Your affectionate well-wisher,

'WALCHER.

' Vienna, January 27, 1827.
' Vidi Julimauser of Freiburg.'

---

* '"Nachthelle" does not mean here somnambulism, clairvoyance,
slept-off debauchery, &c., but a poem by Seidl, music by Schubert,
for an infernally high tenor, with chorus, for which I am engaged as a
second tenor, and for which I have ordered a magnificent F from the
baker at Baden, who is said to make the best.

' N.B.—Don't forget Kleile, and to-morrow you might with ease get to
Kiesewetter.'

(The 'Zur Plunzen' was originally Bogner's Café, in the Singergasse;
' Julimauser ' is Jenger.)

Minnesänger'). In the province of classical chamber music, Schubert, by his two stringed quartetts, written at this time, proved most convincingly his right and title to a place in the foremost rank of chief musicians.

These are the stringed quartetts in D minor and G major, delicate and refined compositions of the true Schubert stamp, containing a wealth of charming melodies, and breathing that spirit of romance which greets us in almost all of the more important creations of this master's genius. If he was urged to make this effort by a circle of musical friends,[1] it is admitted on the other hand—and several declarations made by him (such as the letter to L. Kupelwieser, of the year 1824) all point to the same conclusion—that he had spontaneously set himself the task of proving his increasing earnestness and advanced powers as a writer in this particular branch of his art.

In truth, both these stringed quartetts are far in advance of works of a similar class which preceded

---

[1] These were the brothers Carl and Franz Hacker (violin and viola); the first died in the year 1830, the last Oberlandesgerichtsrath at Vienna, Franz Hauer (at that time Surgeon to the Factory 'in the Oed'), and Bauer, the violoncello-player at the Hofoperntheater. Of these two quartetts only that in D minor was performed in public. At Hacker's lodgings (Schönlaterngasse, No. 673), it was given under the direction of Schubert himself, who made the alterations and curtailments he judged necessary on the freshly copied parts. Randhartinger and Holzapfel were both present on the first occasion, on January 29, 1826; some days afterwards it was rehearsed again, and played as a new work on February 1, at the house of Hofcapellsänger Josef Barth.

them, and for intrinsic artistic worth the stringed quartett in C, composed later (in the year 1828), is the only thing that can be compared with them. With what successful ease our master accomplished his task, we may judge from the short interval which elapsed from the time he began and finished his G Quartett. Within ten days, Schubert, the musical magician, had conjured up one of his most beautiful compositions. The Rondeau brillant in B minor (Op 70), certainly the most valuable of all the duetts Schubert wrote for the pianoforte and violin, belongs to this period.[1]

At the end of this year, Schubert had the satisfaction of receiving a congratulatory address with a present of a hundred gulden (Viennese currency) from the committee of the Amateur Society, ' for the repeated proofs he had given of his interest in the prosperity of the Institute.'

The address was thus worded :—

' You have given the Society of Amateurs of the Imperial city repeated proofs of your sympathy and the interest you take in its welfare, and devoted your

---

[1] The Rondeau was published by the firm of Artaria in Vienna; the autograph copy was in their hands until it passed into those of Herr Balsch, a Russian nobleman. Slawik, the violinist from Prague, played the duett with Herr Bocklet at a party given by Artaria, and Schubert was present. But this violin-player à la Paganini neither succeeded with this piece nor with the Fantasia (Op. 159), which he performed at the Redoutensaal in the year 1828. He played brilliantly, but lacked purity of tone.

distinguished talents as a composer to the benefit of
this Institution, and you also have been a special bene-
factor to the Conservatorium. The Society, capable of
appreciating the full value of your remarkable powers
as a composer, wishes to convey to you some appropriate token of its gratitude and esteem, and begs
your acceptance of the enclosed present, not as a payment, but an acknowledgment on the part of the
Society of the obligations it is under to you, for the
zeal and interest you have taken in its welfare.

'From the leading Committee for the Amateur Society of the Austrian Kaiserstaat.

'KIESEWETTER, *manu propriâ.*

'Vienna: Oct. 12, 1826.'

Amongst the 'proofs of sympathy' here alluded to
must be meant two vocal concerted pieces which Schubert, in the years 1820–1822, at the request of Frln.
Josefine Fröhlich, had written for the pupils of the
Conservatorium, and which were at that time frequently
performed at the evening musical soirées.

In gratitude for the homage thus paid him by the
Musikverein, Franz presented that body, in the year
1828, with his Grand Symphony in C, which, however,
was rejected by the orchestral players of the Society at
that time as being impracticable.

CHAPTER XV.

(1827.)

THE PACHLER FAMILY IN GRATZ—CORRESPONDENCE OF JENGER AND
SCHUBERT WITH MARIE PACHLER—JENGER AND SCHUBERT VISIT
GRATZ--THE RETURN HOME—JENGER'S AND SCHUBERT'S LETTERS TO
MARIE AND FAUST PACHLER—COMPOSITIONS: DANCE MUSIC; SONGS,
THE 'ALT-SCHOTTISCHE BALLADE,' PART-SONG, THE SECOND PART
OF THE 'WINTERREISE,' THE B-FLAT TRIO, 'DEUTSCHE MESSE'—
LETTERS FROM PROBST AND RUCHLITZ TO SCHUBERT.

WE have already stated that Schubert's travelling excursions were limited to two into Hungary (1818 and
1824), and two others to Upper Austria (1819 and
1825). These must be supplemented by a journey to
Gratz in the year 1827, when he and Jenger were most
hospitably received in the house of Dr. Carl Pachler.

The family of Pachler, whose name we first came
across in our observations on the Opera of ' Alfonso
und Estrella,' and which now comes suddenly to the
front, as marking an episode illustrative of Schubert's
closing career, consisted of the master of the house,
the lady, and one son, Faust, who at the time of Schubert's visit was in his eighth year.[1]

---

[1] For an account of Schubert's connection with the Pachlers I am indebted to the kindness of Herr Dr. Faust Pachler, ' Scriptor ' in the
Imperial Library, Vienna.

Carl Pachler was the youngest son of a brewer, whose family, having migrated from the Tyrol to Styria, had taken up their permanent residence there. After the death of his mother, who had carried on as a widow the joint business of a brewery and an hotel, Carl came into the property; but his duties in Gratz and elsewhere as an advocate fully occupying his time, he let the business to a managing agent. In his capacity as citizen 'Braumeister,' he had the honour of being elected First Colonel of the local Volunteer Corps, the resuscitation of which regiment had been owing to his personal intercession with the Emperor of Austria.

In the year 1816 (he was then in his twenty-sixth year), he married Marie Leopoldine Koschak, daughter of Dr. Adalbert Koschak, of Gratz, a man well known for his love of music and society. Marie Pachler was, by the universal consent of all who knew her, a lady remarkable for beauty and various accomplishments, and notably for her musical gifts. As early as her ninth year she had tried her hand at composition, and played Beethoven's sonatas with wonderful intelligence, vouched for by Beethoven himself, who made her acquaintance at Vienna in 1817. She received her earliest education under her parents' roof, and Julius Schneller, at that time Professor of History in Gratz, seems to have been very influential in developing her intellectual capacities.[1] This gentleman seems to have

---

[1] Professor Schneller, prosecuted by the 'Censursbehörde,' left Gratz

contrived to bring his pupil and Beethoven together. In the year 1827, Beethoven was expected as a visitor to the Pachlers: his death, which happened in the March of that year, destroyed that hope, and thence it happened that Franz Schubert came in his stead, accompanied by his friend Jenger, who had intended to join Beethoven in a similar capacity.[1]

Dr. Pachler's popularity, the intellectual refinement and musical accomplishments of his wife, who from childhood had only been prevented by force of circumstances from following art as a profession, made the house not only the scene of constant hospitalities, but a rallying-point for nearly every person of note who might happen to be either staying at Gratz or passing through the place. The famous singers and actors, during their ' starring' times, used to visit there; Schubert, Teltscher, and Schönstein lived there, and everyone who went away recommended some new comer to replace him. The poet Gottfried Ritter v. Leitner,

---

in the year 1823, and went to Freiburg in Breisgau, where he died as Professor of Philosophy in the year 1834.

[1] In 1825, when Jenger was removed from his official post at Gratz to Vienna, Madame Pachler sent him (favoured by Strasser) a letter of introduction to Beethoven, and by Rettich, the actor (an intimate friend of the Pachler family), a second letter, which Jenger, in November 1826, delivered to Beethoven. Jenger wrote thereupon to Madame Pachler, that Beethoven had spoken with delight of her musical gifts, and added, it would be the better plan for him to visit her at Gratz than to meet her in Upper Austria at her brother's place. He hoped, he said, he should visit her at Gratz.

who had been introduced to the family in the year 1825, belonged to this select circle, and such of his poems as Schubert set to music in the years 1827 and 1828 were adapted by the composer upon the recommendation of Madame Marie Pachler.

Of such materials was the family composed, in the midst of which Schubert passed a number of happy days only a short time before his death ; and so attractive had his sojourn among the Pachlers been to him, that he calculated on the possibility of repeating his visit the very next year.[1] He and Jenger were expected at Gratz in the summer of 1826, but they never came. In the autumn of 1827, both, however, realised their friends' wishes.

A journey to the capital of Styria was in those days no trifling matter; but all sorts of unforeseen difficulties acted as obstacles to Jenger and Schubert, for the first had official duties thrust on him, and the ' pecuniary horizon ' of the latter was in a chronic state of gloom. It took a whole year, as we gather from the following correspondence, to make up their minds and resolve on action.

In a letter dated August 1, 1826, and written to

---

[1] Dr. Faust Pachler, a son of Dr. Carl Pachler, is still living. The latter died in the year 1850, aged sixty, and his wife, Marie P., five years later, at the age of sixty-one. Leitner, originally Secretary 'bei den steirischen Ständen,' afterwards retired on a pension, and now lives in complete retirement at Gratz. Anselm Hüttenbrenner has also taken up his permanent residence at Gratz.

Marie Pachler, Jenger laments he cannot get away
from Vienna, adding: 'I may possibly leave in the autumn; but if not, our friend Schubert at all events,
and the painter Teltscher, will, my dear madam, put
in an appearance.' Schubert, however, never came, and
Jenger held out fair hopes and promises for the next
year. In a letter of December 29, 1826, he writes:—
'Friend Schubert has determined on travelling next
year to Gratz; but if I don't accompany him, the plan
is sure to fall through—as it has this year.'

On January 12, 1827, he writes again to Madame
Pachler:—'Schubert, without knowing you, gracious
lady, sends you every assurance of his devotion, and is
delighted to make the acquaintance of so earnest a
worshipper of Beethoven. God grant that our unani-
mous wish to come to Gratz this year be fulfilled.'

And on May 25:—'The best plan, I think, would be
to set out for Gratz at the beginning of the month of
September. I am sure to bring Schubert with me,
and also a second friend, Teltscher, the lithographer.'

On June 12, Schubert himself began a correspondence with the following letter:—

'Most gracious Lady,—Although I am at a loss to
account for my deserving at your hands the friendly
invitation forwarded me in a letter sent to Jenger,
and without ever supposing it will be in my power to
make any kind of return for your kindness, yet I
cannot but accept an invitation which will not only

enable me at last to see Gratz, the praises of which place have become so familiar to me, but also to have the honour of becoming personally acquainted with you. I remain, with every sentiment of respect,

‘Your most obedient servant,

‘FRANZ SCHUBERT.’

On June 16, Jenger wrote again, in answer to a letter of Madame Pachler, of the 7th of the same month :—

‘Our friend Schubert was completely charmed with your kind invitation, and the enclosed note from him contains his expressions of gratitude, and a promise to avail himself of this kind invitation.[1] We are eagerly looking forward to our excursion to dear Styria, and I hope, gracious lady, that you will be pleased with my travelling-companion. We will once again live on music, and Schubert shall intertwine with our musical gar-lands many a new and dainty Liedchen. Our friend Dr. Carl, too, is bound in every way to be satisfied with us. We shall provide the best of beer and wine for any-one that comes.’

The wish of the two friends was soon about to be realised. On August 30, 1827, Jenger announced to the wife of Dr. Pachler the intended journey in the following words :—

‘Next Sunday, September 2, my friend Schubert and

---

[1] Schubert's letter of the 12th of June.

I start by the Eilwagon at 9.30 P.M., and hope by the favour of God to be with you at Gratz on Monday evening at nine o'clock. We are already eagerly reckoning on our pleasurable visit.'

The Pachler family were on the *qui vive* on Schubert's account, and Faust, at that time a little boy of seven years old, was all excitement and expectation, and begged hard, when bed-time came, to be kept up to see the arrival of both the guests. He was not allowed, however, to make his bow to the travellers until next morning at breakfast, when Schubert (whose portrait had been shown to the child previously) appeared in a green coat and white pantaloons.

The visit at Gratz was enlivened by delightful music and frequent excursions amongst the beautiful scenes in the neighbourhood. The Pachlers, at that time, did not invariably live in the country, and excursions from the city were often organised—to Wildbach, for instance, a small estate belonging to a widow lady, Mme. Massegg, Dr. Carl Pachler's aunt, and mother of six blooming grown-up daughters, to Hallerschlössel again, on the ‘ Ruckerlberg,’ a favourite halting-place of the Pachlers; and Jenger and Anselm Hüttenbrenner, as well as Schubert, used to join them on these occasions.[1] With regard to these picnics and excursions, where mirth and

---

[1] The place where the ‘Hallerschlössel’ is situated is called Sparbersbach; the ‘Schlössel’ was at that time (1827) tenanted by friends of the Pachler family.

good humour and the society of pretty women were the order of the day, nothing further need be said than that upon every occasion a good deal of wine was consumed, and that neither Jenger nor Schubert could be called bad hands at that part of the ceremonies.[1] Indoors there was no lack of musical entertainment, the costs of which were almost exclusively defrayed by the two guests of the Pachler family, for Schubert (in the absence of any singer) sang his own Lieder (amongst others the 'Wanderer an den Mond'), and played pianoforte duetts with Jenger.

The cheerful, happy visit to Gratz continued until the last week in September; for on the 27th of that month we find Jenger writing from Vienna to his hospitable and esteemed hostess in Styria thus :—

'By the happy Styrian, Josef Hüttenbrenner, starting to-morrow morning from this place to Gratz, we—

---

[1] As a souvenir of the visit to Wildbach, we find a sketch on a stable-door, a portrait of Schubert himself. This possibly may have been his own production, or he may have sent it afterwards. On these excursions the three friends, Schubert, Jenger, and A. Hüttenbrenner, travelled in one carriage, the Pachlers in another. When the party met at Sparbersbach, they were joined by a pretty young widow, to whose charms Jenger (and very likely Schubert also) was not insensible. The following play-bill shows pretty plainly that matters had gone as far as prostration and tumbling down on the knee—perhaps to entreat a kiss from the fair widow. The title of the piece is ' Der Fussfall im Haller-schlössel, oder Zwilchen's mi nit so ! ' Characters: Harengos (Dr. Haring, owner of the Hallerschlössel), Pachleros (Dr. Carl Pachler), Schwammerl (nickname for the fat Schubert), Schilcherl (A. Hüttenbrenner, so called from his passion for the ' Schilcher wine ').

friend Schwammerl and I—beg to convey to you, most
excellent and dear lady, and to Dr. Carl also, our sincere
and hearty thanks for all the kindness and goodness
you showed us. We can never forget that kindness,
—it is unlikely we should, for Schubert and I seldom
have passed such happy days as we did in dear Gratz
and the country near it, and notably at Wildbach,
amongst the dear good people there. I can't say, in
my own case, matters are very cheerful here as yet,
seeing that I must pull away like a galley-slave; and
yet I cannot get on or make any way. Compared with
the twenty days just passed, it is scarcely bearable; and
yet, I suppose, all will come right again. A short account of our return home, dear lady, might possibly
have some small interest for you, so I begin at Fürstenfeld, for friend Karrer will be sure to have told you
that the parting from our good friends was a somewhat
melancholy business, and that the skies themselves
seemed to sympathise with our woe.'

A description is then given in the letter of their
journey home, which we here briefly glance at.

At Fürstenfeld, Wittmann the Bürgermeisterin received the travellers; on September 21 they visited the
Calvarienberg, drove back after taking their dinner, and
arrived at eight o'clock at Hartberg, where they passed
the night under the roof of Zschok, the district judge.
On the 22nd, at the early hour of 5 A.M., they set out

again on their journey, breakfasted at the Pinga, crossed
the mountain, which is one of the Styrian boundaries,
and from the summit of which they waved their caps,
and shouted adieus and cheers for all their dear good
friends in Styria, and drove past Aspang, Pitten, Wal-
bersbach, Sebenstein, to Schleinz, where they passed
the night and the following Sunday very agreeably, at
the house of a merchant of the name of Stehmann.
On the following Monday, accompanied by their host
and two other friends, they continued their homeward
journey to Vienna. There they arrived at ten o'clock
in the evening, and parted company under the ' Tuchlauben,' in front of Schubert's lodgings, at the ' Blauer
Igel,' with the determination to send letters describing
their doings to their dear friends in Gratz.

Schubert accordingly supplemented Jenger's letter
to Madame Pachler with a few lines to her husband,
which cannot be said to be complimentary to the society
at Vienna :—

' Honoured Sir,—I begin to find out already that I was
far too happy and comfortable in Gratz, and that Vienna
and I don't exactly suit one another. Certainly it is
rather big, but on that account empty of all heart, sincerity, candour, genuine thoughts, and feelings, rational
talk, and utterly lacking in intellectual achievements.
One cannot ascertain exactly whether people are clever
or stupid, there's such a deal of petty, poor gossip—real
cheerfulness one seldom if ever comes across. It is very

possible, no doubt, that I have myself to blame, being so very slow in the art of thawing. In Gratz I soon learned to appreciate the absence of all artifice and conventional ways; had I stayed longer, I should of course have been more profoundly penetrated with the happiness of such perfect freedom from all constraint. Coming to particulars, I shall never forget the happy time passed with your dear wife, the sturdy Pachleros, and the small Faust. Those were the happiest days I have passed for a long time. In the hope of my being able some day to express my gratitude in a fitting manner, I remain, with the greatest respect, yours most obediently,   FRANZ SCHUBERT.

'N.B.—I hope to be able to send the libretto in a few days.'[1]

The day before Schubert set off from Gratz, Madame Pachler wrote a letter to Jenger, which he found at Vienna, and in which she asked him to prevail on Schubert to write a pianoforte duett, to be played by herself and the small Faust, on the anniversary of her husband's birthday and nameday.[2]

Schubert accordingly composed a small march with trio,[3] and sent the composition, accompanied by the following letter, to Madame Pachler :—

---

[1] Doubtless that of 'Alfonso und Estrella.'

[2] She had already spoken to Schubert on the subject, and the purport of this letter was merely to remind him of his promise.

[3] Josef v. Spaun, of Vienna, has a copy of this music.

'Herewith I forward the four-hand piece for the small Faust. I'm afraid it will not meet with your approval, as I don't feel myself particularly well qualified for writing things in this style. I hope you are both in a better state of health than I am ; the pains in my head, a common disorder with me, have returned. Pray congratulate Dr. Carl very heartily from me on his fête-day, and let him know that I have not been able as yet to get back from that lazy fellow, Gottdank, my libretto, which I let him have to read through months and months ago. I remain, with great respect,

'Your most obedient

'FRANZ SCHUBERT.

Vienna: October 12, 1827.'

At the same time Jenger wrote thus to Faust Pachler :—

'Dear little Friend,—You will see by this letter how carefully I have executed the commission you gave me. Therefore study it zealously, and think on the 4th day of next month of friend Schwammerl and me. Say everything pretty you can think of for us to your dear father on his nameday. We intend to be with you in spirit on that anniversary. Write to me soon again. Your letter has pleased me greatly; but I only received it on the 10th of this month through our friend Gometz.'[1]

[1] Gometz, like Jenger, had a military appointment in Gratz, and afterwards came to Vienna as 'Hofkriegsrath;' he is still acting

Schubert marked his visit to Styria by writing a
deal of dance music, which was engraved with the titles
'Grätzer Galoppe' and 'Grätzer Wälzer.' The 'Valses
nobles' and 'Originaltänze' also belong to this time;[1]
the Lied 'Heimliches Lieben' and the 'Old Scottish
Ballad,' by Herder, were both (at the suggestion of the
lady of the house) written whilst Schubert was staying
with the Pachlers. The Lieder 'Im Wald' and 'Auf
der Bruck' were first published in Gratz,[2] and the songs,
'Das Weinen,' and 'Vor meiner Wiege,' by Leitner,
'Heimliches Lieben,' and 'Silvia,' were dedicated to the
lady he so highly esteemed, Madame Marie Pachler.[3]
Madame Pachler was extremely pleased with the 'Old
Scottish Ballad' of Herder, and Jenger was obliged
to have a copy made for her. The ballad—a duett between mother and son—is treated in the strophe form;

officially. Madame Pachler, fearing Schubert would forget his promised
composition, probably made her little Faust write a begging letter.
Schubert wrote the small piece between the 10th and 12th of October.

[1] The 'Grätzer Tänze' and 'Valses nobles,' with other music of a
similar class, were published by Haslinger & Diabelli.

[2] They were lithographed and printed by J. Franz Kaiser, in Gratz,
and published at the same place by Kienreich, to whom Schubert seems
to have presented the music as a compliment. Both the Lieder had
been written originally in the year 1825; they were published by Haslinger in the year 1828.

[3] 'Heimliches Lieben' is not, as the ordinary printed catalogue
affirms, by Leitner, but was one of a number of miscellaneous poems
sent to Madame Pachler by a friend of the family. The Pachlers delighted in Leitner's poetry, and the lady of the house lost no opportunity of calling Schubert's attention to the poem. On October 26, 1827,

although not a lengthy work, it is full of character, and of the genuine Schubert stamp.[1]

Other Lieder of this time have an importance of their own, and have been popular for a long time. Of concerted vocal music we may instance the comic trio, 'Der Hochzeitsbraten,' 'Schlachtgesang,' by Klopstock, for double chorus;[2] the 'Ständchen,' by Grillparzer, 'Nachtgesang im Wald,'[3] and an Italian Cantata in

Jenger wrote to her thus :—'I received this morning early a few lines from you with the small parcel which I gave at once to friend Schwammerl, and here you have his acknowledgment of the receipt.' The packet contained probably the first edition of Leitner's poems. In the following year the dedication business was arranged. Irene Kiesewetter undertook on the occasion to represent Madame Pachler. The latter seems to have delayed her consent to the acceptance of the honour, and Schubert, either indignant at the delay or from carelessness, neglected to send a copy with the dedication to Gratz, so that Madame Pachler was obliged to buy the copy at the ordinary price. Schubert inserted 'Silvia' in the series (Op. 106) in place of the 'Ballade,' which he thought too gloomy in character.

[1] The 'Ballade' appeared at Gratz separately engraved, for Schubert was unwilling to associate so melancholy a work with the other songs he had dedicated to Madame Pachler. Herr v. Spina has the manuscript, and Freiherr v. Spaun a copy, in which, however, the prelude of five bars is omitted, and in the mother's song there is a slight alteration, probably one of Vogl's 'improvements.' The ballad, a short time ago, was published by Spina as No. 5 of the 'Liederkranz.' C. Loewe has set the same much-belaboured poem.

[2] Herr Spina has the manuscript. In the year 1829 Franz Roser introduced this trio with an instrumental accompaniment at a dramatic performance in the Josefstadt Theatre.

[3] This beautiful chorus was given for the first time in public on May 3, 1827, at a concert given by Herr Lewy, and with much applause. The rehearsals were held at Dornbach.

honour of Fräulein Irene K.,[1] for a quartett of male
voices with an accompaniment for two pianos.[2]

In the October of this year, and therefore immediately after his return home, Franz finished his
mournful 'Winterreise'[3]—a curious contrast to the
cheerful pictures with which he had stored his mind
before returning home from the Styrian mountains,
but one of those significant facts which serve to
characterise in a striking manner Schubert's creative
powers as entirely dissociated from contact with the
outer world.

In the following month was written the Trio in E-
flat, a work which added considerably to his fame in the
department of classical chamber music, and one fitted
to take rank amongst works of a similar class by the
greatest masters. The Trio in E-flat, like that in B-flat,

[1] Doubtless Irene Kiesewetter, afterwards Madame Prokesch v. Osten.
The cantata, judging by the text, is an occasional composition in the
form of a congratulatory ode on the restored health of the lady, and it
was probably written for Italian singers. Famous Italian singers,
Lablache for instance, used to visit there, and Herr Bocklet once improvised there on a subject given him by Lablache. Schubert was known
to the family, and received invitations to the musical entertainments.

[2] The composition begins in C major ¾. The men's chorus, concluding with the words—

> Evviva dunque la bella Irene,
> La delizia del nostro amor,

precedes a full chorus for mixed voices. The cantata is not yet printed.
Frh. v. Spaun has a copy.

[3] Beginning with 'Die Krähe,' and including the cycle of the last ten
Lieder.

its earlier predecessor, is one of the few instrumental compositions by Schubert which, during the master's lifetime, was given with distinguished applause at private parties, and at public concerts also, by musicians who were enthusiastic worshippers of Schubert's genius.[1]

But Schubert's activity during this period was by no means exhausted, for church and pianoforte music came in for their share of attention. He wrote the 'Deutsche Messe' to words for a chorus, with organ or instrumental accompaniment,[2] compiled by Professor Johann Filipp Neumann (writer of the Opera 'Sakuntala'), and, as an opening movement, the 'Lord's Prayer,' for general chorus and instrumental accompaniment. These sacred compositions are melodious, and conspicuous for a grave simplicity. With respect to chamber music, he wrote

[1] The MS. of the E-flat Trio is now in the possession of the Countess Rosa v. Almasy, in Vienna. It was bequeathed to her by the Countess Folliot v. Crenneville (*née* Countess Esterhazy), her aunt, and formerly a pupil of Schubert's. The two trios used to be played by Carl Maria v. Bocklet (piano), Schuppanzigh (violin), and Linke (cello). On one of these occasions (at the Spauns') Bocklet seized Schubert's hand and kissed it, calling out to the party present, that they knew not what a treasure they possessed in Schubert.

[2] The hautboy, clarionet, horn, trumpet, and organ, or double-bass are employed. The Mass consists of an introit, gloria, credo, offertorium, sanctus, post offertorium, Agnus Dei, and final chorus. The accompaniment of the Lord's Prayer is the same as that of the Mass. A copy of this sacred work is in the possession of Josef v. Spaun. Schubert wrote this Mass for the audience of the Polytechnic in Vienna; it is sometimes given by men's voices with an organ accompaniment Ferdinand Schubert arranged from it a series of three-part sacred songs for the use of the 'Normalschüler.'

the pianoforte pieces styled by the publishers 'Impromptus (III.–VIII., Op. 142),' and two occasional pieces.[1]

We must here insert two letters bearing on musical matters, and written to Schubert in the year we are now considering. The first of these, a business letter, and nothing more, is from H. A. Probst, the music publisher, at Leipsic, and bears date January 15. Schubert had sent him some manuscripts to be disposed of. The second, dated November 7, is from Hofrath Friedrich Rochlitz, a sincere admirer of Schubert's, whose services as a composer he was anxious to secure for the illustration of his own poems. Probst's letter, declining Schubert's offers, runs thus:—

'I have only lately received your manuscripts by Artaria & Co. Much pleasure as I should have felt in inserting your name in my catalogue, I am compelled, for the present, to deny myself that gratification, as I am overloaded with work by my publication of Kalkbrenner's "Œuvres Complets." And I must confess that the sum of 80 florins for each work seemed to me a rather stiff price. I merely keep the works, awaiting your order for their disposal, and am, with the greatest respect,' &c., &c.

---

[1] An Allegretto, dedicated to Herr Ferd. Walcher on his departure, and headed 'Zur Erinnerung,' bearing date April 26. The original copy is with Hofrath Walcher, in Vienna, and the March with Trio (in G) for the little boy Faust, son of Madame Pachler (written in October).

The next letter, from Rochlitz to the Bard of Vienna, is also on the subject of music, but written in an entirely different strain :—

' Respected Sir,—You know the high esteem and regard I feel for you and your works. Herr Haslinger has told you how grateful I am for your settings of my three songs,[1] and how I wish that you should illustrate, by your lovely music, some larger work of mine. I am told you are not disinclined to do so. Permit me, then, to approach the subject at once. The poem I have in my mind's eye is " Der erste Ton." You will find it in the fifth volume of my collected works. Haslinger has them. And here I will give you my ideas of what would be appropriate music : only pray do not suppose that I wish to write down a sort of prescription (I have no right to do so), only take what I say merely as a hint for your consideration, and after you have considered it, do of course as you feel disposed, whether or not you happen to agree with me entirely, partially, or not at all. Overture : a short sharp chord, ff., to begin with, and then, possibly, a long sustained passage for clarionet or horn, with pauses. Then, opening calmly and gradually, clothed in music becoming gloomier as it proceeds, and more intricate in character, treated harmonically rather than melodiously—a sort of·chaos, which only

---

[1] 'Almide,' 'An die Laute,' 'Zur guten Nacht' (contained in Op. 81).

by degrees developes and becomes brighter. Whether
the overture should conclude thus, or an Allegro follow,
I cannot determine. If you choose the latter, only
let it have meaning, with plenty of power and brilliancy; and yet I would have the weak finale taken
out of the first movement. Next, let there be unaccompanied declamation as far as the words "Wirken
gegeben." At this point let the orchestra come in with
soft and long-drawn-out chords, and the dialogue, with
only short musical interludes to fill in the pauses, be
retained up to the word "Erdenreich." Here, a long
and gloomy musical interlude; a shorter and gentler
one after the word "Gott;" the following movement,
until "selbst gefällt," without any music; the "Nun
schweigen," until "bis soll ich sein," little more than
accompanying chords, with brief musical interludes;
then a more prolonged entr'acte, after which, with the
words "Nun schliesst," the music begins to wax louder
and more animated in character. After the words
"Wiederhall sie nach," the instruments should be in
full swing, and thus prepare an introduction for the
great, brilliant, and majestic chorus, "Drum Preis Dir,"
which can be made as long and effective as the composer pleases; the last lines, however, should, as the
wind-up of the whole work, be of a gentle and mild
character, without any change of time or key. Now if
the music be treated by so intellectual a master and
deep thinker as yourself, and the declamation be given

to such a man as your Anschütz, I promise myself a great result, and such as every connoisseur or ordinary hearer must honour and approve of. Still, I repeat again, all this is merely my raw scheme; the choice and determination are with you. For the rest, I rejoice in being brought into closer associations with you, and that I have the opportunity of refreshing my mind by exchanging ideas with you. Should the work be accomplished, and I obtain it, my next care will be to secure as perfect a performance as possible. With all esteem and devotion, I am, &c.,

'ROCHLITZ.'[1]

[1] We see by a letter from Rochlitz to the music-publisher Tobias Haslinger (dated September 10, 1822), that Beethoven at that time was asked if he was not disposed to set to music the poem ' Der erste Ton.' ' I should, of course, be exceedingly pleased,' writes Rochlitz to his friend, ' if one of my poems were to inspire the glorious Beethoven to write some appropriate music, and if I am not mistaken the subject of all others to suit him would be "Der erste Ton." My wish is really not the prompting of conceit or an excess of self-complacency. I am far beyond such considerations, but I am satisfied he would find here room and materials to the overflow for his rich fancy and wondrous powers of colour.' Beethoven, however, did not fall in with this suggestion, for on December 28, 1822, Rochlitz wrote to Haslinger on the subject :—' Beethoven is not wrong in reminding me that the musical treatment of the " Erster Ton " would possibly recall Haydn's " Creation." But surely one might avoid this by adopting a totally different style of treatment; for instance, let the poem be used as a declamatory piece with instrumental music for interludes (melodramatic): this has indeed already been done (by C. M. v. Weber in the year 1808), but the music was not good; our artist, however, is unwilling to treat the subject again, although Weber's music is hardly known at all, and of all men on the earth, none need fear less than he a collision with Weber. In the event

To this flattering letter Schubert might be supposed
to have sent either an evasive answer or a direct point-
blank refusal. It is a fact, however, that Schubert had
as little to do with adapting the poem to music as
Beethoven.[1] The didactic character of the work, perhaps also the warning and reminder about Haydn's
'Creation,' may have caused Schubert to regard in a
hostile point of view a poem sensible enough intrin-
sically; but anyhow, Schubert, usually so easily pleased,
would not be induced to try the strength of his musical
powers on such a subject.[2]

of Beethoven agreeing after all to undertake the work, the pruning-
knife might be used most advantageously, and considerable cuts be
made.' Then follows a sketch of a musical and declamatory treatment:
—'There being only three instrumental interludes' (continues Rochlitz),
'these might be made somewhat lengthy movements, and the whole
colour predominating in each would avoid the faintest reminder of the
" Creation." '

[1] 'Der glorreiche Augenblick,' a cantata by Weissenbach, set to
music by Beethoven, was performed at Vienna in 1814, on the occasion
of the Congress festivities, with fresh words adapted by Rochlitz, and
entitled 'Preis der Tonkunst.' (Schindler's 'Biography of Beethoven,'
vol. ii. p. 152, where it is also stated that Rochlitz had, in the year
1822, asked Beethoven to set the same poem to music.)

[2] Frhr. v. Schönstein told me that Schubert carried about with him
for several weeks the 'Nächtliche Heerschau,' by Zedlitz, the latter
having given him his libretto, and expressed a wish that Schubert should
write the music for it. At last Schubert gave him back the manuscript,
declaring he did not feel equal to the undertaking; he had not the courage
to apply himself to the task, he felt he could not clothe the poem with
good and fitting music. Felix Mendelssohn, too, was desired (by Madame
v. Pereira, in Vienna) to set the same poem, but he refused, observing,
that a descriptive poem cannot well be set to music. (See 'Mendelssohn's

The year 1827, with which this chapter closes, may be (like the year 1825) reckoned among the happiest episodes of Schubert's life and progress. Penetrated with the lofty consciousness of his mission as a great art-creator, he aspired to more exalted efforts, as we gather from his larger works of this period, and he experienced, for the last time, the happiness of a free unfettered enjoyment of Nature's beauties and the charms of simple friendly companions, who met him half way with entire abandonment of ceremony and conventional restraints. In such blessings his modest unaffected disposition found its full refreshment and content, and this he expressed feelingly, but briefly, as his manner was, in some passages in his letters. Within the short interval of a year after this brief but happy episode in his existence, Schubert had fulfilled his earthly mission, and the cold grave had closed over the artist who had but just stepped on the threshold of manhood.

Letters,' vol. i.) The ' Nächtliche Heerschau' found at a later period a musical exponent in the person of Emil Titl.

CHAPTER XVI.

(1828.)

SCHUBERT'S POWERS AS A COMPOSER IN THEIR ZENITH—A LETTER
FROM FRANZ TO A. HÜTTENBRENNER—SCHUBERT GIVES A CON-
CERT—LETTERS FROM PROBST, THE SCHOTT FIRM, SCHIKH, TRA-
WEGER, MOSEWIUS, AND BRÜGGEMANN—A LETTER FROM JENGER TO
MARIE PACHLER—FRANZ PROPOSES A SECOND EXCURSION TO GRATZ—
LETTERS FROM PROBST AND SCHOTT—SCHUBERT'S ANSWER TO PROBST
—THE JOURNEY TO GRATZ GIVEN UP — AN INVITATION FROM A.
SCHINDLER TO SCHUBERT TO VISIT PESTH—FRANZ LACHNER—A
BUSINESS LETTER FROM THE SCHOTTS—LAST COMPOSITIONS: THE C
SYMPHONY, 'MIRIAM'S WAR-SONG,' THE C QUINTETT, THE E-FLAT
MASS — SACRED 'COMPOSITIONS, SONGS,' THE 'SCHWANENGESANG'—
SCHUBERT'S ILLNESS—IS VISITED BY SIMON SECHTER—THE PHYSI-
CIANS DRS. RINNA AND BEHRING—A LETTER FROM THE FATHER
TO FERDINAND SCHUBERT—SCHUBERT'S DEATH—NOTICE IN THE
PAPERS—THE FUNERAL—FERDINAND'S LETTER TO HIS FATHER—THE
BODY TAKEN TO WÄHRING—MOURNING FOR SCHUBERT—PERFORM-
ANCE OF THE REQUIEM BY A. HÜTTENBRENNER IN THE AUGUSTINER-
KIRCHE—CONCERT IN AID OF THE MEMORIAL—THE INSCRIPTION ON
THE GRAVE—PORTRAITS OF SCHUBERT.

SCHUBERT had returned home from Styria invigorated
and hardened for the fresh exertions that awaited him.
He already thought of repeating his excursion either to
that quarter, or to Upper Austria,[1] on a visit to some

---

[1] Thus Jenger writes on January 28 to Madame Marie v. Pachler:—
' Irene Kiesewetter has recovered from her bad illness, and thinks of

intimate friend, hoping by exercise and change of air
to restore his health, which had suffered from constant
attacks of headache. Although of late years these
sufferings had become more obstinate in character, yet
not the slightest symptom of that catastrophe appeared
which was destined after a few months to overwhelm
the sufferer.

Schubert's power as a creative composer during the
late period, if not marked by a greater wealth and
prodigality of genius, showed more depth and intensity
than hitherto; for, putting aside the Lied, his special
department, in which his genius had culminated to the
highest point, he had broken ground in new fields in
his 'Winterreise,' and the short interval still allotted
him witnessed the origin of his finest and ripest works
'n instrumental music and the development of other
styles of music than those he had more exclusively
cultivated. The completion of his Symphony in C
enabled him to give convincing proof of what he
could do with grand orchestral works, and several of
his pianoforte works and chamber compositions of

accompanying her mother on an excursion to Gratz. Should this take
place, Schwammerl and I shall be taken as guides on the journey, and
thus we may have a chance of seeing you all in a few months.' This
journey, in consequence of the death of a relation of Kiesewetter's, never
came off. But on April 26, Jenger wrote again to Gratz:—'The little
volume of songs by friend Schubert, which he dedicates to you, is
already in the Emperor's hands; when Schubert and I come to you, and
that will doubtless be at the end of August, we will take care to bring
with us some copies.'

this date surpass any of his previous efforts. The fact of his continued and onward course of development in all styles of a composer's art can hardly be questioned.

Shortly after the beginning of this year (January 18) Schubert wrote a letter to Anselm Hüttenbrenner in Gratz. It bears a pleasing testimony to Franz's attachment to his family, and—what is a rare incident—we have a brief account of the performance of one of his compositions. The letter runs thus :—

'Dearest Friend,—You will be surprised at my writing at all. So am I ; but, if I do write, it is from motives of self-interest. Now, just listen. The place of drawing-master at the Normal-Hauptschule at Gratz is, I see, vacant, and candidates are summoned. My brother Carl, whom you possibly know, would like to get the post. He is a clever landscape-painter as well as a good draughtsman. If you could help me in this matter I should be eternally obliged to you. My brother is a married man, with children : to obtain a regular salaried appointment would be extremely agreeable to him. I hope matters are prosperous with yourself, as well as with your family and your brothers. Greet every one for me very heartily. Lately a trio of mine[1] for pianoforte, violin, and violoncello, was played at Schuppanzigh's, and pleased very much. It was exquisitely

---

[1] The Trio in E-flat.

played by Bocklet, Schuppanzigh, and Linke. Have you done nothing new ?[1] By the by, why don't the two songs appear?[2] Confound it ! what a nuisance it is ! I repeat my former request,[3] and only bear in mind that any kindness done to my brother I look on as done to myself. Hoping for agreeable news from you, I remain, till death, your devoted friend,

'FRANZ SCHUBERT.'

Schubert's compositions, especially those of the vocal order, had, since the appearance of the 'Erl-King,' been given with applause at various concerts, the composer usually accompanying at the piano.[4] Schubert, modest and unassuming, if not culpably inert where his own interests were involved, had not as yet given any concerts on his own account, although his store of new and valuable works would have sufficed to furnish ample

---

[1] Schubert liked some of Anselm Hüttenbrenner's compositions, specially ' Der Abend,' a vocal quartett. Rochlitz wrote on January 9, 1825, to T. Haslinger, at Vienna :—'That Sonata of the Styrian Musikverein was assuredly written by Anselm Hüttenbrenner. I am delighted to hear anything good from you of that excellent artist,' &c.

[2] ' Im Wald' and ' Auf der Bruck,' which were to be published by Kienreich, in Gratz. Ten days later, Jenger wrote to Madame Pachler : ' Anselm Hüttenbrenner is a careless dog for not hurrying Schubert's two Lieder at Kienreich's, so that they may be at last engraved.'

[3] Schubert also applied to Dr. Pachler in the same matter.

[4] Thus, at the concert given by Frl. Salomon (1827), at another by J. Lewy (the younger), on April 20, 1828, when Schubert accompanied his Lied ' Am Strom.'

materials for several evening concerts. Large numbers of Lieder were issued at short intervals by the publishers, and in dealing with their offers Schubert was withheld from making ventures on his own account; but he yielded at last to solicitations on all sides, and consented to give a private concert in the hall of the Musikverein. This took place on March 26, 1828, and the programme consisted entirely of Schubert's compositions. The hall was crowded to overflowing, and the success so brilliant, that a repetition of this successful effort was determined on when a fitting opportunity should present itself. This was, however, fated to be his first and last concert: the two later Schubert concerts were only intended to raise a sum to defray the costs of a memorial to the deceased composer.

It has been already mentioned that Schubert made attempts during the last three years of his life to enter into business arrangements with foreign publishers for the sale of his works, his idea being that this step would ensure a larger circulation of his works, and that probably he could make more advantageous terms with foreigners than he could count on with native publishers. A series of letters which came to him in course of the year 1828, from different parts of Germany, relative to business matters in connection with the sale and wider extension of his musical works, only proves that his hopes were but partially fulfilled, and the result of his efforts was limited merely to the sale of his Trio in E.

(This was effected with Probst, in Leipsic.) The recognition of his artistic merits by the most esteemed and valued connoisseurs and lovers of music must have pleased him all the more from having to submit to disappointments of a practical kind, nor should the moral satisfaction he received by way of compensation be undervalued.

As regards his business dealings with music publishers in Germany, we have a letter from Probst, of Leipsic, dated February 9, and to the following effect :—

' I am heartily sorry that the difference in our views before my journey to Vienna rendered your highly appreciated overtures for the publication of your works at our firm impracticable. Last year, when I enjoyed the privilege of your personal acquaintance, I happened to mention that it would be extremely agreeable to me to receive some novelties in the way of composition from you : this wish you promised to gratify. Since that time I have learned to know your new songs, "Zügenglöcklein," "Auf dem Wasser," and several others; and I am more than ever convinced of your progress as a composer, and that your fancies have developed into brighter and more exquisite forms. Further, I have been exceedingly pleased with several of your works for four hands; for instance, the four Polonaises, Op. 75, the variations on the Müllerlied, Op. 82 ; and I am satisfied that the attempt to spread your name and fame throughout the rest of Germany and the North would be a successful one. I would gladly lend a helping hand to the wider recognition of such talents as yours.

'Have the goodness, therefore, when you have finished anything successfully—song, romance, vocal concerted piece; I care not what it be, as long as it be not too difficult of comprehension, without compromising in any way your individuality of style—to let me have them ; send me also some pieces for four hands in the same genre. You have only to let Herr Lähne, of Artaria & Company, have the manuscripts ; he will forward them to me without delay. With regard to the honorarium, we shall soon come to terms on that point. I only desire to be met fairly ; you will find me straightforward and honest in my dealing, as long as your works are such that I can take a genuine delight in them myself. The prices of the Vienna publishers can serve as the easiest guide and standard for us in our dealings. Herr Lähne would expect a fitting remuneration for the loss of his time on your account.

'I must request of you personally to try over with the greatest care the works you intend for me, without first communicating with local publishers, and to let such business matters be transacted simply between ourselves as contracting parties. I most solemnly assure you that you shall have no cause to repent, should you honour me with your friendly confidence, and, by a careful selection of your best compositions, give me an opportunity of working zealously for your reputation. I subscribe myself, with every sentiment of hearty esteem,

'Your obedient servant,

'H. A. PROBST.'

The following letter, bearing the same date as the former, came from the firm of 'Schott's Söhne,' at Mayence:—

'Sir,—You have already for several years been well known to us by your admirable compositions, and we had long since entertained hopes of publishing some of your works, but we have been too exclusively occupied with the publication of the works (Op. 121–128 and 131) of the late Beethoven, many of them being compositions of a very elaborate kind. We are now, however, free to the extent of being able to ask you for some works of yours to be published by our firm. Pianoforte works or vocal pieces, either solo or concerted, with or without pianoforte accompaniment, will always be welcomed by us. Be good enough to fix your terms of payment, and we will have you paid at Vienna by Herr Franck & Co.

'We must call your attention to the fact, that we have also an establishment in Paris, where we can always help to make your compositions known.

'If you have a great deal of music in hand, and would

be good enough to send us a catalogue, we shall be very glad to receive it.

'With great esteem, we beg to remain, &c.,

'B. SCHOTT'S SONS.'

Schubert answered this letter, and his letter led to another from the same firm, written on February 29:—

'Sir,—We are greatly pleased with your prompt answer to ours of February 8. We are enabled to gather from the contents of your letter what you have actually in store in the way of manuscript music, and would come to terms with you at once for all your works collectively, had we not to fulfil contracts and obligations which we entered into some time since. Your works are all so attractive to a publisher that it is difficult to make a selection.

'Please send us the following works catalogued by yourself :—

'1. Trio for pianoforte, violin, and violoncello.

'2. Four Impromptus for pianoforte.

'3. Fantasia for pianoforte à *quatre mains.*

'4. Fantasia for piano and violin.

'5. Four-part Choruses for men's voices.

'6. Five-part Songs for men's voices.

'7. War Song for double chorus.

'8. "Hochzeitsbraten," comic Trio.

'These works we will publish by degrees, and put out

as soon as possible, and afterwards ask you for your more recently composed music.

'You will fix on as moderate terms as you can, consistently with what is fair dealing, and allow us to quit ourselves of our obligations to you after the publication of each of your works, by sending a draft to Vienna. Be good enough to let us know how many copies you wish for distribution amongst your friends.

'Will you deliver the enclosed packet for Herr Andreas Landschütz, pianoforte and instrument-maker (Mariahilf, No. 16, near the "Rothen Breze"); it is an order for him to send us two pianos: we shall thus save the postage. But do as you please in the matter of sending. Be good enough to further also a packet enclosed for Herr Ferdinand Cammeretto, instrument-maker (Laimgrube, No. 68, beim weissen Ochsen); he usually makes us a monthly consignment of pianos, and is a very punctual accurate man in the way of business.

'Calculating on your sending as we desire, we are, with great respect and esteem, &c.,

'B. SCHOTT'S SONS.'

A number of Schubert's admirers at Vienna tried to persuade Schikh, the editor of the 'Modenzeitung,' to insert in his journal a complimentary address to the great composer. Schikh, however, refused the address, as ill suited to publication, and forwarded the original document, headed by a preface of his own, 'to the famous composer' Franz Schubert:—

'Most esteemed Friend,—A contribution for insertion in the columns of the "Wiener Zeitschrift" has been sent me by a circle of fervent admirers of your famous compositions. Joining heart and soul as I do in the worship of your great and noble gifts, as well as in the desire expressed in this appeal, still the address is, in my judgment, ill suited for publication, and I have no doubt at all that you will be equally convinced with me that I have acted properly.[1] Now, to promote as far as I can the object of people personally unknown to me, I allow myself the pleasure of sending you a document which concerns you personally, in the hope of being able to justify myself before the circle of musical amateurs, by adopting the present line of conduct, although unable to carry out the first proposal contained in their petition. Pray accept the assurance of my sincere friendship and respect, with which I remain

'Your most constant friend,

'SCHIKH.'

Franz intended, as we have already stated, to pass the summer of this year in his beloved Upper Austria, and afterwards to pay a second visit to Gratz. His in-

---

[1] Schikh had argued quite correctly.

tention became known to Herr Traweger, in Gmunden, with whom Franz, in the year 1825, had passed some happy days; and in delight at his anticipated visit, he wrote to Schubert on May 19 the following character-istic letter of visitation :—

'Dear friend Schubert,—Zierer [1] informed me you wished once again to visit Gmunden, and he proposed asking me my prices for board and maintenance, and desired me to write on this subject to you. You put me in a difficulty; and if I did not know you, and your perfectly candid straightforward way of dealing, and had I no apprehension of your not coming to me after all, I should ask for nothing at all. Lest, however, it should ever occur to you that you could be a burden to anyone, and in order that you may remain with-out let or hindrance just as long as you please, just listen to me. For your room, which you have already lived in, for your three meals a day, pay me at the rate of fifty kreuzers per day, and anything you drink let it be an extra. I must conclude, otherwise I shall miss the post. Write as soon as you can, to say if you are content with my offer.

'Your sincere friend,

'FERDINAND TRAWEGER.'

---

[1] Zierer was personally acquainted with Schubert, and had, shortly before his departure to Italy, heard him express a wish to return once more to Gmunden. At Naples he received the news of Schubert's death.

The visit to Gmunden never came off, for Schubert, after the year 1825, never went again to Upper Austria.

The following letter, dated June 8, written to him by Mosewius in Breslau, and favoured by a musical friend, must have gratified him exceedingly.[1] We gather from the contents of this letter some idea of the increasing influence and attractions which Schubert's music was acquiring beyond the borders of his own country. The letter is as follows :—

'Most honoured Sir,—I take the liberty of forwarding you by my countryman Herr Kühn, a music-teacher, this letter, and avail myself of the opportunity of asking your good services for my friend, who intends passing some time in Vienna, with the idea of cultivating his talents as a musical composer. I am heartily glad to have been told by Haslinger of your welfare, and that you are reaping the success you are so fairly entitled to. Your numerous compositions bear witness to your continued industry, and these valuable works are acquiring more and more recognition and honour amongst our hitherto prejudiced and one-sided North-

---

[1] Mosewius (Johann Theodor), born at Königsberg in 1788, died at Breslau in 1861. In early days he was a distinguished vocalist and actor. In 1825 he quitted the stage, and founded a singing-school in Breslau. In the year 1827 he received the appointment of second music-teacher at the University, as well as the directorship of the Royal Institute for Church Music ; in 1829 he was made the first music-director at the University. Some cantatas and occasional vocal pieces by him have become popular.

erners. It will be of small moment to you to hear that I am one of your ardent worshippers, and that your "Müllerlieder" (to particularise) have enabled me to get an insight of the peculiar individualities of your style. I am eagerly longing for every production of your muse, and have been truly edified with your "Winterreise." You will already have heard that I have given up my former post; I am now appointed Music Director and Academic Teacher at the University in this place; and as the Government has confided to my keeping the direction of the Royal Institute for Church Music, I find plenty of opportunity for a sphere of activity. Possibly I may have the pleasure of seeing you again very soon, and of being able to repeat, by word of mouth, the assurance that I am, with all sub-mission and the profoundest respect,

'Your friend and admirer,

'MOSEWIUS.'

The two following letters from Brüggemann, of Halberstadt, are of a business nature. In one we find repeated hints and reminders given to Schubert to compose short and easily executed works. It does not seem, however, that Schubert paid any particular heed to the suggestion thus offered. This is the first letter :—

'Respected Sir,—Some months ago a collection of pianoforte compositions was published by us in monthly numbers; half of these were original, and half arrangements and adaptations. I venture most respectfully to ask if you feel inclined to support the above-mentioned undertaking, by furnishing contributions for the pianoforte without accompaniment. The original contributions must not be too difficult—nay, they can be as slight as possible. Their style must of course be left entirely to the respected writers; their actual length need not exceed two sheets, seeing that one " Heft " consists only of three sheets : smaller things, such as slight rondos, dance music, &c., are all suitable to our publication. M. D. Mühling, of Magdeburg, superintends as editor : his name will be a sufficient guarantee to you that nothing is taken which would be unworthy to figure side by side with your valuable contributions.[1] Should you be inclined to fulfil the wish herein expressed, let me ask you to send an affirmative answer as soon as you can, and your terms as to payment, which shall always be made punctually and promptly. Should you have anything in hand which you think suitable for the object I have here alluded to, be good enough to let me have it with your answer. I must remark once more that the whole scope of the undertaking makes it advisable that your

---

[1] August Mühling, born at Raguhne in 1781, was elected, in 1823, orchestral and concert director at Magdeburg, besides organist at the Ulrichskirche. He was a capable musician in almost every style, the operatic excepted.

contributions be made up of pleasing music, and such as will be within easy grasp of an ordinary performer.

'Your devoted servant,

'BRÜGGEMANN.

'Halberstadt: June 21, 1828.'

Schubert wrote an answer accepting this proposal; for on August 10, 1828, he received from Brüggemann the following lines :—

'Honoured Sir,—I am very glad to hear you feel inclined to write some compositions for Mühling's Museum, and I am on the look-out for some agreeable despatches and musical consignments from you. To remove every possible misunderstanding, I beg to re-mark, that the longest contributions must not contain more than two sheets, and that I can only accept of un-accompanied pieces for two hands. Be good enough to let me know your terms for everything you send, and you shall be paid promptly by Herr Jasper, the book-seller. Please send the manuscripts by the post-waggon. As it is my intention some time hence to publish compositions on a grander scale, I shall be very pleased if you can find yourself able to make reason-able offers with a view to such publications.

'With the greatest respect,

'Your obedient servant,

'BRÜGGEMANN.'

The trip to Gratz, which he had intended to make in the summer, had been previously postponed until the beginning of the autumn. Jenger could not get a furlough, and Schubert had no money. The former announced this state of things to Madame Marie Pachler in the following letter, dated July 4, 1828 :—

'The absence of two of my subordinates for the purpose of taking the waters at Baden, added to the not very brilliant state of the finances of my friend Schubert, who begs to send all sorts of good wishes to you and his friend Dr. Carl, will prevent us both from accepting your kind invitation to visit you at Gratz. Schubert, besides, has the project of passing a part of the summer in Gmunden and the neighbourhood, where he has received a number of invitations ; but hitherto, the pecuniary difficulties before alluded to have prevented him from carrying out his project. He is still here at present, working zealously at a new Mass [probably the grand Mass in E-flat], and is only on the look-out—come from what quarter it may— for the cash necessary to support his immediate flight to Upper Austria. Under these circumstances our excursion might possibly come off, as it did last year, at the beginning of the month of September. With regard to our domicile, whether we shall put up with you at Hallerschlössel or at your house in town, we cockney Viennese no doubt should much prefer the first,

God only grant that we may settle ourselves down at either one or the other of these places! All the rest follows as a matter of course. In the event, however, of my not being able to come to you this year, I will at all events send friend Schubert to you, who told me this very day how he delighted in the prospect of being able to pass some weeks in your neighbourhood.'

This visit likewise Schubert was forced to abandon; and instead of finding in the healthy air of Styria, and the circle of his devoted friends, the Pachlers, the probable remedy for bodily and mental sufferings, he chose the fatal alternative of lodging in a newly-built house, the damp chilly atmosphere of which may have laid the seeds of his last fatal illness.

Of all his finished compositions that which chiefly engrossed his attention was the E-flat Trio, the publication of which he worked at with a zeal greater than ordinary—a proof of the attachment he felt for this particular work. He seems to have offered this to the Schotts, at Mayence, about this time for publication, for they wrote to him on April 28 as follows:—

'Your esteemed favour of the 10th of April gives us information respecting the payment you expect for your manuscripts. We gather from your letter that you wished, as soon as possible, to have them engraved; and, under these circumstances, we ask beforehand only for the impromptus and the five-part songs for men's voices; for these we acknowledge ourselves indebted to you in the sum of sixty florins. The Trio is probably a work on a large scale, and as we have only a short time since published several trios, we must defer to some later opportunity, for ordinary prudential reasons, dealing with this kind of composition : we do not think that the publication of your Trio now would advance your interests. As soon as we have finished the printing of the works described by you, we shall be at liberty to ask something else of you. We greet you with all respect.

' B. Schott's Sons.'

Meanwhile Schubert had, on April 10, applied to Herr A. Probst, of Leipsic, in the same business, and received from him, on April 15, 1828, the following answer :—

' A violent attack of fever compels me to avail myself of a friend's services to answer your honoured letter of the 10th of the present month.

' I accept the Trio you have been so good as to offer me, at the price of 20 florins 60 kreuzers, which you will receive by the annexed three cheques, duly noted and numbered. I hope, however, that you will comply with my request to send, at your earliest convenience, some choice morceaux in the way of songs, or pianoforte pieces *à quatre mains*, for a trio at best is but an article which keeps up the credit of the firm, and we very seldom make any profit out of it. Be good enough to send the manuscript, under cover, to Herr Robert Lähne, of the firm of Artaria & Company; and, for the future, you can always adopt this plan of sending things to me, and escape the burthen of unnecessary costs of transit.

'By the Trio, mentioned in the outset of my letter, must certainly not be understood the Fantasia which was given on February 5, at Herr Slawick's concert in the Kärnthnerthor Theatre, the criticism on which in the Leipsic "Musicalische Zeitung," No. 14, p. 223, is anything but favourable.[1]

'I took the heartiest interest in the brilliant success of your concert on March 26, and only trust that for the future your talents will meet with the fullest recognition.

'I am now waiting for your Trio, and beg to remain, with much esteem and friendship,

'Yours, &c.,

'H. A. Probst.'

At last the manuscript Trio was sent to Leipsic.
On July 18, Probst writes once more to Schubert:—

'I have only to-day received your favour of May 10, with the Trio; and it must not surprise you, worthy

---

[1] It is said there that Schubert, in this composition, entirely 'galloped away with himself' (*vergaloppirt*). The Fantasia is Op. 159.

friend, should this work be published at a somewhat later period than you probably expected. It has just been taken in hand, and can be finished in about six weeks. Meantime be good enough to let me have

' 1. The title, with some sort of dedication, and, further,

' 2. The number of the work, if you will be so good as to supply it; as I should like to follow your instructions and wishes in this matter to the letter. All your other proposals in respect of this work shall be carried out to the best of my power.

' As soon as I have finished, I will send you by post the six copies you stipulated for. I shall, at a later period, have the honour of telling you my opinion of the music.

'Meantime I remain, with all esteem,

' Your obedient servant,

' H. A. PROBST.'

Schubert answered these questions, on August 1, by this curt but resolute letter:—

' Sir,—The number of the Trio is 100. I most earnestly beg of you that the printed impression may be correct—this I am exceedingly anxious about. This work will be dedicated to none but those who take delight in it—that is the most profitable dedication of any.

' With all respect,

' FRANZ SCHUBERT.'

Meanwhile, the grand journey to Gratz came once more upon the tapis, as there seemed some probability of his financial difficulties being relieved.

On September 6, Jenger writes to his hospitable hostess in Gratz:—

'Friend Schubert and I settled down on the first of this month in our new quarters, and this will account for the answer to your last kind letter of the 28th of last month having not arrived at Gratz within the eight days assigned as the limit for my writing. Schubert never turned up, either in his old quarters or his new ones " auf der Wieden." At last I met and spoke to him yesterday evening at the Burgtheater; and I am now in a position to announce to you, dear friend, that our friend Schwammerl expects shortly an improvement in his finances, and reckons confidently on such an event; this being so, he will forthwith accept your kind invitation, arrive at your house in Gratz, and bring with him a new operetta. In any case you may expect, eight days before his arrival at Gratz, to hear definitely either from him or me. Of course he wished me to accompany him on the journey, but I cannot be spared. In the event of Schubert staying with you up to the end of October, I might possibly come for eight days to Gratz, to see my old loves once again, and to fetch back friend Schwammerl. Every day I have a look at my last year's diary, and revel in the recollection of those happy days.

On the 10th, 11th, and 12th, I shall think of the happy party at Wildbach.'

The hope of escaping the difficulty alluded to was never realised. The second part of the 'Winterreise' had been completed, and yet the publication of this valuable work had not relieved the pressure of Schubert's money difficulties. Accordingly the trip to Gratz was definitively abandoned.

On Sept. 25, Jenger received from Schubert the following letter, containing his reasons for refusal:—

' I have already handed over to Haslinger the second part of the " Winterreise." It's all over with my journey to Gratz for this year, for my pecuniary, like the weather prospects, are downright gloomy and unfavourable. I accept with pleasure the invitation to Dr. Menz,[1] as I should be very glad to hear Baron Schönstein sing. On Saturday afternoon you can meet me at Bogner's Coffee-house, Singerstrasse, between four and five o'clock.

'Your friend,

' SCHUBERT.

'My address is "Neue Wieden, Firmians-Gasse, No. 694, second floor, right-hand side."'

The following letter from Leipsic, on October 6,

---

[1] Dr. Menz, I have been informed, was owner of the house on the Kohlmarkt, where the firm of Haslinger now stands. Jenger lived there for a considerable time.

refers to the Trio in E-flat, the publication of which Schubert looked forward to with such impatience :—

'In answer to your favours of the 1st of August and the 2nd of the present month, I must offer my apologies for the Trio, Op. 100, not yet being delivered to you. My journey to France and Holland has necessitated some slight delay, and the work, too, is rather an arduous one. Meantime the music has been engraved, the corrections have been done as carefully as possible, and by our next parcel we send the work in a complete state by Diabelli & Company to you. Of your new compositions, the Lieder would best suit my purpose, and I must ask you to send me them. I should also like to have some easy pianoforte pieces à *quatre mains*, such as your variations on the Müllerlied from "Marie."[1] Would not Himmel's subject, "An Alexis," admit of an equally graceful setting and arrangement?[2]

'With sincere respect,

'Your obedient servant,

'H. A. PROBST.'

Schubert was never destined to set eyes again upon

[1] The variations for four hands on the theme from the Opera 'Marie,' of Herold.

[2] Himmel (Friedrich Heinrich), born at Treuenbritzen, in Brandenburg, in the year 1765, and died at Berlin in 1814, a pupil of Naumann, was Chamber Composer to King Friedrich Wilhelm II. He wrote several operas for Italy, and brought them out at Vienna and Naples, also at Stockholm, St. Petersburg, and Berlin. On the whole, there are more

the mountains of Styria or Upper Austria; and the rapid progress of his disease compelled him to give up also an excursion to the capital of Hungary—a scheme proposed to him under the most favourable auspices.

Franz Lachner,[1] a great friend of Schubert's, and officiating at that time as Capellmeister at the Kärnthnerthor Theatre, received an invitation, in the June of 1828, from Anton Schindler, whose sister was a public vocalist at Pesth, to come to that city and there bring out on the stage his first effort in the dramatic field, the Opera of 'Die Bürgschaft.' With a view to that object, Lachner set out on his journey to Pesth towards the end of September; but before taking leave of Schubert, he obtained from him a promise that, if possible, he would be present at the production of the opera. As the performance was imminent, Schindler, who knew his man, endeavoured to ensure, if possible, Schubert's attendance by the following well-intentioned letter (dated October 11):—

'My dear good friend Schubert,—Our friend Lachner is so absorbed with the arrangements of his opera, that I take on myself the duty of inviting your attendance on the all-important day when the great work will be first given in public. This is fixed for

than eighty works of this composer in existence. They are chiefly vocal—Cantatas, Psalms, Masses, and the like.

[1] I am indebted to this gentleman, now Hofcapellmeister at Munich, for the information.

the 25th or 27th of the present month; and I invite
you not only in his name, but in that of my sister
and myself jointly. We wish to give you a hearty,
friendly welcome here, and receive you with all due
respect and honour. We are all here under one roof,
and sit at one table; and look forward to your unhesitatingly filling the place intended for you, which
we hope you will occupy as soon as possible. Make
your arrangements, therefore, for starting by the Eil-
wagen not later than the 22nd of this month, and
only give us two days' warning by writing, if we are to
expect you here without fail on the 24th of this month.
Since your name is so thoroughly well spoken of here,
we propose the following scheme:—You must make up
your mind to give a private concert here, where your
vocal compositions must form the staple of the programme. People reckon here on a complete success;
and, as it is very well known that your bashfulness
and easy-going way prevent any excess of activity and
zeal on your part, let me tell you, confidently, that
you will find the people here cheerfully and zealously
co-operating to support you on their own shoulders,
whatever amount of dead weight you may carry. Still,
you must do something also, by way of contributing to
a successful result; *et quidem*, bring some half-dozen
letters of introduction both from and to your aristocratic
friends. Lachner thinks there should be something
from the Esterhazy family, and so do I. Say a word, for

instance, to our honest friend Pinterics, and he will
take very good care to get letters of recommendation
from his patron Prince. Above all, take care to have
a letter to the Countess Tölöky, the head of the noble
Frauenverein here, and a great patroness of art. Don't
let the thing worry you in any way, for, as a matter
of fact, there is no care or anxiety to be felt in the
matter. You have but to give your letters here, when
we find it necessary, and then *basta*! To net safely
into your pockets 100 florins in this way, is not a
thing to be despised; besides this, other advantages
may accrue in good time. Well, then, up! be stirring!
don't waste time in thinking about it, and don't say no.
None of your excuses, mind! You will be backed up
here and strenuously supported. There's a young amateur here, who has a fine tenor voice, and sings your
Lieder delightfully; then there are the gentlemen from
the theatre, and my sister also, so that you have only
to sit down, arrange your fat stomach, and accompany every song. Your vocal pieces for mixed voices
are sure to be effective: many of them are well known
here. Write nothing new—it is not wanted!

'And so, God be with you! We all expect that you
will be as accommodating as possible, and not show
yourself a refractory animal. To our speedy merry
meeting, then, in the land of moustaches! This from
your sincere friend,

'ANTON SCHINDLER.'

Lachner added a postscript to this letter, telling his friend he expected him at Pesth on October 20 at the latest.

Schubert made no answer, nor was he present at the public performance at Pesth. When that was over (it may have been some time in the early part of November), Lachner travelled back to Vienna, and visited his friend, who had already been suffering from illness for three weeks past. He conversed with him for the space of two hours, and these were the last they ever spent together. About this time, Lachner was commissioned by the director of the theatres—Count Gallenberg—to make a tour through Germany, with a view of getting singers for the Opera at Vienna. At Darmstadt (in a letter written by their mutual friend Treitschke), he received the news of Schubert's death.

We have one more business letter from the Schotts at Mayence, and the last of the series arranged before me in chronological order. It is dated October 30, and was sent to Schubert a little over a fortnight before his death.

The letter is as follows :—

' Your much-esteemed letters of May 28 and October 2 have come safely to hand. I postponed an answer to your first letter, because we had an opportunity of sending the Impromptus to Paris by the same way as we received them ourselves.

'These were sent back to us; and we were given to understand that as "Kleinigkeiten" these works were too difficult, and would find no sale in France. Pray accept our apologies for this.

'We shall soon publish the Quintett (Op. 114), but we must needs remark that this small work is rated at too extravagant a price. The whole of the pianoforte part does not occupy more than six printed pages, and we fancy there must be a mistake somewhere, in our being charged with sixty florins for this composition. We make you an offer of thirty florins for it; and, after receiving your answer, will pay that amount forthwith, or you may draw on us, if you please, for the sum.

'The pianoforte piece (Op. 101) we did not think too highly assessed; but its uselessness, as far as a sale in France is concerned, was very annoying to us.

'Be good enough to send us any occasional composition you may have written, if it be less difficult and still have plenty of brilliancy.

'We are, with all respect and good will,

'B. SCHOTT'S SONS.

'P.S.—To avoid all delay, we hereby send you a cheque for thirty florins on Heilmann's heir, with our letter of advice enclosed. If you reject our proposal, please return the cheque. We will enclose the Impromptus in our first parcel to Herr Haslinger.

'THE ABOVE.'

Schubert's activity during the last year of his life, when we look back on the number and importance of his original compositions, is quite wonderful. It seemed as though, haunted by a presentiment of his approaching end, he wished to gather up and concentrate all his powers, as it were, for a final grasp at the laurels in those fields of the musical art where he had not been permitted hitherto to triumph. The grand Symphony in C, the Mass in E-flat, the fine stringed Quartett in C, the Cantata 'Miriam's War Song,' in which Schubert's individuality is associated with Händel's majesty—the last three pianoforte sonatas which he wished to dedicate to Himmel [1]—the eight-voiced 'Hymn to the Holy Ghost,' all of these brilliant works arose, one after another, in rapid succession. With these must be associated a sacred Air for tenor solo with chorus; a Tantum ergo; the Cantata 'Glaube, Hoffnung und Liebe;'[2] the 92nd Psalm,[3] in five parts,

[1] They were afterwards dedicated by the publishers to Robert Schumann.

[2] The Cantata, with verses by Friedrich Reil, was written by Schubert for the consecration of a new bell at the church of the Holy Trinity, in the Alservorstadt (September 2, 1828), as a chorus for men's voices, ending by a chorus for all voices, with an accompaniment of wind instruments (hautboys, clarionets, bassoons, horns, and trumpets). The poem consists of six lines, the music, after a short introduction, leading to a slow solemn chorus for men's voices. The whole piece contains but twenty-six bars of simple melodious church music.

[3] The Psalm, translated into German by Wirth, and the translation adapted to the music, was written for two baritones, soprano, alto, and bass, and is still unpublished. Freiherr v. Spaun and Madame Lumpe,

to Hebrew words; pianoforte pieces for four hands—amongst them the well-known Grand Rondeau (Op. 107), a pleasant and easily-executed piece, which (in June) he composed by desire of Herr Artaria; and lastly, several Lieder: 'Am Strom,'[1] 'Der Hirt auf dem Felsen,'[2] and a part of the so-called 'Schwanengesang.'

Schubert, after finishing his Symphony in C, presented it to the Committee of the Musikverein at Vienna, for public performance.[3] The parts were actually written out and distributed, and the work of

of Vienna, have copies. The original is in the hands of the Cantor of the Israelitish Synagogue in Vienna, Herr Julius Sulzer; the Psalm is printed in Sulzer's 'Schir Zion.'

[1] 'Am Strom,' by Rellstab, with a pianoforte and horn obligato (for the violoncello also), was written for the French horn-player J. Lewy (at that time settled in Dresden). On April 20, 1828, he gave this at a concert in the small Redoutensaal, Schubert accompanying on the piano a famous amateur from Dresden.

[2] Schubert, shortly before his death, wrote (so I am informed by Spaun) the 'Hirt auf dem Felsen' at the desire of Anna Milder, the operatic singer, and expressly for her. The clarionet obligato seems also to have been written specially for a particular artist. This song was very variously criticised after its publication. By some papers at Vienna it was praised to the skies, by others cried down as a sentimental, exaggerated, phrase-full piece; by others the operatic style of the ending was severely spoken of. The undeniably mongrel character of the work is accounted for by the fact that it was intended for a dramatic singer, who wanted a compound of Lied and bravura. Judged from this point of view, and remembering it was written to order, we are justified in thinking this a charming work.

[3] The original, in the possession of the Musikverein at Vienna, bears date March 1828.

rehearsals was actually set on foot; but the Symphony was soon laid aside, as being too long and too difficult, and Schubert advised them to accept and perform his Sixth Symphony (also in C). The composer, who, on presenting his great Symphony, thus expressed himself to a friend, 'that he hoped now to hear nothing more about Lieder, that from henceforth he should confine himself to Opera and Symphony,' took great delight in the production of his new work; though the substitution of No. 6 was a poor consolation for the disappointment of his just hopes. But not even this small satisfaction was to be allowed him, for the Symphony was never performed in public until after his death.

The 'Schwanengesang' contains songs by Rellstab, Heine, and G. Seidl's 'Taubenpost.' Rellstab's memoirs, 'Aus meinem Leben,' published at Berlin in 1861, give us a detailed account of the origin of the seven songs.

Rellstab had come to Vienna in the year 1825, from an ardent wish to see Beethoven, and to induce him to set one of his opera librettos, of which he had a dozen in store and fit for use. But having learnt from Beethoven's intimate friends that over-reading did not agree with him, Rellstab carried off not only his copies of the librettos, but also what he thought the best and choicest of his small lyrical poems, each carefully and neatly written out, to the composer, who at that time

K 2

was living on the fourth story in the Krugerstrasse,
No. 767.   The poems, observes Rellstab, were very varied in rhythm and meaning, and if, as it might very
well be, one of them happened to chime with Beethoven's fancies, it might have moved him to breathe
upon it the spirit of his immortal music.[1]

Rellstab received the manuscript after Beethoven's
death, at the hands of Anton Schindler, who had laid
the poems aside, and apart from Beethoven's artistic
relics.   Some of the songs were marked with pencil
notes ; these were the songs which Beethoven liked best,
' and which he then handed over to Schubert to set to

---

[1] In connection with this story we may cite the following letter of
Rellstab's.   The original, without date or the name of the person
addressed, is now lying before me :—

'Most honoured Sir,—I send you herewith some songs which I have
had copied fairly for you ; some others, written in the same vein, will
shortly follow.   They have perhaps this novelty about them, that they
form in themselves a connected series, and have reference to happiness, unity, separation, death, and hope on the other side of the
grave, without pointing to any definite incidents.

' I should wish that these poems might succeed so far in winning your
approval as to move you to set them to music, and that, for this purpose, we should come to terms with a firm conducted on a principle of
advancing, as far as possible, the interests of true and the highest art,
the composer's inspiration to be considered the first law.

' Day and night I am thinking of an opera for you; nor do I doubt of
finding a subject which shall satisfy all the claims of a composer, a
poet, and the many-headed public,

'With the deepest respect,
'M. L. RELLSTAB.'

Herr Alexander W. Thayer, the musical biographer, thinks it certain
that this letter was addressed to Beethoven.

music,' as he felt too ill to do so himself.[1] Schubert accordingly set them to music before the poems appeared in print.

The composition of the songs from Heine is said, on the authority of Freiherr v. Schönstein, to belong to an earlier period; they have therefore been wrongly catalogued by publishers as part of the collection which originally appeared under the title of 'Schwanengesang.'

When Schubert was living at Herr Schober's, but several years before his death, he was visited one day by Herr v. Schönstein, and that gentleman happened to find a volume of Heine's songs, which lay on Schubert's table, so interesting, that he begged the book of him. Schubert gave it to him, adding, 'he should probably not want the volume any more.' This observation, coupled with the circumstance that all these pages, containing poetry adapted by Schubert to music, had been turned down at the corners, and the well-known fact that Schubert (although often wrongly) thought much of his music unworthy of publication, and laid it aside in consequence, makes it very probable that the six Lieder were first composed at this period.[2]

[1] The poems were therefore given to Schubert, but, according to Schindler, not until after Beethoven's death.

[2] But not before the year 1824, as Heine's book of songs was not known before that time. The 'Schwanengesang' was published by Haslinger, on May 4, 1829, and thus announced in the 'Wiener Zeitung':—'The last offerings of Schubert's noble gifts are made to the

Schubert's last song, the veritable 'Song of the Swan,' was 'Die Taubenpost,' by G. Seidl, composed in October, a few weeks before his death.

Death, with gentle but premonitory steps, had, in the September of this year, stolen on him, and a brief time was to elapse, when, as in Mozart's case, a few quieter days had given hopes of restoration to health, and then death's relentless grasp was to carry off his victim.

The following accounts, by his brother Ferdinand and Herr v. Schober, give us some particulars of Schubert's last days on earth :—

At the beginning of September, Franz left Schober's house and went to his brother Ferdinand, who, after leaving the suburb of St. Ulrich, had settled in a new street attached to the Wieden suburb. The house which the brothers occupied had unfortunately been quite recently built, and Franz had moved into that quarter by advice of the Court physician, Dr. v. Rinna, thinking from such a starting-point he could get away with less worry and loss of time than would have been possible from the heart of the city; he hoped also, by air and exercise, to get some alleviation of his sufferings caused by constant giddiness and rush of blood to the head. The lodgings he had vacated at Schober's were for the future retained on his account.

numerous worshippers of Schubert's classic muse under the above title. These are the musical poems written in August 1828 (?), shortly before the composer's death.'

At this time Schubert began to sicken, and physicians were called in. For a while he seemed to be getting better. At the beginning of October, accompanied by Ferdinand and two friends, he made a short excursion to Unter-Waltersdorf, and from thence to Eisenstadt, where he lingered for some time, pilgrim-like, at the grave of Josef Haydn. During these five days' journey he was very moderate in the way of eating and drinking, but for all that his good spirits and cheerfulness never failed him.

On returning to Vienna, however, his illness became more alarming. One evening, at the end of October, he was dining at an hotel,[1] and had hardly swallowed the first morsel of fish, when he suddenly threw down the knife and fork on his plate, declaring the food was absolutely odious to him, and tasted like poison. From that moment Franz took little else but medicine. He tried to cheer himself by fresh air and exercise, and occasionally took walks in the neighbourhood. Early on the morning of November 3, he walked from the Neu-Wieden to Hernals, to attend a performance of a Latin Requiem composed by Ferdinand. This was the last music he ever heard. After divine service he again walked for three hours; but on his return home, complained greatly of fatigue.

---

[1] This was the already-mentioned 'Zum rothen Kreuz' (at Himmel-pfortgrund), where Franz used often to be with Ferdinand and several friends.

He seems, however, soon afterwards to have partially recovered, and to have entertained no apprehension of any serious illness, for on November 4 he called with Lanz, a pianoforte-teacher still living at Vienna, on the Court organist Sechter, for the purpose of discussing with the latter the subject of some studies in fugue writing, for which he desired Sechter's assistance. They agreed to go through together the exercises by Marpurg[1] so far as that work might serve their purpose, and fixed on the time and number of hours which Schubert proposed to devote to such a purpose. The

---

[1] Marpurg (Friedrich Wilhelm), born at Seehausen, in the Altmark, in the year 1718, died, as Director of Lotteries, at Berlin, in the year 1795. He was one of the most famous musical theorists of his day. Dr. Hauer told me in a letter that Schubert wished much in the last years of his life to become more intimate with Händel. 'How often' (thus runs the passage in Dr. Hauer's letter) 'he would say: "Dear Hauer, do come and let us study Händel together."' In the monthly number of the 'Wiener Musikverein' (for the year 1829), and in Seifried's 'Family Diary' (1838), it is observed that Schubert, in the last months of his life, worked hard under Sechter—an assertion Sechter contradicts. Others affirm that Schubert wished, as early as 1824, to study under Sechter, but was finally dissuaded from his purpose. J. Mayrhofer remarks on this subject :—'Schubert, with no deep knowledge of counterpoint and thorough-bass, remained, strictly speaking, a great natural genius. A few months before his death, he began to take lessons of Sechter; the famous Salieri, therefore, does not seem to have gone systematically through his severe course of study with him, although he examined, praised, and improved Schubert's earlier efforts.' A. Schindler thinks that, 'had Schubert gone through the necessary drilling with Salieri, he would not have wanted any lessons in counterpoint from Sechter. Salieri's instruction was confined to lessons in part-writing.' (From Alois Fuchs' 'Memoranda.')

project, Sechter says, was never realised, for Schubert's steadily increasing illness soon confined him entirely to his sick-bed. The history of our composer's life was thus robbed of one of the strangest spectacles— that of Herr Sechter and Franz Schubert absorbed in a joint musical labour.

On November 11, Schubert's increasing weakness compelled him to keep to his bed. He felt, he said, no actual pain, but sleeplessness and depression reduced the once strong and healthy man to a state of great misery.

At first Dr. Rinna treated him, and Schubert wrote a letter about him (the last he ever did write) to Schober, a personal friend of the physician. Unfortunately, Dr. Rinna himself fell ill, and a doctor of the name of Behring undertook his duty as a deputy, and sent daily bulletins of Schubert's health to his friend Schober.

During his illness, which lasted only nine days, Schubert was very particular about taking his medicines at the time prescribed, and for this purpose kept a watch hanging on a chair close by his bedside. During the first few days he tried to get up and spend a couple of hours in correcting the proof-sheets of the second part of his 'Winterreise.' On the 16th, the doctors had a consultation; they thought that the symptoms showed the likelihood of an imminent attack of nervous fever, still all hopes of recovery were not yet gone. Several of his friends (Spaun, Bauernfeld,[1] Lachner,[2] J. Hüttenbrenner) visited him; others were kept back from fear of infection. On the evening of the 17th, he raved more continuously, having hitherto suffered only at times and slightly from mental wanderings.

The evening before his death, he addressed his brother with the words : ' Ferdinand ! put your ear close to my mouth,' and added, in a mysterious tone, ' Brother, what are they doing with me ? ' His brother answered, ' They are taking great care of you, and doing all they can to make you well again; the doctor assures us you will soon be well again, only you must be patient, and keep to your bed just yet.' The whole day long he wanted to get up, and laboured under the constant delusion that he was in some strange room. Two hours later, the doctor appeared, and spoke to him in the same way as Ferdinand had done. But Schubert looked earnestly at him, clutched at the wall with his poor weak hand, and said slowly and in earnest tones : ' Here, here is my end.'

---

[1] Bauernfeld mentions in his ' Sketches,' that Schubert on his deathbed expressed to him an earnest wish for a new libretto for an opera.

[2] Franz Lachner told me : ' Schubert, when I visited him the last time before I left, was in full possession of all his senses, and I conversed several hours with my dearest friend and most unassuming and modest of artists. He told me of his several plans for the future, and looked forward with eager delight to his recovery that he might finish his Opera " Der Graf von Gleichen," for which Bauernfeld had written words. He had sketched out a large part of this opera.'

On the same day, probably at some early hour in the
morning, the elder Schubert had written to his son
Ferdinand as follows :—

'Dear son Ferdinand,—The days of trouble and hea-
viness are lowering heavily upon us. The dangerous
illness of our beloved Franz weighs heavily on our
souls. All that we can do in this sad time is to seek
comfort from our Heavenly Father, and bear every sorrow appointed us by a wise Providence with firm sub-
mission to His holy will. The result will convince us of
the wisdom and goodness of God. Be of courage, then,
and put your trust in Him. He will strengthen you
that you sink not under this sorrow; His blessing will
keep a yet happy future in store for you. Take every
possible precaution that our dear Franz have administered to him at once the holy Sacraments given to the
dying, and I live in a cheerful hope that the Almighty
will strengthen and preserve him.

'Thy father, afflicted and yet strengthened by trust
in God,

'FRANZ.'

On the afternoon of the same day the father announced to the public the news of his son's death in
the following obituary notice :—

'Yesterday afternoon, at three o'clock on Wednesday,
my beloved son Franz Schubert, artist and composer,
died after a short illness, and having received the

holy Sacraments of the Church. He died at the age of thirty-two. We beg to announce to our dear friends and neighbours that the body of the deceased will be taken on the 21st of this month, at half-past two in the afternoon, from the house standing No. 694 in the new street [1] on the Neuen-Wieden, to be buried near the bishop's stall in the parish church of St. Josef in Margarethen, where the holy rites will be administered.'

'FRANZ SCHUBERT,

' School-teacher in the Rossau.

' Vienna : November 20, 1828.'

Dressed in the ordinary garb of a hermit of the time, a wreath of laurel twisted round the temples, and his face still unchanged by death, Schubert, more like a sleeping than a dead man, rested on his bier, which, in the course of the first day after his death, had been decked by the passing crowds of visitors with wreaths and garlands.

The funeral took place at the time appointed for the ceremony. The weather was unfavourable, but besides the friends and admirers of the deceased, there followed a numerous and sympathising crowd of people, who wished to follow the composer to the grave. The coffin was borne away from the house of death by young

---

[1] This was afterwards called Lumpertgasse (after a former burgo-master of Vienna), and now goes by the name of Kettenbrückengasse. The house in which Schubert died is No. 6, and belongs to Frau Therese Gauglitz.

men (officials and students). Franz v. Schober had been selected by Schubert's relatives as chief mourner, and the verses given in the Appendix of this work were set by him to Schubert's melody, 'Pax vobiscum.' At the small parish church a body of singers, conducted by the Domcapellmeister Gänsbacher, executed a funeral motett of his own composing and the before-cited 'Pax vobiscum,' with an accompaniment of wind instruments. Prayers were then offered, and the body carried to the cemetery in Währing, where, after another commendatory prayer, it was consigned to the grave.[1]

The family, acting on a fresh impression made on their minds by a remarkable expression which came from Schubert on his death-bed, while still in a state of consciousness, had determined that Schubert's mortal remains should rest in this churchyard, a spot resembling a fair and kindly garden. This is alluded to in the following letter, written by Ferdinand Schubert to his father:—

'Dearest Father,—A great number of people are anxious that the body of our dear Franz should be buried in the churchyard at Währing. I certainly am

---

[1] Eight brothers and sisters were living at the time of Schubert's death. Ferdinand, at that time Professor at St. Anna; Ignaz, school-assistant at the Himmelpfortgrund; Carl, painter at the Himmelpfortgrund; Theresia, wife of the Professor at the Imperial Institute for Orphans; Maria, Josefa, Andreas, and Anton (aged, at the time of their brother's death, 14, 13, 5, and 3 years respectively).

one of that number, and am particularly anxious this
should be so, as I believe Franz himself induced me
to think of Währing for his resting-place. The evening before he died he said to me, half consciously,
" I implore you to carry me to my room, and don't
leave me in this corner under the earth. What !
do I deserve no place above the earth?" I answered
him: "Dear Franz, be calm, trust your brother Ferdinand, who loves you so dearly, whom you have
ever trusted: You are in your own room, the same
you always had, and you are lying in your own bed."
Then Franz added: "No, it is not true; Beethoven
is not laid here." Is not this an index, so to speak,
of his heartfelt wish to rest by the side of Beethoven,
whom he so deeply reverenced? I have, therefore,
spoken to Rieder, and ascertained the cost of remov-
ing the body—it will amount to about seventy florins
—a large sum, a very large sum; but very little
for .the honour of Franz's resting-place! For my
part, I can spare temporarily the sum of forty florins,
for yesterday fifty were paid to me. For the rest, I
believe we may expect that all the expenses incidental to his illness and burial will be met by what
has been left. If you, my dear father, agree with
me in these sentiments, I can assure you my mind
will be relieved of a heavy load. But you must at
once make up your mind, and let me know by the
bearer of this letter, so that I can make arrangements

for the arrival of the hearse. You must also take care to give notice to-day in the forenoon to the clergyman at Währing.

'Your afflicted son,

'November 21, 1828, 6 A.M. 'FERDINAND.

'P.S.—Should not the ladies all appear in mourning? The manager of the funeral thinks he need not provide crape, as it is not usually worn at the funerals of unmarried people, and because the pall-bearers have red cloaks and flowers.'

The father agreed to the proposal, and Schubert's wish, which, although uttered in fever and delirium, was believed to have been his earnest and longing desire—to rest in death by the side of Beethoven—was actually fulfilled, for only three graves separate his resting-place from that of one who was to Schubert the type of all grandeur and majesty in the art of music.[1]

The sorrow for Schubert, called away so suddenly from life and labour, was as sincere as it was universal. Several of his friends and acquaintances expressed their sorrow in poems or musical compositions.[2] In the

---

[1] These are the graves of the two O'Donnells and that of Schlechta-Hardtmuth. Schubert's grave is marked 223, Beethoven's 290.

[2] A. Hüttenbrenner wrote a pianoforte piece (Grave in F minor) entitled 'Nachruf,' the Abbé Stadler a fugue (in C minor) for organ or piano, on the musical characters discoverable in Schubert's name, and the Court organist, Sechter, also wrote a fugue in the same key for piano or organ, 'dedicated to the memory of Franz Schubert, too early taken from us.' All these compositions appeared in print.

public journals of the day several memoirs and accounts
of the deceased were published,[1] and at Linz, where
Schubert's name was exceedingly popular, a funeral
ceremony, with music and orations, took place on
December 25, 1828, in the saloon of the Abbé Luigi
Tomazolli, professor of elocution, and an active pro-
moter of music. At Vienna, soon after Schubert's
death, his sorrowing friends and admirers agreed to
have a solemn requiem performed at one of the
churches, and also determined to raise a monument to
his memory. On this subject Jenger wrote the following letter, on November 26, 1828, to Josef Hüttenbrenner[2] :—

'Dear Friend,—Yesterday I spoke to Schober on the
subject of a requiem for Schubert; he entirely agrees
with me, but his circumstances do not admit his taking
a lead in the matter, and he is of opinion that, on the

[1] An obituary notice, by Freiherr v. Zedlitz, printed in the 'Wiener
Zeitschrift' of November 25, 1828, concludes with the following words:—
'Schubert was loved and honoured as a man by all who were admitted
to his friendship; his private life, as is usually the case with all such
thorough artists, was thoroughly noble and estimable.' A second
account, by Blahetka, appeared in the 'Theater-Zeitung,' at Vienna, on
December 27, 1828. Of the poems we may mention 'Am Vortag von
Franz Schubert's Begräbniss,' by Seidl; 'An Schubert's Sarge,' by Franz
v. Schober, &c., &c.

[2] Jenger wrote also to the Pachlers, expressing a wish that Hüttenbrenner's 'Requiem' should be performed. His correspondence at
this time with Dr. Pachler, which referred to Schubert's compositions
left at Gratz, as well as the last days of his life on earth, were unfortunately burnt after Dr. Pachler's death by the desire of their owner.

subject of the requiem and the cost of a monument, both Schubert's father and his brother Ferdinand should be consulted, and he would like to hear what they have to say on the subject. Do this, therefore, and let me have information as soon as possible. Schober thinks that it would be well to spend as little as possible upon the requiem, that a larger sum of money may be realised for the monument and Schubert's private grave, which have to be purchased.

'Talk this matter over with Piringer,[1] so that we may ascertain the probable cost of the requiem. The whole of the money would have to be deducted from the sums already paid by the subscribers, but we shall draw on the fund as little as possible.

'Schober says he thinks a requiem will also be given at St. Joseph's. Should this be so, surely that in the Augustine Church would be unnecessary. I should like, however, one to be performed there. Meantime I shall take care to tell Schober to have subscription-lists lithographed and distributed in the best music-shops, as well as amongst the friends of the deceased. When the notice is ready for the " Zeitung " [2] let me see it.

'Your friend,

'JENGER.'

[1] Piringer was the conductor of the 'Concerts Spirituels,' founded by Franz Xaver Gebauer in Vienna. These were held in the Landständischen Saale.

[2] An appeal was made in the 'Theater-Zeitung' for December 20, 1828. A subscription-list lay open at the office for the Society of

On December 16, Josef Hüttenbrenner petitioned
the Government for permission to celebrate a requiem,
and two days afterwards received an answer in the
affirmative.

On December 23, the Requiem for double chorus,
composed by Anselm Hüttenbrenner (director of the
Styrian Musikverein), was given by the friends and
admirers of the deceased musician at the Augustiner
Hofkirche, and a large number of artists attended the
performance. The Kirchenmusik-Verein had already,
on November 27, performed Mozart's Requiem in
Schubert's honour. It was said before that a wish had
been expressed by professional artists and amateurs
that Schubert's grave should be distinguished by some
monument or stone memorial. Schubert's relatives
having no means at their disposal to defray the expense, Frl. Anna Fröhlich made arrangements for a
concert on January 30, 1829, in the hall of the Musikverein, and half of the proceeds were to go to the
expenses of the proposed memorial.[1]

Musical Connoisseurs, at Vienna, and in every music-shop and em-
porium of art; there were also lists made out in the provinces. Sig-
natures might be attached up to the end of January 1829.

[1] The programme of the concert consisted of the following pieces :—
'Miriam's War Song,' the solo part by Tieze ; Variations for the flute,
by Gabrielsky, performed by Bogner ; 'Taubenpost' and 'Aufenthalt,'
by Vogl ; Trio in E-flat, played by Bocklet, Böhm, and Linke ; 'Die
Allmacht,' by Pyrker, sung by Schoberlechner ; 'Am Strom,' with
violoncello obligato, by Tieze and Linke ; and the first Finale from 'Don
Juan,' the solo parts by Fr. Kiefstein, Jekel, and Sack, and Herren
Tieze, Lugano, Schoberlechner, and Nejebse.

The success of the concert was so brilliant that it had to be repeated; and the proceeds of the two performances, coupled with subscriptions from some friends, sufficed to defray the costs of the requiem and the memorial.[1]

The Committee entrusted Schubert's friend, Franz v. Schober, with the selection of the particular kind of memorial. Schober, acting under the advice of the architect Förster, sketched a design, and also finished a bust which had been begun by the sculptor Arnold. Wasserburger, a master mason, finished the grave-stone; the bust is the work of the academic sculptor Franz Dialler. Franz Grillparzer wrote the following epitaph :—

> Death has here entombed a rich treasure,
> But still more glorious hopes.
> Here lies Franz Schubert,
> Born on the 31st January, 1797,
> Died on the 19th November, 1828,
> Aged 31 years.[2]

---

[1] The net result was 360 florins 46 kreuzers ; Grillparzer, Jenger, and Frl. Fröhlich undertook the management of the business part of the arrangements.

[2] The words of the second line of this epitaph met originally, and also very lately, with the sharpest criticism. At the close of a review of one of Schubert's pianoforte compositions, R. Schumann says :— 'He was able with a calm look to confront the approach of death. And although on the slab over his grave we read of a wealthy treasure being buried with him, but hopes yet more glorious and unfulfilled, let us with gratitude only reflect on the first of these declarations.' (R.

Schubert's features are known everywhere by the portraits so widely circulated. Of the most successful we may point especially to—

An engraving by Passini, after a sketch by Wilhelm

Schumann's ' Gesammelte Schriften,' vol. ii. p. 240.) Schumann wrote these words in the year 1838; the epitaph was composed in 1829. Nowadays, when the largest part of Schubert's treasures has been revealed to us, this epitaph by Grillparzer, which gave offence so many years ago, sounds to our ears still more strangely, and we may hope that over Schubert's future resting-place there will be nothing carved but the name of the composer. As the simple ' Beethoven ' over that great man's grave, the word ' Schubert ' will speak volumes. At the time when Grillparzer wrote the words, Schubert's rich legacy of song had not made its way in the great world, and the poet in those words gave simple utterance to the thoughts which thousands, on hearing the news of the young composer's death, had fearlessly expressed as the language of their fondest hopes. Nay, even Schumann himself has adopted this idea so scouted and repudiated by others, when he goes on to say:—' To indulge in subtle speculations as to what he might have attained to, is utterly valueless.' People may indulge in all sorts of views as to what the value of the epitaph may be, but the fact remains uncontradicted that Schubert's musical development was one ever advancing as years rolled on, and the most remarkable of his creations (the Lied excepted) belong mainly to the last period of his life, and even in the ' Winterreise ' he opened out a new vein of invention. Schubert himself, a few months before his death, declared ' he would confine himself exclusively to opera and symphony;' on his dying bed he employed the time in sketching out plans of grander works, and at that time his mental powers showed no signs of decay. But ' it is idle to indulge in subtle speculations as to what he might possibly have attained to,' and if an artist, whose writings have won immortality for their author, be permitted to count his earthly mission fulfilled, this undoubtedly is the case with Schubert, and in this sense is in entire harmony with Schumann's concluding words:—' He has done enough, and praised be he who, like Schubert, has striven and accomplished.'

Rieder ;[1] a lithograph by Clarot,[2] at Vienna, also after a drawing by Rieder, which, in fact, was the model for the different portraits afterwards made.

There is a painted miniature in possession of Herr Hofrath Josef v. Spaun, of Vienna. A drawing (June 10, 1821) found in 1862, concealed in the portfolio of Professor Leopold Kupelwieser, was a sketch made by Kupelwieser himself. This is the property of the Kupel-wieser family. Small plaster casts of the bust were also sold by Haslinger.

---

[1] To be bought at Josef Czerny's, in Vienna, Am Graben, No. 134, price 1 florin 12 kreuzers.

[2] At Artaria & Co.'s, in Vienna, for 36 kreuzers.

CHAPTER XVII.

CHARACTERISTICS OF SCHUBERT.

ON SOME FEATURES IN SCHUBERT'S CHARACTER—HIS APPEARANCE—
DISPOSITION—SCHINDLER'S AND MAYRHOFER'S VIEWS RESPECTING
HIM—HIS INDUSTRY AND PRODUCTIVENESS—MUSICAL READINESS—HIS
BEHAVIOUR IN SOCIETY—FONDNESS FOR STRONG DRINKS—TRAIN
OF THOUGHT IN CONNECTION WITH THE 'WINTERREISE'—FRANZ
V. SCHOBER AND GRILLPARZER ON SCHUBERT'S INFLUENCE AND
CHARACTER.

THE presence and personal appearance of the composer
were anything but attractive.

His round and puffy face, low forehead, projecting
lips, bushy eyebrows, stumpy nose, and short curly hair,
gave him that negro look which corresponds with that
conveyed by the bust which is to be found at the
Währing churchyard.[1]   He was under the average

---

[1] When the mortal remains of Beethoven and Schubert were disin-
terred in October 1863, the skull of the latter, which was in a good state
of preservation, was cleansed and washed, and the doctors and hospital
attendants who were present were astonished at its delicate, almost
womanly organisation.   Neither on Beethoven's nor on Schubert's head
were discovered the marks of a musical organisation stamped on those
parts where one would ordinarily expect to find them.   We have yet to
wait for a publication of the result of the measurements taken of both
the skulls. (See 'Actenmässige Darstellung der Ausgrabung und Wieder-
beisetzung der irdischen Reste von Beethoven und Schubert.' Gerold:
Vienna, 1863.)

height, round-backed and shouldered, with plump arms and hands, and short fingers. The expression of his face was neither intellectual nor pleasing, and it was only when music or conversation interested him, and especially if Beethoven was the topic, that his eye began to brighten and his features light up with animation. However uncomely, nay, almost repulsive, his exterior,[1] the spiritual and hidden part of the man was noble and abundantly endowed. All of Schubert's intimate friends agree that he was blessed with a good disposition, that he was a good son, fondly attached to all his family, a firm friend, always ready to do a good turn for any he loved, free from all envy and hatred, high-minded, and an enthusiastic worshipper of nature and the art which was sacred to him. There was a calmness in his demeanour and a cheerfulness, the result of an easily pleased and contented spirit, which, coupled with his innocent humour and fondness for companionship, made him very attractive to men of similar disposition with his own.[2]

Franz Schubert made no famous journeys, like

---

[1] 'The most complete contrast to Mayrhofer,' remarks W. Chezy, in his 'Recollections,' 'was seen in the person of the short, stumpy composer, whose exterior was like a mass of tallow (*Talglumpen*), but whose beaming eyes nevertheless betrayed at the first glance the depth of the fire therein concealed.'

[2] For these traits of Schubert's character I am indebted to verbal and written statements of Spaun, Schober, L. Sonnleithner, Kupelwieser, Bauernfeld, A. Schindler, Mayrhofer, Stadler, and Madame Anna Fröhlich.

Mozart and Händel before him, and other great composers who succeeded him; he never appeared before
crowned heads or produced his works before royal
courts, acquiring thereby an enlarged understanding
of the world, and a greater knowledge of mankind.
Nor, like his great compeer Beethoven, was he versed
in ancient and modern literature or knowledge of State
affairs; nor, again, like Mendelssohn and Schumann, did
he enjoy that modern culture and versatility which gave
such a catholicity to the studies of those famous men;
his education under his father's roof never advanced
beyond the ordinary routine of the necessary elements
of knowledge, and the time he spent at the Convict
was dedicated more exclusively to composing than the
study of classic authors, history, geography, &c.

Still, it would be incorrect to assert that his education was generally defective, and that the many beautiful things he gave to the world were the unreasoning
efforts of a dreamlike imagination.

The few letters we possess, and notably those of his
later days, prove that their author's heart and understanding were both in the right place.

These letters are conspicuous for a plain good sense
and healthy understanding, and a freedom from all
conceit and false sentimentalism, which are valuable
makeweights in an estimate of Schubert's character;
and if he was wanting in what we call the higher
branches of education, it must not be forgotten that his

yearnings for composition in the early days of his youth made him familiar with the noblest poetry, both native and foreign, and that such men as Franz v. Schober, Mayrhofer, Vogl, and many others, must have had an enduring intellectual influence over his thoughts and character.

'It is true' (says A. Schindler) 'that we do not meet in Schubert's life with mountain or valley, but only a level plain, over which he moves with an invariably steady and equal step. The evenness of his disposition, too, which resembled the smooth surface of a mirror, was with difficulty ruffled by external matters—his spirit and actions were in complete harmony with each other. It must be confessed, that his days glided away as well befitted the life of a citizen born in poverty and dying in poverty. Until he was twelve years old he remained under his father's roof; from that time forward to his sixteenth year he was a chorister at the Imperial Convict and a pupil at the Gymnasium, then for three years assistant-teacher to his father at the Lichtenthal, finally a pianoforte-player—well worthy of imitation—and a composer writing just as he pleased, and thereby free and independent, as his publishers paid him fifteen florins for every sheet (*Heft*) of songs and fifteen for a pianoforte work. As in the case of other musicians, the indigence of Schubert's early days diminished the force of the so-called noble passions and the pressure of artificial wants. Family troubles

and anxieties of all kinds, incidental to the married
condition of a poor man, never hindered the soaring
flight of his genius; he stood alone in his own magic
circle, disturbed by no prosaic family hindrances. For
the last eight years of his life he had given up teach-
ing music,[1] and thereby put a stop to a thankless task,
and one which he found most irksome. He made no
journeys, for one cannot dignify by that name the short
excursions he made to Upper Austria. One reason for
Schubert's gifts remaining so long hidden from the
eyes of mankind during the lifetime of their possessor,
was his peculiar obstinate and unyielding temperament
—qualities which, without prejudice to his outspoken
sense of the value of independence, made him turn a
deaf ear to the good and practical advice on the part of
many well-meaning friends.

'This characteristic wilfulness and obstinacy, which
were repeatedly shown in Schubert's social dealings
with other men, are by no means to be ascribed to an
overweening sense of artistic self-consciousness, or an
over-estimate of his peculiar gifts. Schubert's devotion
to the great classical representatives of his art, his ceaseless mental activity, afford convincing proofs against
such a supposition. Emulation, springing from motives
of self-interest and ambition, which are no small
stimulus to the activity and energy of artists, were

---

[1] Schubert had, before the year 1820, given up all pupils, excepting
the Esterhazys.

ideas utterly foreign to Schubert ; the privacy which he clung to as far as was possible, and his course of life generally, speak loudly enough for the purity of his aims. He was no doubt sensitive to blame, however carefully sugared over, but, on the other hand, he was still more callous and indifferent to extravagant assertions of praise; he remained strictly impassive when this or that work of his was the subject of compliment, and his face betrayed no emotion on such occasions.' [1]

Falsehood and envy were absolutely unknown to him (says J. Mayrhofer); his character was a compound of tenderness and solidity, loveableness and sincerity, sociability and melancholy. Modest, open, a man of childlike simplicity, he had patrons and friends devoted to his interests and the success of his works, nor can it be doubted that this was but the earnest of the universal recognition which he would have met with had his life been prolonged, and of the more assured and posthumous fame of an artist, carried off in the early vigour of his genius.

When we consider the astonishing number of the mere published compositions of Schubert, we feel convinced that their author, overtaken by death in his thirty-second year, must have worked with a facility

---

[1] This statement must be reduced to its fair proportions, and Schindler's statements respecting Schubert accepted always with some caution, as Beethoven's 'familiar friend' falls occasionally into the language of exaggeration, and never had any intimate relationship with Schubert.

as surprising as his activity was ceaseless, especially as there is no lack of corrections on the face of his scores.

In truth, Schubert was a man of extraordinary industry and practical power, and it may with justice be said of him, that he utilised nobly and faithfully the talent committed to his charge.

As a rule, Franz began his daily work in the early hours of the morning, sitting upon his bed and writing,[1] thus he would work incessantly up to break-fast-time; after that he became absorbed in his musical studies, and often, when some idea seized him, eye-witnesses, we are told, could guess, from his flashing eye and altered tone of voice, that the spirit was at work within him. Schubert, in one sense, was an intensely active worker, for whilst drawing incessantly upon his creative powers, he sought at once to perpetuate and fix on paper the full treasures of his musical fancies. For that which in ordinary parlance passes for work, and especially for all mechanical labour, Schubert had no taste whatever; and this, taken in connection with some irregularities and unpunctuality at rehearsals, induced him to refuse offers, the acceptance of which would have deprived him of being master of his time.

The other part of the day was, as a rule, given up to

---

[1] Spaun says that Schubert sometimes passed the night at his house, and that even during sleep he would keep his spectacles on his nose ; of a morning, often in a half-dressed condition, he would go to the piano and improvise.

the pleasures of social companionship, and in fine
weather he used to make excursions in the country
with his friends and neighbours. If at such times he
felt thoroughly happy with his friends, and very averse
to parting with the lovely scene and pleasant wine
before him, he would ignore some invitation he had
accepted for the evening, and hence arose some short-
lived unpleasantnesses between Schubert and his acquaintances. When his work was over for the day, it
needed but the faintest suggestion to call and wake
up his sleepless spirit, as we know by the story of the
' Ständchen.'

' If fruitfulness,' says Robert Schumann, ' be a characteristic of genius, Schubert is certainly one of the
greatest. By degrees he might have set to music the
whole body of German literature, and if Telemann [1]
requires that an ordinary composer should, if the neces-
sity arose, be able to set a printed programme to music,
he would have found what he wanted in Schubert. In
whatever direction he wished his music to flow, there
it gushed forth in streams; Æschylus, Klopstock, both
so hard to set to music, yielded to his treatment, just
as he brought out the deepest utterances from the flowing easy strains of W. Müller and others.' Whoever
proposed any subject to Schubert for musical treatment, might rely on the quickest possible despatch on

[1] Telemann (Georg Filipp), born at Magdeburg, in 1681, died 1767,
one of the most productive composers in the world.

the part of the composer, if he liked the subject.
Thus the familiar song of 'The Wanderer' was written
in an incredibly short space of time; the same was the
case with the 'Zwerg' and 'Erlkönig,' which, after
reading through the ballad several times in succession,
he set so rapidly to music, that the very notes seemed to
tumble over one another.

The following anecdote testifies to the lightning-like
rapidity of his comprehension, as well as to the pleasure he took in carrying out the wishes of others.

Fräulein Anna Fröhlich, teacher of singing at the
Conservatorium, at whose suggestion Schubert had written some beautiful choruses for sopranos, intended
giving a birthday serenade in the garden of Herr Gosmar
at Unterdöbling, near Vienna. The heroine on the occasion was her pupil Louise Gosmar (afterwards Fr.
v. Sonnleithner), and the fête was given in the summer of 1827. Grillparzer had composed for the occasion a poem entitled: 'Zögernd leise in des Dunkels
nächt'ger Stille,' and the lady gave the lines to her
friend the composer, with a request that he would
set the poem to music for her sister Josefine (mezzo
soprano) and a chorus of ladies. Schubert took the
poem in hand, withdrew to the window-sill, put his
spectacles on his forehead, as he was wont to do if
looking closely at anything, read the verses twice
through with great attention, and then said with a
smile: ' I have it, it's done already, and it will do very

well.' A day or two after he brought the beautiful
composition. By a mistake, the piece was written for
alto solo and chorus of men, and on Fräulein Frölich's
calling Schubert's attention to this, he took away the
manuscript and brought it back again next day reset
in the mode and key the lady wished for. The effect
of this serenade, sung in the clear moonlight and in
the open air, was enchanting. Numbers of the dwellers at Döbling stood and listened at the garden gate.
Schubert (as usual) was not present at the performance.
On another occasion Schubert, whilst lying in bed,
wrote off in hot haste an occasional trio for Umlauff
which the latter had ordered, and the composer had
completely forgotten, having lost the poem in question.
Many such instances of Schubert's power of musical
improvisation could be quoted.

The enthusiasm of his friends, and the steadily increasing applause of the public, so intoxicating to
many, and leading men to an overweening estimate
of their gifts, never for a moment disconcerted Schubert, and the honourable distinction paid to him by
many eminent in rank, intellect, and artistic fame,
never led him to an immoderate excess of self-consciousness. Amongst the musical artists who took
a lively interest in Schubert, we find C. M. Weber,
Hummel, and Lablache the singer; to the last of these
he dedicated three Italian songs. Theodore Körner
happened to be at Vienna in the years 1811–1813, at

the very time when Schubert made up his mind to devote himself exclusively to art, and the poet (I have Spaun's authority for this) strengthened Schubert in this resolution.

Schubert was often drawn into musical circles in the society at Vienna,[1] and it frequently happened that whilst the performers, instrumental and vocal, were loaded with compliments, not a thought was given to the little insignificant man who sat at the piano accompanying his own songs with an earnestness and depth of expression comparatively lost on his audience. But the unassuming artist was all the more callous to such coldness and neglect, when the applause with which his own composition was greeted was at last directed to the composer himself. At meetings of this kind, and especially in the more refined circles, where he would sometimes, out of pure good nature, accompany his own Lieder, he was very shy and chary of talk. Whilst sitting at the piano, his face became very serious, and directly the piece ended he used to withdraw to an adjoining room. Indifferent to praise and applause, he shrank from compliments, and felt quite wretched if his friends expressed themselves satisfied with what they had heard.[2]

---

[1] At one of these musical gatherings Lablache took the second bass part in the 'Gondelfahrer;' and at a soirée given by Franz v. Lascny, Hummel, to Schubert's great delight, extemporised on the song, 'Der blinde Knabe,' just after Vogl had sung it to the assembled company.

[2] At a party given in the house of the Princess Kinsky, a number of

It was a very different thing when he found himself free of all conventional chains and propriety; his tongue would then be loosed in the merriest humour and talk, and he would indulge in wit and practical jokes, many of which could be told by M. Schwind. Amongst other strange drolleries of Schubert was his parody of the 'Erl-King,' which he would sing through the teeth of a comb, to the amusement of his audience. If sometimes he kept quietly to himself, at others he would join in the merriment around him. His laugh was not that of ordinary mirth, it consisted of a hoarse suppressed chuckle.

He never danced, but occasionally, at parties given by his intimate friends, he would sit down to the piano, and extemporise for hours together the most lovely dance music. He repeated such pieces as pleased him, so as to fix them in his memory and write them down at leisure.

His modesty went hand in hand with the respect he felt for the musical performances of others, even in the Lieder department, where none before him or since his time have attained such undisputed mastery. In his early years he was devoted to Zumsteeg's Lieder, his

his Lieder had been sung, and no one troubled himself with a thought about Schubert. At last the lady of the house stepped forward to say some kind words, and at the same time excuse the behaviour of her guests. Schubert answered the Princess, that she need not trouble herself, he was used to it, and felt all the more at ease if he remained unnoticed.

favourites being 'Kolmal,' 'Maria Stuart,' 'Die Erwartung,' and 'Der stille Toggenburg;' he took such
great delight in Kreutzer's 'Wanderlieder,' that, in
reply to some flatterers who wished to run down the
composer at Schubert's expense, he declared that he
liked the songs uncommonly, and he only wished he
had written them himself.

It is a well-known fact that Schubert was a genuine
believer in wine; nay, there are people who would
libel him as a confirmed drunkard, probably because of
a few harmless excesses in the way of potations, of
which no doubt our composer was guilty.

Franz liked good wine. In spite of the protestations
of friends anxious about his health, he refused to thin
his potations with water; and not having a strong
head, it happened that at the wine-shop with a party
of merry fellows, or in private houses, if the right
sort of vintage was on the table, our friend would
occasionally overshoot the mark, and then either become boisterous and violent, or, when the wine had
completely fuddled him, slink off to a corner, where not
a syllable, in his maudlin state, could be got from him.[1]

---

[1] It is well known that Beethoven had to endure the reproach of
being a drinker, in consequence of some exceptional departures from his
usual abstemious habits. These occurred (according to Schindler) in
the year 1826. Wilhelm Chezy, who had been introduced by Ernst v.
Feuchtersleben to the round table, at which Schubert and his companions were wont to assemble, in Bogner's coffee-house, thus expresses
himself in his 'Recollections of my Life' (vol. ii. p. 292):—' Unhappily,

If plenty of good wine stood upon the table, people had to watch Franz very carefully : there is no exception to the testimony given on this point by all those persons who make no secret of Schubert's weakness and had plenty of opportunity of observing him on such occasions. One is disposed to set down to a too frequent indulgence in wine the cause of the pains and rushes of blood to the head, to which Schubert was subject in the

Schubert's thirsty inclinations led him astray to following those bad courses which generally admit of no return—at all events, of none consistent with health ; the conversion is not at all times of the same importance as the reversion, especially when one follows the example of the familiar old devil, and sits down to booze in solitude. But Schubert could never succeed in getting so far on the path of conversion, and he died in his three and thirtieth year. He took a certain—shall I call it pride? in the accidents which befell him in his wild career at times. Anyhow he turned them to some good account. He set the charming "Müllerlieder" in the midst of griefs of a very different kind to those which he immortalised in music, as the utterances of the poor miller's boy with his despised love. He was surely as fond of wine as any young worshipper of the loveliest art. But when the blood of the grape glowed within his veins, he was not violent, but liked to retire to a secluded corner, and there nurse himself comfortably into a passion ; he became a laughing tyrant, who would destroy everything he could without making a noise—glasses, plates, cups, &c.—and sit simpering and screwing up his eyes into the smallest possible compass.' At a wine-shop, when he had drunk more than he ought, he used, when the time of reckoning came, to put his hand quietly under the table, and the Kellner had to guess, by the number of fingers held up by their owner, the quantity of pints consumed. A friend of Schubert's mentions the so-called 'Vertrunkenen Quartett,' a quartett for men's voices, before writing which Schubert had steeped himself in liquor. He certainly was damaged by his potations on this occasion. At that time (1827) he was living on the Bastei.

last years of his life, and even the illness to which he so quickly succumbed must at least in part be ascribed to his fondness for strong liquors. Schubert's 'drunken habits' are reduced to these facts; but the most convincing proof that sobriety was his rule and intemperance an exception, lies in the solidity and number of works produced by him, unquestionably when all his faculties and powers were absolutely at his command—works which a man could never have accomplished, had he not made a proper use of the scant measure of existence accorded to him.

Schubert can claim, equally with many other gifted men, that right so often withheld, of being measured in respect of his moral worth by no other standard than that used as a test for the ordinary run of mankind, whose faults and weaknesses are often unnoticed, or at all events sparingly condemned, whereas the same failings in men of lofty genius are taken to be the leading features of their character, and that which is a mere human weakness is only too gladly construed into vice.

He was somewhat indifferent to the charms of the fair sex, nor, as so frequently happens with those gifted with a vivid fancy, was Schubert a victim of excessive passion. He revelled in sentimental friendships, and yet was no stranger to tender passion. We have instanced one heart affair, and there may have been possibly others; but they were all of a fleeting nature, and far from making any lasting impression on him. With regard to attachments of this kind, Schubert (so Von Schober told me) was exceedingly reserved, even to his most intimate friends.

Schubert usually kept away from the performances of his own works. He liked working in solitude, but his task once over, he longed for companionship and sociability, and only thoroughly relished hospitality, amusements, and social intercourse provided all ceremony and constraint were banished by consent. One of the chief traits of his character was a modesty which, when Schubert came to deal personally with publishers, made him reserved and timid to such a degree, that he failed to reap the full harvest of his labours.

It was only when he felt the pressure of external circumstances, and could not rid his mind of the painful thoughts which would arise after ill-paid performances, that he gave vent to his indignation in words which had a spice of bitterness in them, and betrayed, very probably, the innate consciousness he had of his own value. His naturally shy temperament, and the unpleasant experiences he had encountered from his love of unvarnished truth and plaindealing, kept him all the more apart from the noisy world and its troubles, inasmuch as his aversion to display unfitted him for conflict with the world, and enabled him in the surest way to avoid the danger of being misunderstood by keeping free from collision with society.

In the final years of his short earthly career he

seems to have been more powerfully impressed with a sense of the importance of life than in earlier time, without allowing his natural cheerfulness to be changed to despondency or sluggish inaction. From such conditions of mind his abiding and overflowing redundancy of power as a composer effectually guarded him—at least from any continuance of such moods—and his works of this period are eloquent testimony to the truth of this assertion. The desire awakened in Schubert's heart of securing a settled means of livelihood, the frustration of that hope, and, more than this, a constant state of ill-health—all these matters may have materially conduced to the unhinging and putting out of tune his naturally equable and contented mind. Hence the more melancholy numbers of the 'Winterreise' found a fruitful soil in the fancy of the composer. Whether, as many have asserted, the pressure of Schubert's physical and moral sufferings was aggravated by the composition of these songs, we cannot undertake to decide, and think it far more likely that in occupying himself as a composer in setting that series of poems, the ultimate success of which would have afforded him such real satisfaction, he found a deliverance from morbid and cheerless views of the world around him. This certainly was the case with numbers of his works subsequent to the 'Winterreise'—works which give us no clue to any morbid condition of spirit on the part of their writer.[1]

[1] J. Mayrhofer thus speaks in his 'Recollections of Franz Schubert':—

In the preceding pages we pointed to certain features of Schubert's character, so far as they admitted of delineation from the glimpses we have had of his outer life—glimpses seldom, if ever, differing in scope and extent from those we have of the ordinary every-day life of individuals, and giving us, therefore, no more than the average materials for forming an estimate of his character.

A far more accurate, and of course more valuable picture could have been made of a nature so peculiar and so delicately organised, had we analysed more closely the laboratory and workings of his mind, and, as in many instances of great artistic natures, thrown more light on the mutual relations existing between the outer life and intellectual energies of the composer than we have done in this particular instance. Schubert is, perhaps, a single instance of a great artist whose outer life had no affinity or connection with art. His career was so simple and uneventful, so out of all

'The selection of the "Winterreise" shows the composer had become more serious. He had had a long and severe illness, life was robbed of its roseate hues; for him the winter had set in. The sadness and irony of the poet worked powerfully on him.' Spaun, in his 'Memoirs,' says that Schubert announced to his friends his completion of the 'Winterreise' in the following words:—'You will soon learn the reasons of my growing despondency. I will sing for you at Schober's some awfully gloomy Lieder; they have had a great effect on me.' Schober declares this, like many others, is a made-up story, and, pointing to Schubert's productive powers, affirms that the composer had, in the little library Schober had got together for him, lighted upon some Lieder by Müller, and being attracted by them, as he was with so many other poems, set them to his beautiful music.

proportion with works which he created like a heaven-
sent genius, that we must at last turn to them mainly,
if we would form any estimate of the wealthy treasures
concealed in the mine of Schubert's heart and spirit.
In ordinary life (says Franz Schober of him) the opportunity was only offered to a sacred few, and to those too
only on the rarest occasions, of convincing themselves
of Schubert's entire nobility of soul, and this they
collected from scenes and conversations which cannot
easily be repeated or described.

As a conclusion to these few characteristics of Schubert, we may quote here a poem by Franz Grillparzer,
in which the poet, who knew Schubert intimately, sums
up his friend's influence and individuality as an artist
in the following lines :—

> Schubert heiss ich, Schubert bin ich,
> Und als solcher geb' ich mich.
> Was die Besten je geleistet,
> Ich erkenn' es, ich verehr' es,
> Immer doch bleibt's ausser mir.
> Selbst der Kunst, die Kränze windet,
> Blumen sammelt, wählt und bindet,
> Ich kann ihr nur Blumen bieten,
> Sichte sie, und—wählet ihr.
> Lobt ihr mich, es soll mich freuen,
> Schmäht ihr mich, ich muss es dulden ;
> Schubert heiss ich, Schubert bin ich,
> Mag nicht hindern, kann nicht laden ;
> Geht ihr' gern auf meinen Pfaden,
> Nun wohlan, so folget mir.

CHAPTER XVIII.

GENERAL SURVEY.

REVIEW OF SCHUBERT'S MUSICAL PERFORMANCES—THE GERMAN LIED
—ATTAINS ITS BEST PERIOD IN SCHUBERT'S WORKS—CHARACTERIS-
TICS OF SCHUBERT'S LIEDER—THE 'LIEDERKREISE'—BALLAD—MEN-
DELSSOHN'S AND SCHUMANN'S LIEDER—PART-SONGS—CHORUSES FOR
MALE AND FEMALE VOICES—CANTATAS AND HYMNS—INSTRUMENTAL
MUSIC—PIANOFORTE WORKS—OVERTURES AND SYMPHONIES FOR OR-
CHESTRA—THE GREAT SYMPHONY IN C—CHAMBER MUSIC—SCHUBERT
AS AN OPERATIC COMPOSER—HIS SACRED COMPOSITIONS FOR THE
CHURCH—THE G MASS.

In Franz Schubert the German Lied has found its
greatest and most genial exponent. His efforts were
directed to composition in every known department of
music, but his speciality, and the most splendid legacy
Schubert bequeathed to the world, is the Lied. No
musician has approached, much less surpassed him in
this particular province; on all sides we greet and
venerate him as an undisputed monarch in the Lieder
kingdom. The early beginnings of the 'Lied,' a plant
which found so congenial a soil in the heart of man,
date as far back as the first days of the spread of
Christianity, which first opened up rich mines of spiri-
tualities, and awakened and called forth a love for

song. But centuries were to pass before the Lied had gone through the many chequered phases incidental to its gradual formation, and not until our time did it culminate in that high eminence which enables us to regard it as a distinct and noble province of art, fitted by its peculiar attributes to animate and adorn the universal world of sound.

The history of the development of the German Lied shows that the foundation and starting-point of its progress must be referred to that period when it was first emancipated from the fetters of the old recitations of church music, and the modes adopted by the Minne- and Meistersinger. When once it confided itself to the energetic progressive spirit of the German people, that spirit animated the thriving plant, which straightway blossomed into the Volkslied.[1]

The people then sang its own songs. These passed on traditionally from mouth to mouth, and no one of the people ever thought of riveting by musical signs

[1] The Minnesang flourished from 1100 to 1600. The famous musical contest on the Wartburg took place in the year 1207. One of the last Minnesingers, Oswald von Wolkenstein, died in 1445. Their most flourishing period was between 1300 and 1600. Hans Sachs, the Meistersinger, died in 1576. The Meistersang was not completely put an end to until the year 1839, when the four last remaining members of the Ulm Singing-school divested themselves of their badges as a corporate body. The chief school of the ' Meistersänger' was (according to Wagenseil) in Nuremberg, their place of meeting at Mayence. See A. Reissmann : ' Das deutsche Lied in seiner historischen Entwicklung.' Cassel, 1861. A. W. Ambros : ' Geschichte der Musik,' vol. ii. p. 258.

the favourite national tunes. Musicians, when once made aware of the indestructible power of these stores of melodious treasure, took possession of it, and, by contrapuntal treatment, remodelled the Volkslied into an artistic form—a process which resulted in a smoother and more even form of song, and clothed at times with a more profound meaning and intention as compared with the more spontaneous but less artistic Volkslied. The Lied, however, lost its original character and the stamp of individuality.[1]

The significance of this crisis, characterising a notable turning-point in the onward progress of the Lied, never became fully apparent until, in the historic sequel or opera, cantata, and oratorio, instrumental music had won for itself a considerable independency and power, and gradually referred back the Air to its kindred predecessor, the Lied (uncultivated by masters in the interim), for which processes the rich appliances of

---

[1] A great number of German Volkslieder, energetic, heart-stirring, and animated in their way, were in vogue between 1480 and 1550, and have been admirably set and preserved by the masters of the school of those times, amongst whom were such men as Heinrich Finck, Lorenz Lemlin, Heinrich Isaak, and many others. The nomadic lute-players of the time, who strolled about the country playing the national strains, and the organists using similar themes, are entitled to be mentioned at the same time with these masters. The Volkslied, like a flower of the field, which of a morning blooms in quiet loveliness, and none can say who planted it, was transplanted to the art-garden of loftier music, and there expanded into blossoms of often surprising beauty and fulness. (Ambros: 'Geschichte der Musik,' vol. ii. p. 281.)

dramatic and instrumental music were drawn upon unsparingly.[1]

The Reformation in the sixteenth century gave a fresh and powerful impulse to the movement by important changes made with reference to ecclesiastical music, by the foundation of choral bodies, by the cultivation of solo singing at school and at home, by making the lute an accompanying instrument, and especially by the fostering care bestowed on the Lied, to the cultivation of which composers now applied themselves with renewed energy.[2]

Generally speaking, however, when the influence of music became more and more extended over all Germany, the original Volkslied began to decay. The

---

[1] The Arie, as a pure lyrical expression, rests on the same basis as the Lied, but has a more extensive and significant meaning viewed as a medium for the utterance of some particular emotion. The German masters (Händel, Bach, and Gluck), with their profound knowledge of harmony, glorified and enlarged the borders of the Arie, whereas the Italians aimed at theatrical effects more particularly. Graun, Hasse, Telemann, Benda, Doles, and Quanz were in favour of the Italian style; Marpurg and the pupils of Sebastian Bach clung to the German. Traces of the specialities peculiar to the North German school are to be found even in our own times. See Reissmann : 'Das deutsche Lied.'

[2] Thus, at the commencement of the 17th century, the ' Palmenorden ' arose, in 1643 the ' Zesen'sche deutschgesinnte Gesellschaft ' at Hamburg, and in 1656 the ' Schwanenorden ' on the Elbe—associations having for their object the cultivation and development of German poetry. The chief bards of the ' Palmenorden ' were the Silesians Martin Opitz and Christian Hofmann, as well as Flemming, Gryphius, and Kaspar v. Lohenstein.

progress of musical education and culture limited with increasing strictness the national art of singing to certain prescribed artistic forms, and then arose a new phase, the 'volksthümliche Lied,' standing midway between the 'Volksgesang' proper, and the 'Kunstlied,' and borrowing from the one its easy flow, from the other its more cultivated form and character. If the old Volkslied, by its naïveté and inexhaustible store of rich national humour, assumed an enchanting variety of artistic forms, this variety was naturally increased by artists who understood how to create great works out of the humble tunes common to the nation. It is this very popular element in its noblest significance which, artistically cultivated, has ensured for so many works of the greatest musical composers, and for Schubert as well, a lasting and universal influence— the best security for the enduring powers inherent in the music of such writers.[1]

The north of Germany had, up to the eighteenth

[1] The greatness and the enduring power of Händel's oratorios rest chiefly on the popular element pervading the choruses. Of the influence of the Volksgesang in Haydn's and even Bach's instrumental and vocal music, we need no further illustration here; it is this national essence which gives the immortal freshness of youth and power of attraction to the most finished dramatic works of Mozart, Weber, and others. Ambros remarks, in his 'History of South European Music,' that the Volkslied is of the highest importance; it is, next to Gregorian song, the second chief power. It was the inexhaustible treasure from which the greatest masters of music drew their melodies, which they not only transformed into vocal pieces of consummate art, but on which they constructed their noblest and most enduring musical compositions.

century, appropriated to itself the 'Kunstlied,' and for
a long period an untold number of composers in the
North testified to the active cultivation of the Lied,
whereas throughout the greater part of South Germany,
and specially in Vienna, where the connoisseurs wor-
shipped the Italian style of vocalisation, the value
attributed to the Lied was little more than nominal.
In the North the Italian opera exercised no longer
any great influence. Dramatic art was represented by
the Singspiel, more akin to English opera or French
vaudeville than the music in vogue throughout Italy,
and this Singspiel altered and improved the German
Lied. In the second half of the last century, there
arose in North Germany the first modest beginnings
of German lyric poetry,[1] illustrated by the works of
Gleim, Hagedorn, Jakobi, and many others, with whom
was associated Adam Hiller as a Lieder composer and
the precursor of other men in the same line.[2]

Afterwards, when Herder had revived once more the
old feeling and appreciation of the 'Volkslied,' and a
fresh spring-time for Lieder had dawned with Göthe's
lyric poems, a new period was inaugurated, and melody and accompaniments, more closely fitted to the
meaning of the words, expressed more powerfully the

---

[1] Weisse hoped by his operas to induce the Germans to cultivate part-
singing, and as a fact, the operetta influenced the cultivation of the Lied.

[2] Neefe, Reichhardt, and Gluck also set Klopstock's odes, but to music
of no lasting value. Schubert tried his hand at them, and certainly with
more success.

secret feelings of the human heart than had ever been known before.

In the north of Germany, Klein, Berger, Reichardt, and Zelter [1] (the two last worshippers exclusively of Göthe's poetry) were the last in the series of Lieder composers, at a time when Schubert's star was already in the ascendant; in the South, Haydn, Mozart, and Beethoven were even in the Lied his immediate predecessors. The Lieder composers above mentioned, who belonged to the Berlin school, endeavoured in some of their vocal compositions to unite the essence of the Volkslied with the poetry of a national kind, and to stamp with a more marked individuality the means of musical representations for the newly-born lyrical poems (notably those of Göthe). What those mighty masters, Haydn, Mozart, and Beethoven, created in the way of song bears no relation to their compositions of the operatic and instrumental · kind ; but genius here too insisted on maintaining its rights, and amongst their vocal compositions are found several masterpieces, which, by their beauties of harmony and melody, surpass everything written of this kind before them.

Mozart's Lieder are formed either on the perfectly simple style of the national air, or, in cases where a higher ideal is before the mind of the composer, ex-

---

[1] Zelter, Carl Friedrich, born at Berlin in 1758, and died there in 1832, a few months after Göthe.

tended to a dramatic form.[1] Each single point in the
poem appears represented musically, and stands out in
independent relief, so that we have a form of Lied in.
which music is rendered more absolutely subservient to
illustrate the poet's meaning than is the case with the
composite style of the essentially lyric Lied.

If Mozart, following the bent of his essentially dramatic genius, enlarged the boundaries of the Lied by
giving it a scenic form, to Beethoven was the task
assigned of still further improving and elevating the
Lied to a higher sphere, by adding a groundwork of
richer and grander instrumental harmonies. With
Beethoven the accompaniments of the song attain, in
certain instances, to a copiousness which pointed to the
following stage on which the Lied was about to enter,
when Franz Schubert appeared on the scene.

Beethoven has, moreover (like Josef Haydn) sung
in the adagios of his instrumental music the most

---

[1] Of the forty-one Lieder known to have been written by Mozart (from
which we must eliminate some Ariettas and part-songs), we may point to
'Das Veilchen,' 'Abendempfindung,' 'Trennung,' 'An Chloe,' and 'Unglückliche Liebe,' as pre-eminent for expression and perfection of form.
The Lied 'An Chloe' approaches in form an Italian canzonet, 'Unglückliche Liebe' is full of dramatic passion. All his other Lieder are
musically of no great value, although, of course, not without their particular charm. The poems of Weisse, Hagedorn, Jakobi, Blumauer,
Hermes, Hölty, Günther, Kanitz, and Claudius offered no field for composition on a grander scale, but Mozart seems never to have known
Göthe's lyric poetry, from which the more modern Lieder-singers drew
so largely. The one single Lied of Göthe he ever set to music was
'Das Veilchen.'

lovely Lieder; these are deeper and greater utterances than any of his songs set to actual words—not to mention the fact that these, formed in a great measure upon the model of Mozart, can by no means be adopted as a standard for the valuation of Beethoven's intrinsic greatness.[1]

When the force of lyric poetry had once more revived under a more rigid adherence on the part of musicians to the poet's meaning, and a more intense and conscientious application of suitable forms of musical expression; after the father of instrumental music, Josef Haydn, had written Lieder with instrumental accompaniments to suit the national taste, and Mozart and Beethoven, each in his kind, had elevated the Lied to a position of artistic importance; after many other great and insignificant masters had taken the liveliest interest in its further development—without any single one of them having succeeded in combining every condition requisite to a finished picture of the ideal—

---

[1] The 'Scotch' and 'Irish' Lieder are set to pianoforte and string accompaniments. Of the forty-eight published Lieder and Airs by Beethoven, the foremost rank must be assigned to the 'Spiritual Lieder' (Op. 32), the Cantata (Op. 48), 'Adelaide,' 'Sehnsucht,' 'Wonne der Wehmuth,' 'Mit einem gemalten Band,' 'Das glückliche Land,' 'Der Wachtelschlag,' 'Neue Liebe, neues Leben,' and the lovely 'Liederkreis,' 'An die ferne Geliebte.' Beethoven knew Göthe's lyrics intimately, he set ten of Göthe's poems, and of these 'Sehnsucht' four times. The 'Liederkreis' is a musical poem adopted and improved upon by Schubert in his 'Müllerlieder,' and the 'Winterreise,' Klärchen's Lieder in 'Egmont,' the 'Freudvoll und leidvoll' are cast in a romantic form.'

it was reserved for a son of Southern Germany, the poor child of a schoolmaster of Vienna, so famous for symphony and song, whose organisation was in its particular kind as rich and deep as that of Mozart or Beethoven, to blend by his wonderful gifts the essence of the Volkslied with all the deep meaning and magic charm of vocal and instrumental art, and by a return to the dismembered and now artistically welded together forms of art, to create that masterpiece of artistic work, in the narrow frame of which a whole world is reflected, and the tenderest and most passionate emotions of the human heart, in all their strange and manifold variety, find their full and true expression.

This master, whose gift of invention and wealth of fancy and individuality in the composition of the Lied were utterly independent of all previous models and patterns, is Franz Schubert, and in his music a fair flower, the first time for centuries, blossomed abundantly. At the bare mention of his name, the German Lied, with all its irresistible power, stands out before us. He is the creator of the Lied engrafted on the original stem of the national song, and it is to this popular element, taken in connection with his high artistic finish, that Schubert owes his great power, for—as an enthusiastic worshipper of Schubert expresses it—'by the entire satisfaction of our intellectual requirements and purified taste, he is for ever harping on those " primal sympathies " which bind us throughout our lives to one great whole, to a living union of kindred elements.

Schubert's Lied works by a charm which can only be wrought by genial and original creations; his fancy has unearthed melodies which reveal to the human soul its deepest secrets; and, as new and surprising in their development as they are familiar and confiding in their deep spiritual meanings, they, in a triumphant manner, blend the revelation of the truth with the captivating and beautiful witchery of art. The echoes of his Lieder awake in us a longing for a more lovely home, the bright ideal we have shaped in our own fancy, and sorrow and regret dissolve into a sweet gentle melancholy, such as we derive from a look towards the skies and a feeling that we could wing our way into the bright realms that float above us. He listened to the human voice, which as an art material developes more than any other an unthought-of fulness of expression and beauty, he fathomed its deep secrets, and by the magic charm of exquisite musical accompaniments, gave life and light to every song that flowed from him.'

Prolific a writer as Schubert was, his vocal works are conspicuous for certain qualities denied to other writers. As distinguished from the fragmentary unconnected Lieder of other masters, those of Schubert, by their large number and subtle affinities with each other when written in sets or series, are pre-eminent for their completeness, presenting to us, as they do, in a continual flow of representative images, all the passions akin to the human breast—joy, sorrow, hope, longing, love,

hate, comfort, submission—just as these feelings form
distinct episodes in our mortal life. The number of
Schubert's Lieder already known to the world amounts
to nearly six hundred. Many German, and numbers also
of foreign poets, supplied a greater or less contingent of
poems, and amongst the former, Göthe is pre-eminent
as the one poet whose lyrical poems are universally
allowed to claim the foremost place in the whole cycle of
Schubert's Lieder.[1] The greatest of German poets became also the creator of the modern Lied as it is now
sung. Like Beethoven before him, and Mendelssohn
and Schumann after him, Schubert, in the second period
of his career as composer, became specially enamoured
of Göthe's lyric poems.[2] Göthe's song gushes forth
so spontaneously from the depths of the poet's inmost
soul, that the musician finds ready-made an exquisite
and expressive flow of words, which he forthwith clothes
with sound. The rounded form of Göthe's poetry acted
as a curb to the over-abundant fancy of Schubert, and
his settings of the majority of these poems may be
reckoned among the most perfect specimens of Lied he
ever composed.[3]

---

[1] In his earliest days (1811–1815), Schubert had a preference for
the tender sentimental poetry of Hölty, Mathisson, Kosegarten, Salis,
&c., as they were popular at the time, and were often in the hands of
his comrades at school. At a later period, Mayrhofer, Vogl, and
Schober influenced him in his selection of poems.

[2] He set as many as sixty of Göthe's poems.

[3] Amongst these are the songs from 'Wilhelm Meister,' those also

Schubert's connection with the other prince of German poets, Friedrich v. Schiller, cannot be said to be equally happy. The ideal flights of this master's fancy, the philosophical character which pervades numbers of his smaller poems, render them, as a whole, unsuited for musical treatment, whereas the lyric poems of Göthe came to him, as he himself says, 'unsought and uncalled for; suggested by truth and actuality, they are grounded and rooted therein.' No doubt Schubert, into whose hands Schiller's poems had early fallen, was filled with that eager enthusiasm with which most young people are wont to devour the ballads and the passionate poetry written during the 'storm period' of Schiller's career, and consequently there appeared in the years 1813–1815 those great compositions, 'Die Bürgschaft,' 'Der Taucher,' and 'Ritter Toggenburg,' as well as several other Lieder, which although not to be compared with the songs afterwards set to Göthe's poetry, nevertheless give brilliant testimony to the rare gifts of the young composer. It is plain enough that Schubert at that early period composed single songs, which, by virtue of their high artistic finish, might well belong to the ripest period of his artistic career.[1] The classical poems

from 'Westöstlicher Divan,' 'Ganymed,' 'Schwager Kronos,' 'Rastlose Liebe,' 'Erlkönig,' 'Willkommen und Abschied,' 'Grenzen der Menschheit,' 'Gretchen am Spinnrad,' 'Der Musensohn,' 'Erster Verlust,' 'Wanderers Nachtlied,' 'Geheimes,' &c.

[1] Thus that majestic Lied, 'Thekla, eine Geisterstimme,' belongs to the year 1813, 'Des Mädchen's Klage' (a genuine lyric, and therefore

of Mayrhofer, such as 'Memnon,' 'Atigone und Oedip,'
'Iphigenia,' 'Aus Heliopolis,' 'Filoktet,' 'Orest auf
Tauris,' 'Der entsühnte Orest,' 'Freiwilliges Versinken,'
'Lied des Wanderers an die Dioskuren,' required a
peculiar kind of musical treatment. Schubert, who
had a rare aptitude for hitting off the exact meaning
intended by the poet, and getting at once at the kernel
of the matter, set these works to more heroic styles
than he had applied to the minor lyric pieces, the effect
being admirable in both cases.[1] The above-mentioned
Lieder are selected as being the songs which produced great effect on an audience, when interpreted by
Vogl with his fine dramatic feeling and declamatory
power. To this series must be added the eighteen
Lieder compiled by Franz v. Schober, which were all
set by Schubert at his very best time ; of these the

one of Schiller's most vocal poems) to the year 1815. To this earlier
period belong 'Emma,' 'Hector's Abschied,' 'Der Kampf,' 'Die Erwartung,' 'Laura am Clavier,' 'Entzückung an Laura,' &c. Schubert
has set on the whole over twenty of Schiller's poems, and to these,
in addition to those already named, we must add two others, 'Gruppe
aus dem Tartarus,' and 'Dythirambe,' both admirable as musical compositions.

[1] We may point with admiration to the classic poems of Göthe,
'An Schwager Kronos,' 'Ganymed,' and 'Grenzen der Menschheit.'
Mayrhofer used to say of 'Memnon,' that the poem had never been
thoroughly intelligible to him until Schubert had set it to music.
Of other settings (of Mayrhofer's poems), 'Der zürnenden Diana'
and 'Nachtstück' are conspicuous for grand and thoughtful treatment.
Schubert set some thirty of Mayrhofer's poems, amongst others 'Der
ndelfahrer,' arranged also by the composer as a quartett.

'Jagers Liebeslied,' 'Pilgerweise,' 'Viola,' 'Schatzgräber's Begehr,' 'Todtenmusik,' and the 'Pax vobiscum' of the sacred songs, are amongst the finest and most widely known.[1] Those songs are deserving special notice which the composer threw off at once as a connected series of Lieder, as the poet had originally intended them, or which, if not immediately intertwined one with another, appear, by the uniform way they are treated, to be parts of an entire poem, and treated as a single subject. Such are the 'Müllerlieder,' 'Die Gesänge Ossians,' those to Scott's 'Lady of the Lake,' 'Die geistlichen Lieder,' 'Die Winterreise,' and in part 'Der Schwanengesang.'[2] The first-named embrace that well-known cycle of Lieder set to poems by Wilhelm Müller, entitled 'Die schöne Müllerin.'[3] The cycle of Lieder contains,

[1] The effective comic trio, 'Der Hochzeitsbraten,' and the beautiful quintett for male voices, 'Mondenschein,' are also set to Schober's words.

[2] When the public expressed a wish that Schubert should apply himself to composing Lieder of a more cheerful character, he wrote music for Castelli's 'Echo,' and the so-called 'Refrainlieder' (Op. 95), by G. Seidl, and other works of the same style were to follow. Schubert, however, felt little fitted for this style, and his comic Lieder are amongst the least successful of his works. One of his humorous songs is No. 3 of three Italian canzonets, dedicated to Lablache (Op. 83). The songs set by Schubert to Italian words bear throughout more the character of an Aria than a Lied. This is pre-eminently the case with the 'Traditor deluso' (No. 2 of Op. 83), which begins with a recitative, and expresses admirably the feelings of despair which prey on the mind of the deceived traitor. The form, like that used for Italian soprano airs, is that of Mozart's concert airs.

[3] Wilhelm Müller, born at Dessau, on October 7, 1795, son of a

under the title, 'Die schöne Müllerin, im Winter zu
lesen,' five-and-twenty poems, of which Schubert has set
twenty. Müller's lyrics are naive in character, true in
feeling, and he has much of the intuitive perception
of a genuine poet: it is no matter of surprise that
Schubert felt attracted by such poetry. Beethoven, in
his beautiful Liederkreis, 'An die entfernte Geliebte,'
gave an external unity to a series of poems, each of
which bore some affinity to the poem immediately preceding it; Beethoven, in fact, was the originator of this
particular form of vocal composition. Of Schubert's
Müllerlieder, each number is complete in itself; the
master, with a true poetical conception, being intent on
giving exhaustively to every song an appropriate form
and character, although each Lied forms a part of a
whole, and has therefore a true signification of its own.

tradesman in easy circumstances, studied philology and history at
Berlin in 1812, in the year 1813 fought as a Prussian soldier in the
War of Independence, and in 1814 returned to Berlin to pursue
his studies. In the year 1817 he travelled to Italy, in 1819 was
appointed to the newly organised academy in Dessau, and subsequently
became Imperial librarian. In the year 1827, he returned from a
journey he had taken for the benefit of his health, and died a few days
afterwards at Dessau, on October 1, 1827, at the exact time when
Schubert had set to music the second part of his 'Winterreise.' Müller
was known as one of the best of men, a scholar of very versatile
acquirements, and one of the best lyric poets. He wrote ' Rom und
Römerinnen ' (1820), ' Gedichte aus den hinterlassenen Papieren
eines Waldhornisten' (1821–1824), and 'Lyrische Spaziergänge' (1827).
In the year 1830 Gustav Schwab published a collection of his miscellaneous poems in five volumes.

With heartfelt sympathy we follow the miller in joy and sorrow, hope and despair, joining with him in the melancholy strain at the end of the series in 'Des Baches Wiegenlied.' The 'national' character of these songs (in the best sense of the epithet) has long since made this cycle a priceless treasure, common to all lovers of the genuine Lied.

The great variety and wealth of musical form, ranging from / the simple strophes to the rhythmical and declamatory style, the exquisite character of the accompaniments, so admirably adapted to the intention of the poet, and the richness and individuality of the harmonies, give a very high value to this series of connected Lieder. The finished artistic working up of melodies, national in their origin, national in their essence, is here displayed in Schubert's most genial manner.[1] Of a nature completely different to these are the 'Gesänge Ossians' found amongst Schubert's papers after his death. Some of these, such as 'Loda's Gespenst,' 'Shilrik und Vinvela,' 'Das Mädchen von Inistore,' and 'Kolma's Klage,' belong to the year 1815—to a time, therefore, when Schubert, possibly

---

[1] Thus the Lieder 'Das Wandern' (No. 1) and 'Gute Ruh' (No. 20) are written in strophes, and in the national character; 'Der Feierabend' (No. 5) and 'Der Neugierige' (No. 6) contain recitative passages; in 'Ungeduld' it is the play of rhythm which imparts to that Lied its great charm; in other Lieder, such as 'Morgengruss,' 'Die Liebe,' and 'Die böse Farbe,' we are charmed by the simplicity of the harmony and general treatment.

attracted by Zumsteeg's ballads, with which he was
familiar, applied himself to the composition of works
in this form.[1]   The songs from Ossian, with few exceptions, are, from their epic breadth and the rhapsodic
treatment of the words, more closely akin in character
to the ballad than the Lied.

What Schubert effected in the way of ballad-writing
and 'romance,' which is akin to the same genus of
composition, has already been stated. By the largeness of resources always at his command, by that
intuitive power which enabled him to seize the poet's
meaning, and give to the salient points of the poem
every delicate shade and fit expression, Schubert in
this department far outstripped Zumsteeg and the
Berlin composers, Reichardt and Zelter, who were
probably unknown to him. It is certain that many of
his ballads will endure for all time. Nevertheless it
is equally certain that in spite of the 'Erlkönig' and

[1] Johann Rudolf Zumsteeg, born 1760, in what was formerly the
Ritter Canton Odenwald, received his musical education in the Hofcapelle of the Duke of Würtemberg. He began to compose at an
early period of his life, and was much encouraged by Schiller, who
gladly offered him some of his own songs for music. Zumsteeg wrote
several Lieder, ballads, cantatas, operas, and vocal pieces, besides
instrumental things. In the year 1792 he was made Ducal Capellmeister and Opera-Director, and died on January 27, 1802. He was a
very learned man, but his musical talents. were rather those of a
skilful arranger than an original inventive thinker. His compositions
therefore have in our time a mere historical interest, and even in the
ballad, on which his fame and reputation rested, he was surpassed by
Schubert, Schumann, and Carl Loewe.

other ballads in that particular style, he has never
reached the ideal perfection he attained to in the
lyric Lied. If Schubert, in his masterly delineation
of pictures contained in some of the great ballads,
stands unrivalled for truth, and his deep apprehension
of the various situations before him, still on the whole
the palm in this particular province of art must be
given to Carl Loewe, who, as an inventive composer,
has reached a climax of excellence in his best ballads,
and become the chief representative of that form of
vocal writing.

Of the Ossian songs the two grand poems 'Loda's
Gespenst' and 'Die Nacht' have been treated in the
free rhapsodic form, whilst 'Das Mädchen von Inistore'
and 'Ossians Lied nach dem Falle Nathos' resemble
more the usual form of Lied. 'Kolma's Klage' and
'Kronaar' are in the grand majestic style. All these
pieces have an artistic value of their own; the unearthly
demon and spirit essence pervading the poet's songs,
the gloom and darkness frowning over jagged rocks and
wild heath, and peopled with fantastic weird shapes
and forms, well befitted the musical genius of Schubert,
who identified himself with the pictures before him,
and gave them one and all their appropriate expression.[1]

---

[1] The concluding air in 'Loda's Gespenst,' 'Heil, Morvens König,' is,
I am warranted in saying, not Schubert's composition, but a supple-
ment made by an experienced musical amateur, 'zum Zweck des
Abrundung.'

If Schubert, in the tone-pictures here alluded to, could transport his hearers into a dreamland hitherto unknown to them, by the first musical chords in which he opened his version of the Ossian song, so also in the world of romance did he with equal skill manage that fiery Pegasus, his fancy, in the Lieder composed to Sir Walter Scott's poems.[1]   If the 'geistlichen Lieder' are conspicuous for their devotional feeling, they are unequal in value as works of art.[2]   The second cycle of Lieder, in form and intendment similar to the Müllerlieder, is the well-known Liederkreis by Wilhelm Müller, entitled 'Winterreise.'

The dominant idea in the three sets of Lieder entitled ' Reiselieder,' although they all have reference in common to a restless wandering life in the world, and the longing for some once-loved subject, is varied in particular instances; for whereas in the 'Grosse Wanderschaft' and the Lieder immediately connected with it, as well as in the 'Wanderlieder,' we find a tone of cheerfulness dashed only cursorily here and there by a faint breath of sorrowful regrets, the 'Winterreise' gives us a picture of a heart bleeding from the pangs of despised love, but venturing ever and anon to trifle

[1] Besides the songs from Sir W. Scott's 'Lady of the Lake,' must be reckoned, 'Richard Löwenherz' (from ' Ivanhoe'), songs of Anna Lyle (from the 'Legend of Montrose'), and Norna's song (from the ' Pirate ').

[2] The best of these: 'Pax vobiscum,' ' Vom Mitleiden Maria,' and ' Fest Allerseelen,' were arranged by Herr Herbeck for a mixed chorus, and were published in that form.

with its own misery, and jesting ironically at the returning symptoms of tenderness. A breath of deep
despair and disconsolateness pervades these melancholy
songs, the star of life seems to grow pale, and a cold
cheerless winter is before us. The songs of the 'Winterreise,' written during the last years of Schubert's
life, synchronise with the 'Müllerlieder'; it may be said
of them, that in completeness of lyric expression and
intense finish, in simplicity and the unity sustained
throughout the various fragmentary pieces, they surpass most of Schubert's songs, and that in melody and
pianoforte accompaniment they reveal certain peculiarities which mark a turning-point even in the regular
Lied of Schubert, and project, as it were, the shadow of
that phase now adopted by Lieder-writers following in
the wake of Schubert. The Lied became conspicuous
on the one hand for a certain independence of melody,
and on the other by an excess of pianoforte accompaniment, which by its very preponderance keeps the air
or melody in the background.

We have yet to mention the 'Schwanengesang,' a
connected series of fourteen Lieder, the words by Heine,
Rellstab, and Gabriel Seidl. Heine's first appearance
as a German poet was during the last years of Schubert's life, so that the latter could inaugurate, with
only a few Lieder, that era which began with Heine,
and was illustrated at a later period, in an exhaustive
manner, by two famous song-writers who succeeded

Schubert, Mendelssohn and Schumann, most notably by the latter.[1]

It might well be supposed that the short comprehensive lyrics of Heine were admirably adapted to Schubert's artistic individuality ; and of the loyalty of the composer in following out the poet's intentions, by veiling in a shadowy twilight of song inferences and meanings to be gathered *from* the words rather than expressed *in* the words, the Lieder ' Ihr Bild,' ' Die Stadt,' and the ' Doppelgänger,' with their incomplete, mysterious, and yet profoundly suggestive chords, bear ample witness.   Here, too, we have in conspicuous relief the characteristic pianoforte accompaniment, illustrating the poet's meaning and enhancing the value of the song itself.   Rellstab's Lieder and G. Seidl's ' Taubenpost ' have been mentioned before.   Schubert could play powerfully and impressively on the more cheerful

---

[1] Heine's songs set by Schubert are ' Der Atlas,' ' Ihr Bild,' ' Die Stadt,' ' Am Meer,' ' Der Doppelgänger,' and ' Das Fischermädchen.' In these the devotion of love and a high tragic sentiment find their legitimate and most beautiful expression.   But the highly cultivated Schumann completely mastered Heine, and seized on the scepticism and ironical side of his lyrics with exquisite skill, and in a manner which the sensitive Schubert would never have managed with equal success.   Just as little was it granted to Mendelssohn ever to get beyond a kind of formal beauty and rounded finish in his setting of Heine's Lieder.   On comparing ' Ihr Bild,' ' Allmächtig im Traume,' set alike by Schubert, Schumann, and Mendelssohn, we shall see the different way each composer handled these poems.   Meyerbeer has confessedly set the ' Fischermädchen ' in a fashion differing entirely from Schubert's method. It is certainly the most successful Lied Meyerbeer ever wrote.

strings of his harp, as well as on the sadder ones, and in his happiest inspirations he has been exceeded by none before or after him. In the matter of lovely melody and wealth of musical invention, the 'Schwanengesang' is on the same level with the rest of the Liederkreise.

Deep imbedded in all these groups of songs are to be found every variety of exquisite melody, every phase of dramatic power, and a finish, originality, and depth of musical apprehension which never fail to impress intellectual listeners as being the specialities of Schubert's songs.

The number of Schubert's Lieder actually engraved amounts now to about 360. He wrote, however, as we have already stated, near upon 600 Lieder, some of which are still in manuscript, and others have been copied from the originals.

Amongst the published Lieder are some few, the non-appearance of which would have formed but small subject of regret amongst Schubert's admirers. On the other hand, it is a well-known fact, that many a gem worthy of being brought to light is still concealed;[1]

---

[1] For instance, the ballads composed in the year 1815, and still existing in manuscript, and surely the following pieces (not to mention others) ought to be published:—' Hagar's Klage,' ' Der Jüngling und der Tod,' ' Ihr Grab,' ' Die Sterbende,' ' Täglich zu singen,' ' Daphne am Bach,' ' Vollendung,' ' Mein Frieden,' ' Ammenlied,' ' Es träumen die Wolken' the 'Italienische Canzone,' ' Des Wallfahrtslied' (Lunz). We may here remark, that in the chronologically arranged catalogue of

and if the possessors of unpublished songs were to
make a careful selection, and one that might be accessible to the general public, they would deserve the
gratitude of all lovers of music.

Two masters of the first order who succeeded Schubert had a special predilection for the Lied, and they
have opened out a new vein in a mine which people
had thought was exhausted. Mendelssohn's Lied and
that of Schubert's, as indeed all other works of these
two masters, differ so materially in form and meaning, that no points of comparison between the two
styles can possibly be suggested. Mendelssohn's Lied,
so beautiful in form, so noble in feeling, so full of
national sympathies, bears the stamp of a genuine lyric
character, the essential elements of which are frequently
recurring. Now Schubert's song, on the contrary, dis-
cards the lyric type, when the situation demands it,
and assimilates to itself both epic and dramatic elements; but in wealth of original melody, and in variety
of form and expression, it is as much above the Men-

all these compositions no mention could be made of those where we
have no sure index of the actual time and date they were originally
written. Amongst those pieces omitted for this reason we must mention
' Die Schlacht,' by Schiller, a vocal piece on a large scale with pianoforte accompaniment. The fragments consist of a prelude in the shape
of a march, recitations, and chorus. The vocal part is incomplete; the
march is no other than Schubert's 'Marches héroïques,' without trio
(Op. 27). Herr Josef v. Spaun, of Vienna, possesses a copy of the
work in the handwriting of Ferdinand Schubert.

delssohnian Lied as Schubert's rich fancy and profound
individuality surpass in some respects Mendelssohn's
artistic nature, which, although one of the rarest refinement and enlightenment, was less versatile than
that of his predecessor.[1]

It is quite another case with Robert Schumann, who,
suddenly abandoning pianoforte for vocal writing, produced a great number of songs in unbroken succession,
and gave indisputable proof of his being Schubert's
most genial and gifted disciple. He has elicited, in
truth, songs perfectly original, and expressed all the
phases common to our daily experience, from simple
naïveté, cheerfulness, and emotion to demoniacal wild-
ness, deep pathos, and morbid melancholy. Declamation, rhythm, and wealth of harmony are conspicuous
features in his Lieder. Whereas in Schubert's music
the chief point is always in the melody, Schumann, by
straining after characteristic expression, seeks to compensate for his less abundant wealth of musical invention. In testing one by one the elements, by aid of which
Schumann, as a creative artist, has advanced in this
direction, we may talk of the progress of the Lied and

[1] This cannot be said of the four-part songs 'Lieder im Freien zu
singen,' an exquisite illustration of Mendelssohn's delicate and loving
spirit as an artist, who, thoroughly versed in the choral technicalities of
Bach and Händel, as well as the lesser inspirations of great musicians,
found in this department of art a rich field for activity. In these choral
songs he attained to a greater variety of expression than in any other
style of composition.

the advance made beyond Schubert's time; but viewing
the Lied in its totality and essence, we must not talk
of progress. As little improvement has been made in
this style of music since Schubert, as in the symphony
since Beethoven. For none like Schubert knew how to
embody in passionate and soul-stirring melodies all the
intricate depths and meanings of poetry, none like him
ever adapted word and song with such perfect ease, with
such gentle and yet persuasive force. His song soars
like an eagle aloft, and it is in this perfect freedom
and crystal clearness of fancy that his power remains
invincible, even when contrasted with the Lieder of
Schumann.

Leaving for a while the solo songs, let us look at
his concerted music for mixed voices.

He has written a large number of concerted vocal
pieces, some for male and others for mixed voices, some
unaccompanied, others with instrumental, and frequently
pianoforte accompaniments.[1] If Schubert was not destined to create such an epoch in this particular province of art as in his solo songs, the reason is not to be
traced to any deficiency of powers, but only to external
circumstances, for he has succeeded in producing some

---

[1] The guitar was greatly in request in Schubert's time, as a solo instrument and as an accompaniment also. He wrote several part-
songs with a guitar accompaniment; the vocal quartetts, Op. 11, have
an accompaniment both for the piano and guitar; the 'Gesang der
Geister' and 'Sieg der Deutschen' are accompanied by stringed instruments; there is a horned obligato to the 'Nachtgesang im Wald.'

enchanting masterpieces in this kind, which rank in the first order of vocal works.

Schubert, in his early days, wrote not only instrumental and vocal works, &c., but also part-songs, which, numerically inferior to his other compositions, are also inferior in value. At a later period (1821), he had several friends and acquaintances around him,[1] for whom he would write off a trio or quartett at a moment's notice.[2]

At the time Schubert wrote these pieces, a numerous and well-disciplined chorus, suited to our modern ideas, was never thought of, nor indeed for some years that followed; consequently, there being no incessant demand

[1] The Schubert singers were Tieze, Barth, Umlauff, Götz, Nejebse, Weinkopf, Frühwald, Heitzinger, Rauscher, Ruprecht, Seipelt, and Johann Nestroy.

[2] Amongst the trios figures the well-known 'Die Advokaten,' words by Rustenfeld (the name Engelhart, which appeared on a written copy, is struck out, and that of Rustenfeld substituted), for two tenors and a bass, with pianoforte accompaniment. The style in which 'Die Advokaten' is composed negatives the presumption that Schubert was the author, and as an actual fact, the trio was not his work, but that of a certain Fischer (possibly Anton Fischer, who was born at Augsburg, 1782, lived a long time at Vienna, and wrote there a dozen operas, amongst others 'Raoul der Blaubart'), and was only retouched by Schubert and furnished with a more complete pianoforte accompaniment— the only instance of his undertaking to improve upon a stranger's work. Fischer's composition was engraved by Eder, at Vienna; Wenzel Nejebse, who still survives (one of the quartett party in the Schubert period, 1821–1823, and my authority in this matter) sang for the first time in the years between 1830 and 1840, at the house of Dr. Biela, advocate in Brunn, and a second time at Kameralrath Bannerth's, at Vienna. This gentleman surprised his friends by showing them the Fischer manu-

for choral and concerted vocal pieces, he produced them with an effort, and as a matter of fact, in the majority of instances, and the most popular of his choral songs were only written for special occasions.[1] However (about the year 1820), he composed the already-mentioned chorus for male voices, ' Gesang der Geister über den Wassern,' one of the grandest and most characteristic pieces of its kind, and one which has been admirably received in more recent times. ' Das Dörfchen,' ' Die Nachtigall,' and ' Geist der Liebe,' mark that first period in which Schubert wrote concerted things for musical amateurs, and the success of which in many concert-rooms increased the reputation of the composer, who at that time was but little known. His energies in this field of labour were but short-lived. These very same vocal quartetts, the style of which—especially with reference to the concluding strophes, treated in the canon form—is not adapted to the taste of our time, gradually even in Schubert's days lost their power of attraction, and two more efforts in the same direction failing to succeed, the result was not lost upon the composer, who felt a distaste for continuing to write vocal music in this style. His disinclination on this point was so strong, that Schubert, usually so obliging,

script, whereas they thought they had sung an original composition by Schubert. Josef v. Spaun also remembers Fischer's ' Advokaten,' and the resetting of that piece by Schubert.

[1] For instance, eight singers, with an instrumental accompaniment, performed the ' Gesang der Geister.'

could not bring himself to comply with an offer made ·
by Dr. Leopold von Sonnleithner, to compose for a
concert of the Musikverein a new quartett, 'in a form
differing from any hitherto observed by quartett-
writers,' and he stated the grounds of his refusal in the
following letter:—

'Dear Herr von Sonnleithner,—You yourself know
how it fared with the reception given to my lately-
written quartetts: the people have plenty of them. No
doubt I might succeed in inventing some new form,
but one cannot reckon upon such success as a certainty.
But as my future destiny is a subject of great anxiety
to me, you, who, as I flatter myself, are interested in
my welfare, will own that every step I make in advance
must be a safe and sure one; and I shall not be able to
undertake the commission unless the Romance from
the "Zauberharfe," executed by Jäger,[1] would answer
the purpose of the honourable Society: in that case I
should feel perfectly easy and contented.

'Your most obedient
'F. SCHUBERT.'

Schubert therefore wrote no new quartett for concert
purposes; but whilst he thought with characteristic
modesty 'that he might possibly be successful in dis-
covering new forms,' these already had been stamped

---

[1] This melodrama was brought out on the stage at Vienna in 1820,
and Schubert wrote music for it.

distinctly on his fancy; for the quartetts 'Widerspruch' and 'Der Gondelfahrer,' the quintett 'Mondenschein,' and others written soon after, announced a new phase in Schubert's career, and were the first fruits of still more brilliant results in the art of writing for men's voices.

＼ During the same interval (1820 to 1822) his labours increased in writing part-music for soprano voices. He wrote expressly for a small but well-disciplined female choir, made up of the pupils of the Conservatory at Vienna, and these compositions were frequently performed at the so-called Thursday Concerts, in the old hall of the Musikverein.

On occasions of this sort, when people were determined to do Schubert honour, or a well-disciplined chorus offered some security for the success of a performance, or (as frequently was the case in after times) Grillparzer presented the composer he so highly esteemed with a poem to set to music, Schubert threw himself heart and soul into the work, and proved most convincingly, by his musical offerings, that he could give the world undying testimony of his capacities in this line of composition as well as others. ）

In the last three years of his career he was permitted, both in instrumental music as well as part-song writing, to crown his performances with some compositions of true Schubertian grandeur and individuality. Of such sort are the 'Nachtgesang im Wald,' 'Nachthelle,'

'Ständchen,' and the 'Schlachtgesang' for two choirs, musical poems of the most varied kind, the two first tinged with that thoughtful dreaminess so peculiar to many of this master's works—the 'Ständchen' of exquisite loveliness, the 'Schlachtgesang' breathing a spirit of warlike valour and trust in Heaven. In the first three pieces the pianoforte accompaniment predominates, and constitutes the real strength. Schubert's well-known plan of continuing a rhythmical accompaniment from the beginning to the end here assumed a very prominent form, and gives a peculiar and distinctive charm to the delicate and refined voice-writing.

We must reckon the cantatas and hymns as belonging in a wider sense to compositions written for several voices. Amongst the first—apart from the unknown 'Prometheus' and the Easter Cantata ('Lazarus')—'Miriam's War Song,' the words by Grillparzer, is the most important.

Miriam's hymn of praise to the Almighty after the passage of the Israelites through the Red Sea, and the jubilant cry of the people, redeemed out of bondage, at their own deliverance and the destruction of the enemy—a majestic theme in any case—seems to have inspired the poet as well as the composer; for the former treated this theme successfully as a poem, and the latter set the poem to some of his finest music.

The first strophe, 'Rührt die Zimbel, schlagt die Saiten,' is in broad rhythm, and in some ways mo-

delled on Händel's style. In the second strophe, where
the Lord is represented as a shepherd, with a staff
to guide His people, and 'lead them forth from Egypt
like sheep,' the music breathes a spirit of deep peace
and trust. The third strophe is expressive of awe
at the miracle of the waters standing up on heap
whilst the Israelites pass through. Then we have an
ideal picture of the approach of the enemy, the im-
pending danger, and the destruction of Pharaoh with
his host, and after the sea's calm has returned, the
introductory chorus is again repeated, and this great
tone-picture concludes with a powerful fugue.

Of the psalms and hymns, that 'An den heiligen
Geist' (Op. 154), for an eight-part chorus of male voices
and accompaniment of wind-instruments, is conspicuous
above the others by its grand majestic style; and next
in order are 'Gebet vor der Schlacht,' 'Gott ist mein
Hirt,' 'Gott im Ungewitter,' 'Gott in der Natur,' and
'Hymne an den Unendlichen.'[1] Schubert's originality,
his great powers of arrangement, the exquisite delicacy
and charming modulations of his part-writing, characterise all the most important of his vocal concerted
pieces, and particularly those written when his vital
powers were on the decline: and if for awhile the

[1] The Cantatas published years ago as Op. 146, 158, 157, and 128,
are now as good as unknown; those in honour of Vogel, Salieri, the
elder Schubert, and the 'Italienische Cantata' are still in manuscript;
the Cantata 'Glaube, Hoffnung und Liebe' (1828) only existed in a
few copies. None of these are very remarkable.

laurels did not deck his brow, in honour of the many beautiful gifts he had already showered on the world, they must now be joyfully conceded to him for such master-pieces of art as those just alluded to.

It is a well-known fact that whereas Schubert, as Lieder composer, met during his lifetime with much praise and honour, his instrumental works, with slight exceptions, were comparatively little heeded, and that it took a long time after his death to reconcile the public to his pianoforte works, chamber music, and great instrumental compositions. And yet without doubt Schubert developed as much mental energy in the province of instrumental music as in the minor department of song ; for the earliest of his stringed quartetts synchronise with the earliest of his Lieder. The sacred fire kindling in him, when scarce passed the threshold of boyhood, and guiding him to the discovery and production of melodies which, by their rare beauty, opened out a yet undiscovered world, enabled him also, independently of systematic instruction, to become familiar with the complex forms of instrumental music, and at an early period to create works in the department of chamber music, the performance of which, even in our own time, never fails to interest and to create in particular phrases and passages great effects.[1] The same thing may be said of his other

---

[1] Thus, for example, Schubert's stringed Quartett in B-flat, one of his earliest compositions (1814), given two years ago, for the first time, in

instrumental works.　Franz Schubert, the representative
of the new musical lyric, like other composers, followed
the call of his genius, which drew him away from vocal
to instrumental music, only that with him the influence
of the Lied upon orchestral music was of a more significant kind than in the case of other composers.
The depth and earnestness of his spirit, the wealth and
vigour of his fancy, incited him, in the composition of
his vocal works, to draw largely on instrumental resources, in which the subtilties and intricate thoughts
of men of genius can range with more perfect freedom
than in music where words and phrases act as fetters
and restraints upon the imagination.　His poetic in-
stincts were less adapted to the invention of broad instrumental forms, and the grouping and moulding of
such into a complete shape ; in this plastic power he
was surpassed by men infinitely his inferiors in musical
genius.　Not a few of Schubert's instrumental works,
and amongst them some of the grandest, present a series
of exquisitely wrought-out fancies, and these, steeped
in the peculiar charm and exquisite sensibility of his
music, yet lack that compactness of form and conden-
sation of power which again seem the special heritage
of other masters.　This peculiarity, arising from his
musical organisation, which is put forward by the de-
fenders of the ' strengen Satzes,' and ' grand style ' as a

Vienna by the Hellmesberg party, and then again the G minor Quartett, written in the year 1815.

defect, by no means hindered his coming forward not merely as an original thinker in the field of instrumental discoveries, but as a creator of, in their way, no less perfect orchestral works than those of the great masters—works which will confessedly hold their own amongst the masterpieces of the greatest writers of orchestral music.[1]   In his well-known but slighter efforts, the short pianoforte pieces,[2] he opened out certainly no new path, but one which had long been forsaken, and bestowed on those musical forms, by a free original treatment and the exquisite caprices of his fancy, an artistic value which was fully comprehended by his most gifted successors, especially Mendelssohn, Schumann, and Chopin; his example gave the impulse to a series of similar lyric effusions, in which the first-named of the three composers takes a more decided stand even than Schubert on the side of the Lied, whereas Schumann's fancy-pictures for the pianoforte are stamped almost exclusively with the character of pure instrumental works.[3]   In Schubert's instrumental music, pianoforte pieces for two hands

---

[1] Amongst these we must reckon the Grand Symphony in C,· the stringed Quartetts in G major and D minor, the stringed Quintett in C, the Sonatas Op. 42 and 78, the three last Sonatas, the two Trios, &c.

[2] Impromptus, Moments musicals, Marches, Dance music, Variations, &c.

[3] Let anyone compare Mendelssohn's 'Lieder ohne Worte,' which in truth necessitate no words to illustrate them, and numbers of Schumann's smaller pianoforte pieces.

occupy a very prominent position. Some of them, such
as the Impromptus, Moments musicals, and the entire
body of dance music, are of a narrower and more limited construction than the sonatas and fantasias, which
are dealt with in a larger and more comprehensive
manner. Schubert's pianoforte music, however, in its
totality, is of high artistic value, and ranks amongst
the most important contributions to music of this
description. This assertion is not gainsayed by the
fact of Schubert's pianoforte music being comparatively
rarely performed in public.[1]

No unprejudiced person will ever dream of comparing the pianoforte works of our composer with those
of a similar nature by that monarch in the kingdom of
sound, who has in his sonatas called forth the wondrous
treasures drawn from the great deeps of his artistic
mind. Schubert's efforts in this style of pianoforte
composition cannot, either by their comprehensiveness
or intellectual grasp, be placed by the side of Beethoven's. For all that, they breathe the true spirit
of genius; and if Beethoven, in many of his sonatas,
probes the lowest depths of the human soul, if his

---

[1] During Schubert's lifetime, and even for some considerable period
after his death, the prejudice against him as a pianoforte composer,
coupled with the difficulty of executing his pianoforte works, may have
acted as a deterrent to public players; but these objections in our time
are valueless. This, however, is certain, that the grandest of Schubert's
pianoforte compositions, at least in Vienna, scarcely ever figure in a concert programme.

genius has soared to regions unattainable by other
men, and he has bequeathed to us perfectly unique
works of art, we have in Schubert's pianoforte music
individualities with a special charm of their own, kindling with that fire and passion which perhaps no musical
poet has ever been endowed with to so high a degree as
Schubert.[1] The lyric element is the prominent feature in these tone-poems; the Lied will take no denial,
and emerges in the midst of some passages where we
should the least expect to find it, at times even to the
prejudice of the artistic symmetry of a particular
movement, by the introduction of weak long-drawn-
out phrases and sentimental thoughts; but the rapid
stirring motives, the bold and original modulations,

---

[1] 'Schubert,' says R. Schumann, 'will ever be the favourite musical interpreter of Youth. He shows what a full heart, bold thoughts, and rapid
action and impulse can effect; he tells her of her pet fancies, romantic
histories, loves and adventures; he throws a dash of humour into the
picture, but not so much as to disturb the gentleness and tenderness of
his ideal. Thereby he adds wings to the fancy of his interpreter in a
way unknown to any other composer but Beethoven. Strong sympathies
with that great man are traceable in Schubert, but the latter's individuality would have been just the same had Beethoven never existed;
his specialities would probably have only developed at a later period.
By the side of Beethoven, Schubert's character is effeminate, he is far
more talkative, gentler, and more easily treated; he is a child playing
fearlessly amongst giants. Schubert, like his great contemporary,
employs his forces *en masse*, but bears the same ratio to Beethoven
as a woman to a man—the one commands, the other entreats and per-
suades. But with Beethoven alone does this comparison hold good;
viewed by the side of others, Schubert has plenty of the man about
him—nay, he is the boldest and freest of the modern masters.'

the admixture and treatment of national elements, the soft dreamy inspiration emanating from many of his poetic fancies, win for the great bulk of his piano-forte works an abiding power of attraction.[1] The wealth of musical inventiveness is a lovely feature in these works, and a knowledge of the technicalities of the piano is shown in the application of broken chords, and the use of certain combinations which give to the instrument, when Schubert deals with it, the properties of an almost orchestral significance. The Impromp-tus, Momens musicals, a great deal of dance music (waltzes, 'Allemandes,' country-dances, galoppes and Schottisches, and occasional compositions (many of them of no great value) belong to his pianoforte works of the smaller kind.[2] Amongst these the Im-promptus (Op. 90 and 142, containing eight pieces in all), by their breadth of design and roundness of form, are entitled to a prominent place. Beautiful in every respect are the two Impromptus, No. 1 from Op. 90, and No. 4 from Op. 142 (each in C minor), the first of

[1] One trait, says Robert Schumann, of Beethoven's romanticism, that which may be termed 'den provençalischen,' Schubert brought to the very highest pitch of cultivation. Consciously or unconsciously, a new and not yet developed school relies on this basis; from this school it may be expected that a new era in the history of Art will take its origin.

[2] For instance, the 'Zehn Variationen' (written in 1815), a Scherzo and Trio (1817), Allegretto (in memory of Herr Walcher, 1827), a March with Trio, a lovely Adagio (probably the opening movement of a Sonata), the original of which is in my possession. Spaun and Stadler have also other fragmentary pieces of pianoforte music.

which, beginning with an elegy, becomes in time an animated strain, and closes triumphantly (Allegro scherzando) with an Hungarian air, full of fire, and worked up into the boldest and most masterly harmonies. The other Impromptus, notably that in A-flat (No. 2, Op. 142), are full of originality, and give a new and fresh significance to the technical treatment of the piano. Scarcely less attractive than the works just named are the 'Moments musicals' (6 pieces in 2 series, Op. 93), of which Nos. 4 and 6, by their quaint modulations, full harmonies, and dreamy elegiac expression, have a special charm attached to them. Viewed as a whole, both these works are a rich mine of the lovely fancies and caprice of Schubert, who probably in those extemporised pieces gave himself up without reserve to the play of his genius and fancy.[1]

Of the dance music, the lively Polonaises are good examples of rhythm and delicate construction; but for charming melody and happy musical invention the country dances, Schottisches, &c., are perhaps more

[1] It is hardly to be supposed that Schubert gave these pianoforte works the names they now bear. With reference to both of these first Impromptus, Op. 142, Schumann is of opinion that Schubert certainly did not inscribe them with the title now given them, and that the first is without doubt the first movement of a sonata, and the second the second movement of the same sonata, the concluding portions of which were either never composed or have been lost; the fourth, although certainly not a part of the original work, might have been added as a finale.

conspicuous, although their range is narrower than that of the Polonaises.[1]

With regard to the Fantasias, the famous one in C (Op. 15) is reckoned as one of the most important, if not of the most attractive, of the pianoforte works. The construction of the first and last movement seems certainly rather uncouth, but the work itself is rich in melody and genial touches of inspiration; as a free and inventive play of fancy, it ignores artistic rules and formulæ, even more conspicuously than Schubert's other instrumental works. On the other hand, the whole drift and treatment of the fantasia, with the exception of the intercalated passage for a Lied in the middle of the work, is so inviting for an orchestral adaptation that Franz Liszt, rightly estimating its symphonic character, arranged it for a band in that masterly way he has of doing such things, and in this form the fantasia has been repeatedly performed.

Directly opposed to this is the Fantasia-Sonata in G (Op. 78). A dreamy idyllic character imparted to the two first movements and the trio of the minuett,

---

[1] The ' Erste Walzer ' are thus apostrophised by Schubert's enthusiastic worshipper, Schumann :—' Little fairies, hovering over the earth, no taller than a flower, how I love the " Sehnsuchtswalzer," steeped in a hundred virgin thoughts! How I dislike the three last! which, as æsthetic errors in the main, I can't forgive the composer.' The best of the ' Allemandes ' have been arranged by Herr Johann Herbeck for stringed and wind instruments ; in which form they were repeatedly played with the greatest success at Vienna in 1863.

merging into playfulness only in the final movements, s the feature of this remarkable and refined work, the performance of which demands a fine executant and an artist of exquisite sensibility. One of the favourite and best known of the sonatas is that in A minor (Op. 42). It is also one of the most finished pianoforte works: the first movement, with its sudden halts and pauses, and particularly by the bass unison passages, tells of a certain unrest and gloomy disquiet; the second is a Lied embellished with charming variations; the third, a Scherzo after the Beethoven model, with a lovely trio; the last movement (Rondo), a rapid Hungarian dance tune, conspicuous for the boldness' of its rhythm and modulation. The entire work, from beginning to end, is a masterpiece.

Scarce inferior to this in attraction is the second one, in A minor (Op. 143), dedicated by the publishers to Mendelssohn. The introduction of the first movement and the whole of the last are in the grand style; whilst in the sorrowful Andante we have another of those gloomy fantastic figures common to many of Schubert's profoundest compositions. Here, too, the ingenuity of the pianoforte-player is severely taxed.

Of a totally opposite character to these two sonatas is that bold defiant Sonata in D (Op. 53), dedicated by Schubert to his friend Carl Maria v. Bocklet. It is of all Schubert's sonatas the richest in contrasts and the most difficult to execute, from its peculiarities of rhythm and harmony. Its second movement is certainly one of the most valuable contributions to pianoforte music of modern times.[1]

[1] Schumann thus writes upon the Sonatas in G major, A minor, and D major :—' Not to be prolix, we can only say of all three sonatas that they are "glorious ;" still the Fantasia-Sonata, in form and essence, seems to us Schubert's most perfect work. Here all is organic, everything breathing the same life. Let the unimaginative man, with no gift for solving its enigmas, keep away from the last movement. Very closely related to it is the Sonata in A minor. The first part is so calm, so dreamy, it might move us to tears ; and yet the construction of the two subjects is so light and simple, that we wonder at the magician who has contrasted and interwoven the two subjects with such rare subtlety.

'But what a different kind of vitality gushes forth in the defiant-spirited Sonata in D major—stroke upon stroke hurrying us along with it! And then an Adagio, thoroughly Schubert's own, impulsive, overflowing, impatient of restraint or limit. The last movement hardly dovetails with the whole, and is curious enough. Anyone wanting to take the thing au sérieux, would make himself very ridiculous. Florestan calls it a satire on the Pleyel-Vanhal nightcap style (auf den Pleyel-Vanhal'schen Schlafmützenstyl) ; Eusebius finds in the violently opposed contrasts ugly faces, with which people try to frighten children. There is humour in both these verdicts.

'If Schubert in his Lieder appears, perhaps, more original than in his instrumental compositions, we value the latter as works of the purest art, and as standing in solitary independence of other men's examples. As a pianoforte composer he has surpassed all others, in some respects even Beethoven himself (marvellously acute as the ear of his imagination was, even in the days of his deafness), in this respect, as one who probed to the lowest depths the capacities and powers of the instrument. In Schubert we get from the depths of the piano ideas of all kinds of sounds ; with Beethoven, for the colouring of music, we are obliged to borrow from the horn, the hautboy, &c. This is what we should say, in attempting to analyse generally Schubert's pianoforte works.

'He has music wherein to express the most subtle fancies, thoughts

The Sonatas in E-flat (Op. 122), in B major (Op. 147, dedicated by the publishers to Thalberg), and in A major (Op. 120), are conceived in a less grand style; but all these have characteristic excellencies, and the first is a very remarkable work.

There still remain the three grand Sonatas, dedicated by the publishers to Robert Schumann, besides the Adagio and Rondo (Op. 145) and a partly-finished Sonata in C.

For the first of these works, being Schubert's last-published sonatas, Schumann, so generally enthusiastic on the subject of the Waltzes (Op. 9) of his favourite, never could express the hearty eulogies and admiration he reserved for the other pianoforte works.

'The Sonatas,' says Schumann, 'are, strange to say, designated as Schubert's last work.[1] Possibly, anyone unacquainted with the actual date of their origin would form a different opinion. I myself should probably have set them down to an earlier period of the composer's career, and the Trio in E-flat has always had a

—nay, circumstances and conditions of life. Manifold as are the thoughts and aims of men, yet equally varied are the shades of Schubert's music. What he sees with the eye, touches with the hand, that is metamorphosed into music ; from the very stones he flings spring up, like Deucalion and Pyrrha, living human forms. He, of all Beethoven's successors, was a deadly enemy to all *Philisterei*, the man to carry on the mission of music in the highest sense of the word.'

[1] The publishers state that the sonatas were the 'last things' Schubert wrote, but there is no real proof that they are correct in this assertion.

peculiar value in my eyes, not only as the last work of Schubert's but as a composition of the greatest originality and character. It certainly were more than human to be for ever improving and advancing in each effort in the case of a man who, like Schubert, wrote so much every day of his life; and it may be that these sonatas were the last works he wrote. I never could ascertain whether or not he wrote them on his deathbed; judging from the music, one would be inclined to believe so. However this may be, to me these sonatas seem to differ materially from his other ones, and particularly by a greater simplicity of invention, and by a cheerful surrender of every effort to be thought brilliant and original; whereas he makes very high demands on himself by his drawing out certain general musical ideas, connecting " with links of sweetness " period after period. As though his invention were illimitable, as if he were never embarrassed for what is to follow, his melodious strains ripple on from page to page, only now and then interrupted by a more passionate movement which soon calms down again. This is the impression conveyed to my mind by these sonatas. At last he concludes, joyfully, lightly, and cheerfully, as if he were perfectly well able to begin afresh next day.'

Schumann's musical individuality was powerfully influenced by the rhapsodic character, the bold flights and modulations, the strong contrasts, and the undeniable brilliancy and novelty of the earlier sonatas;

these incidents affected him more than certain qualities which, in our opinion, stamp these works as of
the ripest and most solid order, viz., the beauty and
symmetry of their structure, and the ease and quiet
power with which Schubert has developed his subject.
We would specially call attention to those genuine
artistic works, the Sonatas in C minor and B-flat
major.

The 'Fragment' (Op. 145) consists of an Adagio
(E major ¾) and a Rondo (Allegretto ¾), concluding in
a similar key. The first movement consists of an introduction of a serious character, in a style reminding
one far more of the old masters than of Schubert;[1]
but the last movement is a short but lovely subject,
and stamped with the true Schubert mark. It consists
of two parts, each to be repeated by the executant, and
leads into a new subject in quicker time, full of rapid
passages for both hands. This subject is in some sort
a paraphrase of the second part of the Rondo; it recurs
in the final part of the work, and after a repetition of
the rapid movement, treated in much the same manner as in the first instance, the whole piece concludes
with the first subject of the original theme. The
'Fragment' does not reach to the height of the other

[1] From a catalogue lying before me, of the pianoforte and chamber
compositions of Franz, by his brother Ferdinand, I find only the
'Rondo Allegretto' mentioned, and I am inclined to think that the
introduction is the work of another hand, supplemented with a view of
completing the fragment, and making it more marketable.

sonatas, and is certainly overweighted with difficult
bravura passages; but the introduction and the subject
never fail to impress, and as the latter forms the
burden of the concluding part, the general effect of
the piece is always satisfactory.

The pianoforte Sonata in C has been quite recently
published by Whistling, at Leipsic. It bears the date
April 1825, and was composed in Schubert's best time.
Of the four movements, only the first (Moderato C
major $\frac{4}{4}$) and the Andante (C minor $\frac{6}{8}$) are finished;
the Minuett with Trio (A-flat $\frac{3}{4}$) and the Finale (Rondo
Allegro C major $\frac{4}{4}$) have remained fragments. The
sonata, which is constructed on a grand scale, and
sustains its promise of breadth and largeness in the
first two movements, is not so captivating as the other
pianoforte works of Schubert. The Andante, constructed
on a beautiful flowing theme, is not only the best thing
in the sonata, but one of Schubert's most exquisitely
finished works.[1]

Of the pianoforte pieces for four hands, the Fantasia
in F minor is remarkable for the wealth and beauty of
melody, its startling modulations, and a certain modera-
tion in the treatment of the various themes. Schubert
has written no second work in this style to be compared
with it in the delicate fancies here displayed.

Next in order come the 'Variations on a French

---

[1] A criticism of the greatest part of the pianoforte music will be
found in Nos. 4, 5, and 6 of the 'Deutsche Musikzeitung' of Vienna,
3rd series, 1862. In the 'Niederrheinische Musikzeitung' for 1862,

Air,' dedicated to Beethoven.[1]   The 'Andante favori,'
with variations (Op. 35), is a graceful, highly intellectual work; so are the Marches—especially those
contained in Op. 40 — and the Duett in C (Op.
140).

This last work, in design and development, has many
of the striking characteristics and properties of an
orchestral work (with strains that recall Beethoven's
Symphonies). As such it has been recognised by
Schumann, and the correctness of his views on this
subject is now seldom disputed.[2]   Franz Liszt has set

there is also a treatise on the pianoforte compositions by Schubert, published by Holle, in Wolfenbüttel.

[1] This French Air (with words) is taken from a book of MS. romances
which Schubert discovered in the year 1818, whilst on a visit to the
Esterhazys in Zelész. The music is now in the possession of the
Countess Rosine Almasy, of Vienna.

[2] As usual, Schumann's enthusiasm for his favourite knows no bounds.
His words run thus :—' There was a time when it gave me no pleasure
to speak of Schubert ; I could only talk of him by night to the trees
and stars. Who amongst us, at some time or another, has not been
sentimental ?   Charmed by this new spirit, whose capacities seemed to
me boundless, deaf to everything that could be urged against him, my
thoughts were absorbed in Schubert. As old age advances, and one
becomes more exacting, the circle of favourites becomes narrower and
narrower: it is with us as with them. Of what master could one
throughout life maintain a uniform and precisely the same opinion ?
For the proper appreciation of Bach there are wanted experiences which
youth cannot have; even Mozart's sunny heights are depreciated by
youth, whereas ordinary musical studies are not enough for understanding Beethoven, seeing that in certain years of our life we are more
excited by one of his works than another. We have our preferences,
which shift with the advance of time. Thus much is certain, that a
parity of age signifies a corresponding power of attractiveness in
master and student ; that youthful enthusiasm is best appreciated by

some of the marches for an orchestra, and they have
been performed in public thus arranged.[1]

youth, just as maturity of power is best felt by manhood. Ten years
ago I should unhesitatingly have pronounced these last-published
works as the finest in the world, and, viewed by the productions of
the present time, I still cling to that opinion. But, as compositions
by Schubert, I do not reckon them as members of the same class as
the Quartett in D minor for strings, the Trio in E-flat, and many
of his vocal and pianoforte works. The duett seems to me impreg-
nated with Beethoven's influence, and I considered it to be a symphony arranged for the piano, until the original manuscript, marked
in his own hand as "vierhändige Sonata," was shown to me, and convinced me that I was wrong. Still, I cannot quite give up my former
notion. A man who writes so much as Schubert is not very particular
in dashing down some title at the end of his work, and it may very well
be that he wrote "Sonata" over his work, whilst in his own mind he
considered it a symphony; to this must be added that publishers were
much more likely to be found for a sonata than for a symphony at
a time when Schubert's name first began to be known. Well versed
as I am in his style and manner of treating the piano, and comparing
this work with his other sonatas, most strongly marked with pianoforte
characteristics, I cannot interpret this otherwise than as an orchestral
work. One hears stringed and wind instruments, tutti's solos, flourishes of trumpets, all in the great broad symphonic form—nay, faint
echoes of Beethoven's Symphonies; for instance, in the second movement the Andante of Beethoven's Second Symphony, and in the last,
the finale of the A major Symphony, not to mention other less palpably-
felt passages which seem to me to be lost in the arrangement. All these
facts support my view. I wish also to defend the duett from the objection made to it, as being inconsistent with pianoforte rules, and a work
incapable of being performed on that instrument,—the fact being that
one should look at it from a different point of view, as being a symphony arranged for the piano. Assuming this to be the case, we are
the richer by one symphony.' Joachim has arranged the duett for
instruments, and Spina has the work in this orchestral form. Madame
Clara Schumann has the original MS. of the Sonata.

[1] These marches, Op. 121 and Op. 40, instrumented by Liszt, are

After all that has been said of Schubert's pianoforte music collectively, we need scarcely point to the valuable treasures he has bequeathed to us in the pianoforte works for four hands. But we cannot in common honesty suppress the fact, that in no single style of composition has Schubert given such free play to the wings of his fancy as in these very pianoforte pieces for two performers. In illustration of this, we would refer to the Sonata in B (Op. 30), the ' Divertissement hongrois ' (Op. 54), the ' Lebensstürme ' (Op. 144), and the ' Divertissement' (Op. 63).

Franz Schubert's orchestral compositions consist of occasional overtures, those to his operas, and symphonies.

Of the overtures we have already spoken frequently.[1] Of the symphonies, the first, in D major (composed

performed at Vienna up to the present time, and, taken on the whole, are brilliantly and cleverly set, though with an occasional excess of freedom. No doubt many salient points are brought out in the orchestra, which are far less conspicuous in the pianoforte arrangement; but the marches in their original form are sufficiently interesting to be able to dispense with such an orchestral arrangement.

[1] They consist of the Overtures ' in the Italian style' (in C and D, 1817), written in imitation of Rossini's Overtures, those in B-flat and E minor (written in 1819), and in C minor, which, after Schubert's death, were given with applause at his brother Ferdinand's concert ; besides these, the Overture to ' Alfonso und Estrella ' (Op. 69), which, in the year 1823, was played as a prelude to the Drama of ' Rosamunde,' that to the ' Zauberharfe ' (published incorrectly as the Rosamunde Overture), that to the ' Teufels Lustschloss,' ' Fierrabras,' ' Die Zwillingsbrüder,' ' Die Freunde von Salamanka,' ' Fernando.' The best of these operatic overtures are the two just named, and that to ' Fierrabras.'

in 1813), was written whilst Schubert was still under the influence of the masters who had preceded him, Haydn and Mozart. It could not well have been otherwise. He had become thoroughly conversant with their symphonies during his early days at the Convict; and although his original power was decidedly more conspicuous in his later compositions, yet it is impossible not to recognise the face of Beethoven's mighty influence in these admirable works. A short time before his death, Schubert had determined on writing a grand orchestral work, in order to convince the world of his original powers, and the result was the (seventh) Symphony in C—a work with a history of its own.

In the critical analysis of a symphony (Op. 4) by H. Berlioz, Robert Schumann expressed an opinion, that, with the Ninth Symphony by Beethoven, the mightiest instrumental work yet written, music seemed exhausted, but that Franz Schubert, ' the imaginative painter, whose brush was steeped in sunbeams, and moonlight also, had to Beethoven's nine Muses added a tenth.' This Tenth Symphony was then in existence, but not yet known. The score, since it had been laid aside unused in the year 1828, had slumbered in Ferdinand Schubert's music-room, forgotten and untouched. When Schumann, in the year 1838, visited Vienna, and made a pilgrimage to the graves of the two great musicians, it occurred to him, as he was returning home from the Währing churchyard, that Franz's favourite brother, Ferdinand Schubert, was still existing. 'Whereupon,' (we are quoting his own words) 'I looked him up. He knew me from my enthusiastic veneration for his brother, which I had often expressed in public, and he told me and showed me many things in connection with Franz, which I subsequently, with his permission, published an account of. Finally, he let me see his treasured store of Franz's compositions. On gazing at the piles of music before me, I positively trembled with excess of joy; I did not know where to begin or where to end! Amongst other things, he showed me the scores of several symphonies, many of which have never yet been heard—nay, they have often been laid aside as too difficult or too pompous and bombastic. One must know Vienna, the peculiar circumstances connected with public performances, and the difficulties incidental to raising the means for concerts on a grand scale, in order to find some excuse for the fact, that in the city where Schubert lived and worked, and where his Lieder are so popular, little or next to nothing is known of his grand instrumental works.[1] Who knows how long, too, this symphony, whereof we speak to-day, might

---

[1] The criticism on the C Symphony was written under the still fresh and by no means favourable impression which Schumann carried away on his first visit to Vienna, in the year 1838—a time of the most melancholy stagnation in the world of music.

have remained in dust and darkness, had I not soon
come to an understanding with Ferdinand Schubert,
and arranged with him to send it to Leipsic, either to
the directors of the Gewandhaus concerts, or the conductor himself, whose intuitive powers seldom miss
the discovery of hidden and unassuming beauties in
art, and never those of a palpable kind.   Thus it happened.   The symphony arrived at Leipsic, was heard,
understood, heard again and again, and almost universally admired.   The enterprising firm of Breitkopf
& Härtel bought the work and copyright, and as all
the parts are now complete, we shall probably before
long have the published score in a form we would have
it, for the use and delight of the whole world.'

On March 22, 1839, this new star appeared on
the musical horizon at the last Gewandhaus concert of
the season.   The public listened with rapt attention to
the music, which was given for the first time under
Mendelssohn's direction, and the applause with which
it was greeted was universal.   The critics were loud in
their praises, and whilst Wilhelm Fink, in a detailed
analysis of each movement, tried to direct the public
attention to the high value of the work, Schumann, the
Schubert devotee, and overjoyed at this triumph, expressed himself in the following enthusiastic language:
—'I speak deliberately and plainly: anyone ignorant
of this symphony, knows but little of Schubert, and
this, when it is considered what Schubert has already

contributed to the world of art, must be regarded as a somewhat equivocal compliment. It has been frequently and obtrusively said, to the annoyance of composers, that "after Beethoven they had best refrain from any designs of symphony;" and with partial truth, for, with the exception of some important orchestral works (which, however, were interesting as furnishing an estimate of the intellectual progress of their writers, without exercising any important influence on the mass, none on the progress of civilisation and refinement), nearly all the rest was the colourless reflection of Beethoven's style, not to mention those lame tedious symphony-makers who had the power of reproducing in a passable caricature the powder and perruques of Haydn and Mozart, without the heads belonging to those musicians. Berlioz belongs to France, and is occasionally spoken of as an interesting foreigner and madcap. As I had thought and hoped, and most likely many others with me, that Schubert, so strict in musical forms, so rich and varied in fancy and invention, when dealing with works of the most varied character, would attack the symphony from his own side, and reach that point which, once having attained to, he could reach the hearts of thousands, all this has now been effected in the happiest manner. He certainly never thought of continuing the Ninth Symphony of Beethoven; but, himself a most laborious artist, he created one symphony after another without any delay or break in the series, and that the world should now be examining his Seventh Symphony, without any previous knowledge of its development and its forerunners in the shape of preceding symphonies, is perhaps the one subject of regret connected with this publication, and a fact which in itself may give rise to a misunderstanding of the work itself. It may be that before long the other symphonies will emerge from obscurity; the least important amongst them is sure to have its value as Franz Schubert's work. The Viennese symphony-copyists need not have gone so far in quest of the laurels they needed, seeing they lay sevenfold in Ferdinand Schubert's small study in a suburb of Vienna.[1] Here, at all events, a noble crown was to be given away! This is the oft-repeated story; if in Vienna, for example, you speak of ——, one hears Franz Schubert's praises without end; but when they are by themselves, neither the one nor the other passes for much. However that may be, let us refresh ourselves in the fountains of that spring which gushes full and free from this glorious work. It is true, this Vienna, with its towers of St. Stephen, its beautiful women, its public magnificence, its fair plain girdled with the countless circles of the Danube, and rising gradually into ever higher and loftier hills,

---

[1] An allusion to the 'Prize Symphonies,' proposed by the Musikverein at Vienna in the year 1836, and the victory obtained by Franz Lachner, of Munich, with his Sinfonia Appassionata in C minor.

this Vienna, with all its great memories of the greatest of the German masters, must ever be a fertile theme for a musician's fancy.

'Often, when looking on Vienna from the mountain heights, I thought how many times the restless eye of Beethoven may have scanned that distant Alpine range, how dreamily Mozart may have watched the course of the Danube, which seems to thread its way through every grove and forest, and how often Father Haydn looked at the spire of St. Stephen, and felt unsteady whilst gazing at such a dizzy height. Range in one compact frame the several pictures of the Danube, the cathedral towers and the distant Alpine range, and steep all these images in the holy incense of Catholicism, and you have an ideal of Vienna herself; the exquisite land-scape stands out in bold relief before us, and Fancy will sweep those strings which, but for her, would never have found an echo in our souls. In Schubert's sym-phony, in the transparent, glowing, romantic life therein reflected, I see the city more clearly mirrored than ever, and understand more perfectly than before why such works are native to the scene around me. I will not try to extol and interpret the symphony; men in the different stages of life take such different views of the impressions they derive from artistic fancies, and the youth of eighteen often discovers in a symphony the echo of some world-wide event, where the mature man sees but a local matter, whereas

the musician has never thought of either the one or
the other, and has merely poured forth from his heart
the very best music he could give. But only grant
that we believe that this outer world, to-day fair,
to-morrow dark, may appeal deeply to the inmost
heart of the poet and musician, and that more than
mere lovely melody, something above and beyond sorrow and joy, as these emotions have been pourtrayed
a hundred times in music, lies concealed in this symphony—nay, more, that we are by the music trans-
ported to a region where we can never remember to
have been before—to experience all this we must
listen to symphonies such as this. Here we have, besides masterly power over the musical technicalities
of composition, life in all its phases, colour in exquisite gradations, the minutest accuracy and fitness
of expression, and, permeating the whole work, a spirit
of romance such as we recognise in other works of
Franz Schubert. And this heavenly, long-drawn-out
symphony is like some thick romance of Jean Paul's in
four volumes, which can never end—and, indeed, for the
very best reasons, in order that it may draw along the
reader with it up to the last moment. How refreshing
this feeling of satisfaction of being deceived by the
large wealth of melody, whereas with other composers
one always fears the end, and feels often saddened by
the impotent conclusion. Schubert's easy and brilliant
mastery over the resources of an orchestra would be

unintelligible, if one did not know that six other
symphonies had preceded his last effort, and that he
wrote it in the full maturity of his powers.[1] Those
gifts must be pronounced extraordinary in a man who,
having during his lifetime heard so little of his own
instrumental works, succeeded in so masterly a hand-
ling of the general body of instruments which converse
with one another like human voices and chorus. Except
in numbers of Beethoven's works, I have nowhere found
such an extraordinary and striking resemblance to the
organs of the human voice as in Schubert; it is the
very reverse of Meyerbeer's method of treating the human voice. The complete independence in which the
symphony stands in respect of Beethoven's, is another
sign of its masculine originality. Let anyone observe
how wisely and correctly Schubert's genius developes
itself. In the consciousness of more modest powers, he
avoids all imitation of the grotesque forms, the bold
contrasts we meet with in Beethoven's later works, and
gives us a work in the loveliest form, full of the novel
intricacies of modern treatment, but never deviating
too far from the centre-point, and always returning to
it. This must be patent to anyone who often consi-
ders this particular symphony. At the outset, the brilliancy, the novelty of the instrumentation, the width
and breadth of form, the exquisite interchange of vivid

---

[1] On the score is written, ' March 1828,' and in the following November Schubert died.

emotion, the entire new world in which we are landed all this is as bewildering as any unusual thing we look upon for the first time in our lives; but there ever remains that delicious feeling which we get from some lovely legend or fairy story; we feel above all that the composer was master of his subject, and that the mys- .teries of his music will be made clear to us in time. We derive this impression of certainty from the showy romantic character of the introduction, although all is still wrapped in the deepest mystery. The tran- sition from this to the Allegro is entirely new; the Tempo does not seem to vary; we are landed, we know not how. The analysis of the movements piece by piece is neither a grateful task to ourselves nor others; one would necessarily have to transcribe the entire symphony to give the faintest notion of its intense originality throughout. I cannot, however, pass from the second movement, which addresses us in such ex- quisitely moving strains, without a single word. There is one passage in it, that where the horn is calling as though from a distance, that seems to come to us from another sphere. Here everything else listens, as though some heavenly messenger were hovering around the orchestra.

'The symphony, then, has had an influence on us such as none since Beethoven's have ever exercised. Artists and amateurs joined in extolling its merits, and I heard some words spoken by the master who had studied the work most elaborately, so as to ensure a grand performance and interpretation of so gorgeous a work—words which I should like to have been able to convey to Schubert, as perhaps conveying to him a message which would have given him the sincerest pleasure. Years perhaps will pass before the work becomes naturalised in Germany; I have no fear of its ever being forgotten or overlooked; it bears within its bosom the seeds of immortal growth.' [1]

At last this symphony was given in a complete form at the second public concert at Vienna, on December 15, 1839. At the very first orchestral rehearsal the paid ' artists' refused to attend a sufficient number of times required to ensure a fine performance, and thus it happened that although a performance was announced of the entire symphony, only the two first movements were given, and these were interpolated by an Italian air.[2] After this unhappy attempt, the work once more slumbered for a period of eleven years, until, at the end of the year 1850, it was given in its entirety for the first time at Vienna, under the conductorship of Herr J. Hellmesberger. The applause it met with was but moderate.[3]

[1] When the symphony was repeated on October 29, 1840, he wrote: —' Then we came at last to the symphony, the crowning-point of the evening. A thousand hands were uplifted. Had Schubert looked on with his own eyes, he would have thought himself a wealthy king.'

[2] The other pieces in the concert were, Air from ' Lucia,' sung by Frl. Tuczek, and the Forty-second Psalm by Mendelssohn.

[3] Ferdinand Schubert mentions an attempt made by the Conservatoire in Paris to perform the symphony in 1842, but this, too, was frustrated

In the fatherland of the composer himself, this work,' although recognised by Mendelssohn and Schumann as the most important orchestral work in existence, next to Beethoven's symphonies, and of extraordinary value from the individuality of its form, has not yet met with that success and recognition to which it is so eminently entitled; although it should be stated that, in consequence of repeated performances, it begins to enjoy greater and increasing popularity. The breadth and extension of the several movements (and the general length of the symphony in consequence), the want of form, are invariably urged against this work as objections, and hence the curious result has followed that the symphonic fragments from earlier written symphonies [1]—namely, the extensive Beethovenish Scherzo of the Sixth Symphony, and the final movement of the second in D, were vigorously applauded for the conciseness of their form and stirring nature of their subjects; whereas a similar movement in the 'Seventh'— a work of the profoundest originality, and composed in the

by the indolence of the orchestral players. In the year 1839 Mendelssohn wanted to send it to the Philharmonic Society in London for performance, and made enquiries of Ferdinand Schubert; the latter, however, did not answer Mendelssohn's letter on the subject. Since the year 1850 the symphony has been given on three public occasions at Vienna.

[1] For instance, the two first movements of the 'Tragic Symphony' in C minor (written in 1816), the third movement of the first C Symphony (1818), and the finale of the second Symphony in D, It is curious that in Mendelssohn's published letters no mention occurs of Schubert's symphony.

maturity of Schubert's powers—has not been so fortunate. We have already mentioned the two finished
movements of an hitherto unknown symphony in B
minor, which, since the year 1822, has been in the
possession of Herr Anselm Hüttenbrenner, in Gratz,
and is said to contain many beauties. Also a sketch
of a Symphony in E (1821), which (according to Ferdinand Schubert) passed, in the year 1845, into the
hands of Mendelssohn.[1]

[1] Of the confusion and mistakes made in the dates, the numbers,
and the alleged performances of Schubert's symphonies, the following statement furnishes a striking proof. In the MS. catalogue, compiled by Alois Fuchs, we find mention made of a Sixth Symphony
in C, composed in the year 1816 (!), as having been presented to
Mendelssohn. Ferdinand Schubert mentions a Symphony in C of the
year 1817, and the original date of the Scherzo of the Sixth Symphony
in C is stated in the concert programme of the Musikverein at Vienna
to have been the year 1825. All these statements are incorrect, for Franz
Schubert has written on the original score (in the possession of Dr.
Schneider, of Vienna) the year 1818, which certainly admits the possibility of the work having been begun in the year 1817, the date of the
origin of the symphony according to Ferdinand Schubert. In the year
1839 Ferdinand Schubert sent two of his brother's symphonies to Felix
Mendelssohn-Bartholdy ; one of them the grand Symphony in C, which
was given at Leipsic on March 21, 1839. Of the Seventh Symphony,
Bauernfeld, in his sketch, says it was composed in the year 1825, and
Ferdinand Schubert gives the year 1826 as the date of its origin ;
whereas the date marked on the original score, in possession of the
Musikverein at Vienna, is March 1828. With regard to this work
(supposed to have been written in the year 1826), Ferdinand Schubert
thought it had been produced by Mendelssohn at Leipsic some time
between 1845 and 1847, and that Franz had received a testimonial of
honour for the same from the Amateurs' Society at Vienna—dates and
hypotheses equally incorrect.

We stated at the very outset of this volume that Schubert's efforts were at an early period directed to the province of chamber classical music. The quartetts for stringed instruments which he composed whilst still at the Convict, or immediately after he left it, were performed at his father's house, and some of these still exist in manuscript.[1]

Schubert himself, as we saw in a passage already quoted from one of his letters, regarded these quartetts merely as composition exercises, and thought much less of their intrinsic merits than the relations and friends who heard them performed. At a later period, when he devoted himself almost exclusively to the Lied and pianoforte music, he gave up the study of this particular form of composition for a number of years, but only to labour with increased energy and more successful results, during the latter part of his life, at the production of classical music of a solid artistic value. Whilst on the subject of Schubert's performances in chamber music, we should assign the foremost place to the two Trios (in B-flat and E-flat), the stringed Quartetts in D minor and G major, and the stringed Quintett in C. Both the trios, which were performed in private circles during the lifetime of the composer, are amongst Schubert's best-known works.

[1] Amongst these are: a stringed Quartett in D (November 19, 1812); a second in B-flat, dated August 23, 1814; and one in G minor (March 25, 1815), the MS. of which is in the collection of the Musikverein.

They were written within a short time of each other, and belonging as they do to the last creative period of the composer,[1] are therefore conspicuous for all the peculiar graces and loveliness of Schubert's manner; both these works, indeed, bear on them the stamp of artistic ripeness and intense cultivation. Broader in conception, and more powerfully worked out in form and detail, is the E-flat Trio, when judged as an entire work—a work which the modest artist himself regarded with self-complacency.[2]

[1] The E-flat Trio, as we see from the original in the hands of the Countess Almasy, of Vienna, was written in November 1827, and engraved shortly afterwards at Leipsic. The B-flat Trio, although written before that in E-flat, was engraved at a later period.

[2] After criticising a series of other trios, Schumann says of the one in B-flat :—' One glance at the trio by Schubert, and this poor world of ours reappears fresh and bright. Some ten years since, a trio of Schubert's, like some angry meteor, blazed forth and outshone everything in the musical atmosphere of the time; this was exactly his hundredth work, and shortly afterwards, in November 1828, he died. The trio which has just appeared seems to be older in point of date. In style it betrayed certainly no earlier period, and may have been written shortly before the well-known Trio in E-flat; but they differ from one another in very material ways. The first movement of one of these trios, with its deep scorn and transition to sad passionate longings, is in the other full of lovely maidenlike trust; the Adagio, with a sigh which seems likely to melt into a burst of sorrow, is here cheerful, confident, and virginlike; the Adagio, in which there is a wail of anguish, is here a soft dream of bliss—the ebb and flow of exquisite human tenderness. The Scherzos are like one another, but I give the preference to that in the earlier published of the two trios. I pass no judgment on the final movements. In a word, the Trio in E-flat is more spirited, manly, dramatic; this, on the other hand, is full of anguish, more womanly and lyric in character. May the work be-

The first three movements especially are beautiful in form, but the finale, with a poor subject, and worn threadbare by exceeding length, is not a fit pendent to the preceding movements.[1]

Both the stringed Quartetts in G major and D minor [2] are admirable in every respect; in particular passages the effects are of a startling kind, but in breadth of plan, depth of conception, they are both surpassed by the stringed Quintett in C, a perfect gem in music, of the true Schubert stamp, and in some movements (the Adagio and the Trio of the Scherzo) quite Beethovenish in grandeur.

Next in order we have the stringed Quartett in A minor (Op. 29), and those in E major and E-flat (Op. 125), the first of which is the best, and therefore most frequently performed; three short Sonatas for violin

queathed to us be a precious legacy ! Time, which brings to light such numberless and beautiful things, will not soon reproduce another Schubert.'

[1] The subject of the second movement in the E-flat Trio is, as Dr. L. v. Sonnleithner pointed out to me, a Swedish national melody. The famous sing r, Johann Siboni, at that time director of the Conservatorium in Copenhagen, had a pupil, the tenor-singer Berg, now director of the Conservatoire at Stockholm (Jenny Lind's first teacher) ; and in the years 1827 or 1828 Berg used to travel to Vienna with letters of recommendation to Fräulein Fröhlich, and he used frequently to sing at private parties. Schubert heard then the national Lieder of Sweden, which he liked exceedingly, and asked and obtained a copy of them. One of these he used as a subject in his trio, without concealing the fact of the origin of the subject.

[2] In the D minor Quartett we recognise, as the subject of the Adagio, the melody sung by 'Death' in Schubert's Lied, 'Der Tod und das Mädchen,' varied in the most exquisite manner.

and pianoforte, Duett for piano and flute (Op. 160), a
Notturno for pianoforte, violin, and cello (Op. 148),
the two Duetts for pianoforte and violin in C and A
(Op. 159 and 162), the Rondeau brillant for pianoforte
and violin in B minor (Op. 70), with an introduction
in the grand style, and the most successful of the three
duetts; then the grand Octett composed in the year
1824, of which (as well as Op. 160) we have before
made mention; finally, the melodious but somewhat
spiritless pianoforte Quintett (Op. 114), with the Lied
'Die Forelle' as the theme of the second movement.

The Duett (Op. 159) entitled 'Fantasie,' and the
Notturno, are very difficult to play, and are not very
effective specimens of their class. The first consists
of an introduction (Andante moto, C major $\frac{6}{8}$), leading
to a curiously varied Hungarian motive (Allegretto, A
minor $\frac{2}{4}$). Schubert's beautiful song, 'Sei mir gegrüsst'
(by Rückert), is the theme of the second movement
(Andantino, A-flat $\frac{3}{4}$); the introductory subject reappears, and the whole piece finishes with an Allegro (C
major $\frac{2}{4}$). The 'Fantasie,' certainly one of the composer's least important compositions, if not positively
objectionable, was in such bad odour during Schubert's
lifetime by reason of its 'intricacy,' that the public
and the publishers were as shy of it as though it were
a musical bugbear.

In direct contrast with the duetts here mentioned
are the three short Sonatas for pianoforte and violin

—little known, and written in the year 1816—(Op. 137), distinguished by a surprising simplicity of treatment, but still bearing some traces of the genuine Schubert. The most attractive of the short sonatas is certainly the second, in A minor.

A knowledge of Schubert's chamber music in its entirety and comprehensiveness is, as we shall have occasion to show at the end of this volume, an entirely modern achievement in the composer's native place. People now are no longer satisfied with giving the most perfect performances attainable of works already known, but most praiseworthy efforts have been made to bring to light compositions of the writer's earliest period,[1] and, by unearthing buried and hidden treasures of Schubert's genius, to facilitate a proper appreciation of the writer's versatility in different fields of composition.[2]

We have already given a detailed account of the operas. Taken as a whole, Schubert's dramatic works are still an ' unknown country ; ' for but few of them, and those the least important of their kind, have been performed ; and his two grander operas which have come down to us have not been heard for such

---

[1] For instance, the beautiful stringed Quartett in G minor, which Schubert, as we read on the original score, wrote in the year 1815 in the space of five days (March 25 to April 1), a quartett written in 1814, and other works.

[2] Ferdinand Schubert's memoirs assure us that Schubert wrote a violin concerto, the original being in his possession.

a length of time, that of Schubert's capacity for working successfully in the dramatic field we can form
no distinct opinion. Like nearly all great masters,
Schubert, in his early years, felt an ambition to write
dramatic works, and in his sixteenth year he had
taken in hand the composition of 'Des Teufels Lustschloss.'

In his eighteenth year his activity in the operatic
field kept pace with that of his composition of Lieder,
and produced an extraordinary harvest of musical results.
Then followed a longer pause, interrupted only occasionally by a single detached melodrama and musical vaudeville, until, at the very best period of the composer's
career, arose the two grand Operas, 'Alfonso und Estrella,' 'Fierrabras,' and the Operetta 'Die Verschwornen,'
with which his performances in this department of composition ended. In spite of his unhappy experiences
and the hopelessness of seeing his works given at the
theatres, his ambition to write for the stage remained
in after-life as strong as ever. Many passages in his
correspondence with Schober, Schwind, and Bauernfeld, the well-authenticated confession which he uttered,
after completing his grand Symphony in C, 'that he
intended to devote himself entirely to symphony and
opera,' his longing for an operatic libretto during his
illness, and numbers of schemes and books he had
actually taken in hand, prove to demonstration that,
had his life been spared, the musical world would have

been richer by some grand dramatic works; nay, that Schubert might have appeared as an operatic reformer and the founder of a true German musical drama.[1]

It can hardly be disputed, by unprejudiced persons, that Schubert had the stuff in him requisite for such an undertaking; or even allowing (and several grand numbers in his two romantic operas bear witness to the fact) that he would have failed to master the broader dramatic forms of the operatic style, opposed as these were to his musical organisation, still, in the melodramas that suited him, his grace, ease, facility, and certainty in dealing with the vocal and instrumental parts, might well have enabled him to create some lasting monument in the dramatic style.[2] It may well

[1] A libretto, 'Der Graf von Glenallan,' which Schubert, according to a statement of his brother Ferdinand, intended to set to music, is in my possession; there is an outline, too, of an opera, 'Die Salzbergwerke,' by Graf Maylath. Bauernfeld informs us that 'an instrumental sketch' of the Opera 'Der Graf von Gleichen' (1827) has been found, but I have not succeeded in finding any traces of this work hitherto. 'Der Graf von Gleichen' was also set in the year 1822 by Traugott Maximilian Eberwein, a composer at Weimar (born 1775, died 1831), and the first act was rehearsed at Göthe's house on December 5. (See Ekermann's 'Conversations with Göthe,' vol. iii.) Quite recently (1863) this opera, composed by Dörstling, was performed at Sonderhausen.

[2] The number of good operas in more recent times is very small, but we have heaps of worthless music for the stage. We may well believe that Schubert's operas deserve a trial on the stage; people anyhow would hear new and beautiful music. The theatrical atmosphere is of so peculiar a kind, that many a poor plant thrives in it, whilst the healthiest flowers fade irrecoverably.

be doubted if Schubert's larger operas would satisfy the requirements of our time. Schubert and his friends strove, with good reason, to get them produced on the stage; for they well understood that practical experience is the only passport to future efforts in the dramatic style, and the means of avoiding errors in all works that follow crude undisciplined efforts. At a later period, when the national reaction set in against Italianising the opera, he might have succeeded in realising his hopes and wishes; but his early death completely annihilated every hope of a representation of his operas and operettas, so that his compositions, written expressly for the stage, have fallen into oblivion. It may be stated as a curiosity, and, at the same time, as a proof of what absurdities may be perpetrated by well-meaning but ill-advised counsellors, that, several years ago, a grave proposal was made in an essay in the 'Unterhaltungen am häuslichen Herd,' to make one opera out of disjointed pieces selected from Schubert's eight operas, not one of which was fitted by itself for public performance, and to bring forward this hash of absurdity before the public.

Church music is much indebted to the genius of our composer for the originality and depth of devotional meaning in many of Schubert's sacred compositions. His first Mass was written in the year 1814, the last in the year 1828, a short time before his death. In the interval that elapsed between these two works were written five Masses,[1] two Stabat Maters, a grand Magnificat, a Hallelujah, and a considerable number of contributions to church music.

The intrinsic worth of these compositions is very varying and unequal; for if the Offertoriums, the graduale, &c., seem to have been thrown off carelessly, and are, as artistic productions, comparatively speaking, unimportant, several of the Masses, from the beauty of their form and genuine religious expression, are highly valued by the musical connoisseur. Schubert was not the man to dally long with any department of art without leaving there the unmistakable marks of his genius.

On the whole, the noblest of Schubert's known Masses is that in G, which he composed in his eighteenth year. It is a splendid testimonial to the wonderfully developed maturity of his power, shown (and this is curious enough) in a work of a religious character.[2]

The Kyrie of the G Mass opens in four parts with that simplicity of melody for which Schubert shows his predilection in other works, in order to give

[1] These are the Masses in B-flat and G (1815), in C (1816), in A (1822), and the 'German Mass' (1827).

[2] This Mass (as distinguished from those in A-flat and E-flat) belongs to the small ones. It is set for four voices, with accompaniments for violins, viola, bass, trumpets, and drums *ad libitum*. The longest movement (188 bars) is the Credo. Schubert began the Mass on March 2, and finished it on the 7th of the same month.

himself scope for beautifying and extending by degrees that which seems at first commonplace and insignificant. Although the key of the Kyrie Eleison is G major, the leading sentiment is a mournful and gloomy one, and only assumes a brighter and more cheerful hue when the tonic shifts to its dominant. The first subject, which reminds us of the well-known benediction-hymn, ' Heilig,' is characteristically treated in the key of G major. The melody, given independently to each of the four parts, is written in a minor key ; the wail of the Kyrie rises to tones of sorrowful yearnings, until by chromatic progressions it comes upon the dominant organ point in D. The music again returns to the original key ; the former subject is repeated, in order to close the first part with chords of a peaceful reposeful kind. The Gloria is mostly in the conventional church style ; the Gratias is conspicuous for one of those lovely melodies which Schubert could pour forth so largely from his cornucopia of sound ; the ' Quoniam,' although with beauties of its own, bears the Mozart-Haydn mark, and the whole of this part, somewhat hastily and laboriously treated, and only here and there revealing Schubert's idiosyncrasy, concludes in an unmistakably affected manner. The Credo then follows—a powerful and broadly treated chorale, which, although marked ' piano,' rolls on majestically and powerfully. The contrapuntal treatment of the piece, the working of the other parts

against the chorale, the chorus and orchestral accompaniment to the vocal parts which acquire fresh force
from bar to bar, the deep suggestiveness of various
parts of the Credo, and the gradations from sadness to
jubilant triumph, finally, the beautiful return to the
original theme and perfect development, not to mention
many other noble characteristics, make this sacred
music one of the finest things ever written for the church.
The Sanctus is not specially attractive, but the Benedictus, on the contrary, is a heartfelt song of praise, in
which all the voices, the alto excepted, join in a canon,
which is one of Schubert's loveliest inspirations. On
an equally lofty scale with the Benedictus is the Agnus
Dei, throughout every bar of which runs a melody of
plaintive and expressive character, intertwined with
the alternating strains of the solo quartett. The remarkable succession of keys used in the Agnus, the
characteristic accompaniment (especially the sighing of
the low violas), the mournful unisons blending afterwards with the whole chorus, finally, the joyful Dona
nobis and the concluding Kyrie, ensure for the whole
of the concluding part an unflagging interest on the
part of an appreciative audience.

The Masses in B and A-flat are of no mean value,
even in comparison with the Mass in G. The Gloria
and Agnus, in the first-named of these sacred works,
but especially the Credo, as well as the Incarnatus in
the A-flat Mass, are in every respect far beyond the

ordinary run of church compositions. The Incarnatus, indeed, is one of the noblest movements existing in modern Catholic church music.

Schubert's last grand church composition is the Mass in E-flat. This work, without doubt written at Schubert's best and ripest period, takes rank with the foremost compositions of the kind written at that time. A knowledge of this Mass hitherto has, with some few exceptions, been monopolised by Vienna, outside of which city it has remained almost entirely unknown. Possibly we shall have soon, either in the church or the concert-room, a worthy performance of this work.[1]

[1] The E-flat Mass was performed very badly in the church of St. Ulrich, in Vienna, soon after Franz Schubert's death (in the year 1829). A critic in the 'Allgemeine Musikzeitung' of Leipsic carried away the worst impression of it. The MS. of the work is in the Imperial Library at Berlin.

CHAPTER XIX.

SCHUBERT'S MUSIC BECOMES GRADUALLY KNOWN—HIS MUSIC AT
VIENNA, BERLIN, AND LEIPSIC—HIS SONGS FAMILIAR IN FRANCE,
ENGLAND, ITALY, AND RUSSIA—TRANSCRIPTIONS AND VARIOUS AR-
RANGEMENTS OF THE SONGS—PUBLICATION OF HIS WORKS—FATE
OF MANUSCRIPTS AFTER HIS DEATH—APPRECIATION OF SCHUBERT
QUITE RECENTLY.

SCHUBERT, whose fame in Germany was based by his
acknowledged supremacy in the world of song, became first known to the public world of his native place
by his efforts for the stage. The musical vaudeville
' Die Zwillingsbrüder,' and the melodrama ' Die Zauberharfe,' were the works which extended his reputation
beyond his immediate circle; whereas the ' Erlkönig,'
written about 1815 or 1816, was not heard in public
until the year 1821.

This Lied, which created an epoch in music, was succeeded in the same and the following years by several
other Lieder and concerted vocal pieces, some for the
theatre, some for the concert-room. During Schubert's
lifetime nearly one hundred of his Lieder were published and engraved at Vienna, besides pianoforte works
for solo and duett-players, in which dance music formed
⸴ conspicuous item ; finally, some works for the church

and chamber, nearly all of which were greeted with
hearty recognition and applause by critics, both native
and foreign.

It appeared after Schubert's death that a rich legacy
in the shape of numbers of musical works of all kinds
came into the hands of his brother Ferdinand. The
musical firm of Diabelli & Company (about the year
1830) purchased a large part of these compositions,[1]
and there appeared, to the surprise of everybody, no

[1] The official document (in the hands of Herr Spina, and very kindly
lent me by that gentleman) runs thus :—'We, the undersigned, heirs of
the late Franz Schubert, deceased, of Vienna, declare hereby, that the
art and music firm of A. Diabelli & Company has acquired the property in all the following-mentioned works of the aforesaid Franz
Schubert ; and that, in consequence, the firm of A. Diabelli & Company are to be reckoned the sole and lawful publishers of these works.
These works are the following.' Then follows a catalogue, from which
we gather that the compositions therein enumerated, from Op. 1 to
Op. 153 inclusively, were purchased by the publishing firm of Diabelli,
with the exception of these works :—33, 34, 36, 37, 38, 60, 61, 65,
70, 78, 79, 80, 81, 82, 83, 89, 90, 91, 100, 105, 107, 110, 111,
112, 114, 117, 118, 120, 125, 126, 129, 131, and 141. The first forty
'Lieferungen' of the 'Remains' (issued without reserve), and several
other manuscripts besides (only a part of which, however, has appeared
in print), were also recovered by this firm, namely, fifty-one Lieder,
14 vocal Quartetts, the Canons written in the year 1813, a Cantata for
three voices (in C), the Hymn to the Holy Ghost, the Stabat Mater (in
F), the grand Hallelujah and Magnificat in C, the stringed Quartett in C,
four stringed Quartetts (in C, G, and two in B), a stringed Trio (in B),
two pianoforte Sonatas (in A-flat and A minor), Variations (in F), an
Adagio (in D), &c., a violin Concerto with orchestra (in D), an orchestral
Overture, the Overture to the third act of the 'Zauberharfe,' the Easter
Cantata ('Lazarus'), a Tantum ergo for four voices and orchestra (in E),
and an Offertory (in B) for tenor solo, with chorus and orchestra.

fewer than fifty 'Lieferungen,' consisting of exquisitely poetical musical works, marked in the catalogue as 'Nachlass,' which seemed in point of number and import to vie in popularity with the compositions already known to the world.

Up to the year 1840, over three hundred Lieder had been published; at present the entire collection amounts to some three hundred and sixty.

During his lifetime, and for a long period after his death, Schubert was only generally recognised and esteemed as a great song-writer. 'The complex character of his treatment of harmony,' and other 'adverse circumstances,' conspired to make his dramatic compositions of small value in the judgment of the public; of his pianoforte compositions, his church and chamber music (some few pieces excepted), next to no notice was taken, and the fate of his grand Symphony in C has already been mentioned. In consequence of this, the public performance of his grander works was during his lifetime confined to a few orchestral overtures, the Octett, the stringed Quartett in A minor, the pianoforte Trio in E-flat, and some of the greater choral Cantatas. But for this very reason the Lieder were more frequently given at concerts by artists, and Schubert repeatedly accompanied his own songs on these occasions at the piano.

The first of his vocal quartetts for male voices ('Dörfchen,' 'Nachtigall,' &c. &c.) were very warmly greeted by the public.   Those which immediately followed did not produce a similar effect; but the choruses for female and mixed voices were very successful.   One of the overtures in the Italian style was performed in the year 1818, that in E minor in the year 1821, at the fourth Gesellschaft concert.

A few years after Schubert's death, fragments of his operas, some orchestral pieces, and other compositions, still new to the artistic world, were performed for the first time at Vienna.   They were generally introduced at the private concerts got up by Ferdinand Schubert and the directors of church music in the Alservorstadt, Kirchlehner and Michael Leitermayer, for the benefit of the Institution for Orphans and Widows, or for other charitable objects at Vienna.[1]

With regard to the chamber music, both the pianoforte Trios and the D minor stringed Quartett were very well received, during Schubert's lifetime, in Vienna, and subsequently in other parts of Germany, after having been previously heard at Berlin and Leipsic. Hellmesberger's revival of quartett performances in 1849, at Vienna, was the dawn of a new era for Schubert's classical music, for in addition to several of the

---

[1] In April 1836, Ferdinand Schubert produced at the Musikverein concert the Overture in D, the March and Chorus from ' Fierrabras,' and in the following year, at a concert of his pupils, the last movement of the great Symphony in C—this for the first time.   At last, in the year 1841, the ' Stabat Mater ' (written in 1816), in which Frl. Tuczek and Herren Staudigl and Lutz sang the solos.

less known works, there were many others which either never had been performed, or were unknown to the present generation, and were now first brought before the public, and ever since have, in their turn, formed the special attractions in the concert programmes. In connection with these works Hellmesberger introduced the D minor Quartett, first performed on November 11, 1849, the brilliant success of which led to a performance of the stringed Quintett in C, and other works.

The Trio in E-flat was from the year 1836 a constant item in the concert repertoire of the violinist Zimmermann, the pianoforte-player Deker, and the brothers Stahlknecht and Steiffensand, up to the year 1846, when the quartett soirées were established at Berlin. At that time loud complaints were heard in Berlin that the grand Symphony in C, after only one performance, had been laid aside, and that, generally speaking, Schubert's instrumental compositions had been too little respected. In 1837, for the first time, were heard the pianoforte Quintett in A and the B-flat Trio. Herr Lewy, of Vienna, in the year 1847, played in the B-flat Trio at a matinée musicale given by the violinist Vieuxtemps at St. Petersburg. Quite recently, in the season 1861–1862, the C major Symphony was performed at the concert of the Russian Musical Society, under the direction of Anton Rubinstein—probably this work and the D minor Quartett also were novelties to a Russian audience. The other chamber classical pieces which have been published have never or very seldom been performed in public.

With regard to musical institutions on the Continent, we must note particularly the Leipsic Gewandhaus concerts as those where Schubert's Lieder have been most warmly received.[1] At Leipsic there were admirable artists to execute them. Schubert's concerted vocal pieces remained for a long time uncared for out of Vienna. Even in the composer's native place they were never frequently performed, except during Schubert's lifetime, and then because he had composed them expressly for the pupils of the Conservatoire and for set occasions. After his death there was a pause of several years, broken by short interruptions in the years 1836 and 1838.[2] In more modern times, however, the Männergesangverein at Vienna, soon after the society was founded, resumed the choral songs of Schubert, and the best of these were performed at their concerts in quick succession. These enterprising efforts to popularise the genius of Schubert reached their climax in the year 1858, by a performance of the 'Gesang der Geister über den Wassern,' and some operatic fragments. Other

---

[1] The poet Lenau, on his first visit to Stuttgart, drew the public attention to the treasures of Schubert. I had this information from Herr L. A. Frankl.

[2] In the year 1830 (at the fourth Gesellschaft concert, on March 28), 'Miriam's War Song' was given with instrumental accompaniments by Franz Lachner; in the year 1836 (also at a Gesellschaft concert, February 28) the 'Hymn,' and in 1838 the 'Ständchen.'

vocal societies and schools have arisen in more modern days at Vienna, and given specimens of Schubert's choruses, cantatas, selections from his operas and melodramas, besides several numbers of the 'Stabat Mater,' written in 1816.[1] For the present, but few of Schubert's choral songs have become naturalised outside Vienna.

Schubert's church music has scarcely been heard beyond the walls of Vienna. During his lifetime, his Masses in B-flat and A-flat, and some smaller sacred pieces, were performed once or twice in the churches at Vienna. The grand Mass in E-flat was given in a very unsatisfactory manner shortly after Schubert's death (on November 15, 1829), at the church of Santa Maria Consolatrix, and more recently the Masses in F, G, and B-flat have been given, besides various contributions by Schubert in the shape of church chorales.[2]

---

[1] Fragments were given (in 1857 or 1858) of the Operetta 'Die Verschwornen' and the Cantata 'Lazarus.' In the year 1841 the Cäcilienverein at Prague performed the Shepherd's Chorus from 'Rosamunde,' and in the year 1848 the Twenty-third Psalm was performed at Leipsic, and quite recently the 'Gesang der Geister' at Munich. The well-known chorus, 'Widerspruch,' was given, it seems, for the first time in February 1863, at the Pauliner Verein at Leipsic; and on the occasion of a Schubert festival, the 'Nachtgesang im Wald,' and the Chorus of the Moors and Knights out of 'Fierrabras.' The eight-part hymn does not appear to have been known in Brunswick before the year 1863.

[2] The B-flat Mass was performed at the Dominican and Altlerchenfelder churches in 1861 and 1862. On Good Friday, 1863, after an interval of twenty-two years, the 'Stabat Mater' (1816) was given at

Of Schubert's operas, musical vaudevilles, and melodramas that were ever performed on the stage, all,
with the exception of the Operetta 'Die Verschwornen,'
and the Opera 'Alfonso und Estrella,' have been given
exclusively at Vienna.

Of Schubert's symphonies, the grand one in C, after
coming out of the fiery ordeal of Leipsic with great
brilliancy, went through the round of all Germany.
The Sixth Symphony, and fragments of that in C minor
and D major (1816 and 1815), have been performed
exclusively at Vienna in the years 1828, 1829, and
1860. We have had of late no more public performances of overtures which are pleasing to listen to, but
of no great and permanent musical value.

Schubert's peculiar gifts as a Lieder-composer were
first recognised beyond Austria and Germany, in France,
about the year 1829. A report had once been circulated
that he was to be invited to Paris to write an opera for
the Academy. His Lieder were sung with great delight
in private circles, the German words having been translated into elegant French. The singer Wartel con-

the Altlerchenfelderkirche at Vienna. At Leipsic, at the close of the
year 1862, or the beginning of 1863, the Mass in A-flat was in part
performed, and the same work repeated at the Carolus Kirche in Vienna,
in the year 1863. Robert Führer, a composer, who died a short time
ago at Vienna, dealt dishonestly with the G Mass. He published it as
his own composition at Prague, where he was Capellmeister in St. Veits-
kirche, and dedicated the work to the Archduchess Marie Caroline,
Abbess of the Convent at Hradschin. The Mass was published by the
firm of Marco Berra, at Prague.

tributed greatly to their popularity by the success attending his fine execution of the Lieder. The music-publishers Bellange and Richhault, in Paris, published about a hundred Lieder, besides waltzes, marches, sonatas, duetts, trios and quartetts, overtures, variations, the 'Moments musicals,' and four series of sacred pieces.

In a musical correspondence of that time, we find the following passage relative to the reception of Schubert's music in France:—'Franz Schubert's Lieder are exceedingly popular in Paris; his name is never omitted in any programme of a really important concert.' A collection of his songs with French words, by Émile Deschamps, appeared about that time. As the French felt and fully appreciated the difference between their 'chansons' and the German 'Lied,' they adopt the word 'Lied' as a new French term, and some go so far as to talk of 'le lied,' 'les liedes,' others, 'les lieder,' or 'les lieders.' The collection here alluded to was published as 'Collection de Lieder de François Schubert,' and contained all of Schubert's Lieder then most in fashion in Parisian circles.

In another treatise, devoted to 'Recollections of Paris from 1817 to 1841,' we read this passage:—'The amateurs of the period gained far more from the introduction of Franz Schubert's Lieder than from the style of the modern stage. Their influence was all the more surprising, from the fact of the French having so many years adopted a totally opposite style. Schubert was eminently successful. The depth, the solidity, the absorbing melancholy, all those elements of Schubert's Lieder which can only be felt and not described, were well understood by the French, and, curiously enough, were in certain instances charmingly rendered by the singers. For instance, I shall never forget the impression made on me by Nourrit's singing of the "Erl-King." [1]

In England and North America, Schubert's name is well known. The original English words have, in several instances, been added to the Lieder, and helped to make them universally known in those countries. The 'Ungeduld' has been set to Spanish words, and Lenz found the 'Winterreise' lying upon a pianoforte at Cadiz. Still Schubert's compositions have not become catholic, and the full appreciation of this writer beyond Austria and Germany has hitherto failed to get beyond certain narrow limits.

In North Germany, the Strofenlieder of Reichardt

[1] This famous tenor won great applause by his singing, at a concert of the Conservatoire in the year 1835, the 'Junge Nonne,' with orchestral accompaniment. The taste for German Lieder, engendered by every fresh experience of Schubert's style, proved the power and influence of these new inspirations. Berlioz, and quite recently Felicien David, showed to the world their inclination for the romantic style; but great intentions are not always at once realised. The French imitations of Schubert were less successful than the German. In Italy the knowledge of Schubert's works is confined to some dozen of the Lieder, printed at Milan and Naples. They are chiefly selected as being best suited to the Italian method of singing.

and Zelter carried all before them, and Schubert's triumphs in that part of his native land were not achieved until a long time after his death, when the performance of the Symphony in C at Leipsic first brought the writer into notice. The passion for his Lieder in Vienna was as strong as ever, until a period of musical indolence intervened, and song-writers of a second and third rank, with their weak brainless effusions, got the upper hand for a time. The difficulty of Schubert's accompaniments may have had something to do with it. The reaction, however, did not continue, and the more modern taste returning to the good and genuine, came back, as it were spontaneously, to Schubert's imperishable works. In Vienna and elsewhere, the various transpositions, settings, and arrangements of the Lieder have been common. These are of doubtful value, but have the essential merit of having contributed in their way to an extensive and public recognition of Schubert's melodies.

In the year 1849, a new edition was printed, by Diabelli, of Schubert's Lieder, with German and French words; still more recently a cheap collection of Schubert's compositions by Louis Holle in Wolfenbüttel; by Spina at Vienna, a transposed (Stockhausen) version of the 'Müllerlieder,' with German and French words (the latter by Béranger), and quite lately Hofcapellmeister Randhartinger has undertaken to edit a work, based on the first edition, containing the original readings of the Lieder. There is some talk of Herr Spina's publishing an entire and complete edition of all Schubert's compositions—an undertaking which, if conscientiously carried out, would be hailed with universal satisfaction.

The finest of Schubert's songs have long since been the public property of the whole musical world. The same may be said—but only with reference to a very recent period—of his instrumental compositions, but with much reserve in respect of all his other works.

The appendix at the end of this volume speaks more eloquently than words of the astounding fertility of the master's genius, and justifies the assertion that Schubert in his totality is only known and appreciated by a few. There are all kinds of vocal works, cantatas, overtures, orchestral, opera, and church music, of which hitherto not a single note has ever been heard. For forty years and more have these works remained unused, in some cases mere objects of painful solicitude, as though the musician had written his enchanting music only for himself, and not for ourselves and our children.

It has not been enough that Schubert during his lifetime should be allowed to produce only a tithe of his incessant labours before the public; but even after his death, and in recent times, a kind of fatality seems to have hung over the works he bequeathed to the world. The conduct of those who were the earliest possessors of these works has been conspicuous for an affectionate care of the musician's memory. But some important compositions, or fragments of the larger works, have been irrecoverably lost; valuable manuscripts, quite unique in their way, have perished—nay, over and over again, there has been danger of the entire collection of the posthumous works being scattered to the winds, annihilated, or relegated to a book-chest in some foreign library. After the painful experiences we have been made familiar with in matters of this kind, the utmost caution to prevent new mischief was entirely justifiable.

To rescue from oblivion a number of small as well as great compositions by a publication and popular edition of the manuscripts, seems a task for many reasons reserved for those who are to succeed us. The work should enable posterity to form a correct estimate of Schubert's musical development, and give a detailed account of his achievements.

On the other hand, the cheering fact is patent to all, that people, and Germans more especially, are turning to Schubert's music with increasing interest, and with dispassionate unprejudiced views. A feeling has shown itself on the part of the present generation, as though it were bent on compensating Schubert for the wrong —part consciously, part unconsciously—done to him by his compeers: this atonement will be made all the more cheerfully, as every sacrifice will be thankfully requited and repaid abundantly by the keener appreciation of a neglected composer.

By the side of that artistic path trod by Franz Schubert may bloom, in secrecy, many a fragrant flower yet to be gathered: we may possibly have given a hint here and there where to find them.

CHAPTER XX.

IN the course of our narrative we have already alluded
to the distinctions and honours paid to the composer
during his lifetime. He was made an honorary member of various musical societies, and chosen as one of
the chief representative body of the Musikverein at
Vienna; some flattering letters of recognition of his
musical gifts, and two addresses thanking him for the
dedication of his Lieder, were also sent to him, but
beyond these poor compliments, Schubert was favoured
with no conspicuous marks of public esteem. But his
ambition was quite the other way; he had no desire
for public honours, and would have gladly exchanged
them all for a modest but regularly paid yearly income.

A considerable time after his death a commemoration
festival, in honour of his memory, was celebrated by
the Academies at Vienna; thus, for instance, in the
year 1835, a ceremony of the kind was arranged by

Ernst v. Feuchtersleben, and an ode recited by Franz v. Schober.

More substantial honours were paid to the deceased from that time; people, ill satisfied with vapid talk and fine words, sought to revive the poet's memory by means of his own works, and to establish more widely the influence of that music with which numbers were already familiar.

The Männergesangverein, in the dawn of its prosperity at Vienna, was the first artistic body which, acting under the deep impression received from Schubert's choral songs, so long buried in oblivion, expressed the enthusiastic feelings of every member at a festival congress held in the year 1847, and on November 19, 1850, a solemn commemoration was held on the anniversary of the musician's death.

On February 28, in the year 1851, a Schubert festival was held in the Schubert Salon built by Herr Spina, and inaugurated with a prologue by Bauernfeld, recited by Dawison. A similar ceremony was held on November 25, 1853, to solemnise the twenty-fifth anniversary of Schubert's death, and a poem by Steinhauser called 'Ein Musenkind,' recited on the occasion.[1]

Anton Langer, the editor of a popular newspaper in

[1] The ceremony, in 1847, was arranged by the choral-master, Gustav Barth, and Drs. Flögel and Weiss, members of the Verein. Barth pronounced the oration. The programme of the just-mentioned Schubert Festival consisted of the following musical pieces:—stringed Quartett

Vienna, drew the attention of the public in the August of 1858 to a proposed restoration of the house in which Schubert was born, adding that the time had arrived for distinguishing the birthplace of their famous countryman by the erection of some commemorative tablet, which would be recognised by Germans as well as by foreign visitors.

Suggestions were at once made of opening subscription-lists, and the Vienna Männergesangverein were invited, amongst other bodies, to contribute their mite. But this society professed itself willing and desirous to undertake the business single-handed; subscriptions which had flowed in from various quarters were rejected, and Wasserburger, a sculptor in Vienna, was entrusted with the completion of a memorial. On October 7, 1858, at four o'clock in the afternoon, the memorial tablet was inaugurated in presence of

in D minor, played by Josef Hellmesberger, Durst, Heissler, and Schlesinger; 'Lob der Thränen,' sung by Ander; 'Fantasie zu vier Händen,' played by Pacher and Egghardt; 'Der zürnende Barde' and 'Augenlied,' sung by Staudigl; Fantasie (Op. 159), played by Josef Hellmesberger and Egghardt; vocal Quartett ('Des Tages Weihe'), sung by Frls. Schmidl and Bury, and Herren Schmidbauer and Staudigl. At the later festival were heard the following of Schubert's works:—Quartett in A minor (played by the four gentlemen already named); 'Auf der Donau,' 'Der Schiffer,' 'Der Doppelgänger,' 'Der Wanderer,' and 'Gruppe aus dem Tartarus,' sung by Staudigl; Variations on an original theme, played by Herren Dachs and Fischhof; Impromptu (Op. 142), played by Dachs; and the vocal Quartett, 'Die Nachtigall,' sung by Kloss, Muk, Legat, and Petzelberger. At both these concerts Herr Randhartinger accompanied upon the piano.

the Gesangverein, and numbers of guests invited to the ceremony, amongst whom were all Schubert's family and belongings. An oration was delivered, and several choruses and the Quartett 'Der Lob der Einsamkeit' performed. The musical part of the ceremony was prolonged to the evening of the same day at a Festliedertafel, where the programme consisted entirely of Schubert's compositions.

At a subsequent period, and again quite recently (in January and March 1861, and March 1683), the composer's memory was again honoured by a performance of the Operetta 'Die Verschwornen' and the Easter Cantata 'Lazarus.' [1]

A short time since, the Viennese Männergesangverein once more took the initiative in an undertaking which, if successfully carried out, was to supersede all public proposals hitherto made with respect to a Schubert memorial. This musical society, at their general meeting (on June 6, 1862), unanimously voted the erection of some enduring monument to the great tone-poet of Fatherland. Immediate steps were taken for procuring the necessary means, and the results led to a well-founded hope that at no distant time we shall have some good statue of Franz Schubert erected on a convenient site in his native place, not only to be a lasting ornament and pride of the locality, but a testi-

---

[1] A Schubert festival was held in the year 1861 at Weimar, and also at Bremen.

mony of the gratitude due to those who by deed and counsel have helped to perpetuate Schubert's memory.[1] But whatever success may attend the efforts of Schubert's worshippers and those jealous of the master's fame, the musician himself has in his own works founded a strong, imperishable monument ' ære perennius.'

Emancipated from those formal fetters which, owing to the shifting nature of the public taste, make so many grand works of even the greatest masters appear old-fashioned and out of date, Schubert's profound tone-poems, the fruit of an ever-fresh fancy and inexhaustible invention, will assuredly be reckoned amongst those musical phenomena which, by their innate artistic strength, will bloom in coming ages with perpetual youth. Nor should this be said merely in respect of his Lieder, but also of a large part of his compositions in other styles, for the high flights of Schubert's genius forbid for these as well as the Lieder a premature old age, and ensure them the same happy fate which has befallen the masterpieces of Beethoven himself.

The secret of the special attraction in Schubert's delightful works is their entire originality. What exuberant inventiveness we find in all his music! what vigour and glow! He sets us no difficult enigma to unravel, we are driven to no forced and absurd inter-

[1] In September 1864, the Schubert Monument Fund amounted to 18,600 florins.

pretations of his thoughts and feelings, he does not use his art as an arena for the display of the conflict between his inner and external life. If ever there lived a 'naïf' music-composer in the highest sense of the epithet, that man assuredly was Franz Schubert. Deep earnest calculation and thought was foreign to the quick inventive spirit that burned within him, and herein, it may be, lies the reason why in so many of his creations we miss that concentration of power and exquisite polish which we admire in other masters— qualities which, without prejudice to his individuality, he might have lavished also on the general mass of his compositions. And here we may blame the un- necessary length and breadth or the uncalled-for re- petitions which occur in occasional movements in his instrumental works, and only tend to weaken the effect, whereas the Lieder, more confined by the limits allowed by the words, are, in nearly every instance, free from this reproach.

That the *limæ labor* was a very rare thing with Schubert, is a well-authenticated fact, and evidenced most unmistakably by his own manuscripts.[1] The short span of Schubert's life, of which possibly he may have

---

[1] Taken into connection with this undeniable fact, it will be found that the concluding movements in several of his instrumental works are not on the same exalted level as the preceding movements. Instances of this manifest inequality occur in some of the pianoforte sonatas— the stringed Quintett in C, the final chorus in the Operetta 'Die Ver- schwornen'—which have the character of the last dance of the evening.

had some vague presentiment, did not admit of any·
long and painful elaboration of his works, and the
imperious calls of genius justified his constant efforts
in new fields of artistic enterprise. Within the space
of eighteen years he burned to let loose on the world
all the living powers of music he felt within him. His
artistic resources were so wonderful, that he never had
occasion to fear exhaustion, and instead of polishing
and beautifying his work again and again, he preferred
to strike out something new, immediately after finishing the task before him.

In this respect Franz Schubert was one of the most
extraordinary phenomena that ever appeared in the
art-world; and although men are utterly mistaken in
ascribing his inventive genius and power to a state of
clairvoyance, irrespective of ordinary cultivation, the
characteristic fact still remains, that even men[1] who
were deeply interested in him, and occasionally seized
an opportunity of watching him in his working hours,
tried to explain, by references to supernatural means, a
process incomprehensible to them, but one which was
developed completely in the works of this great composer.

Nearly forty years have passed since the day when
Schubert finished his short earthly career. He blazed
awhile like a meteor on the musical heavens, and
disappeared swiftly; but the light he left behind him

---

[1] Vogl, Schönstein, and Schober.

is as lasting as his appearance in this world was tran
sitory. Nay, in an age of vapid shallow music, he
fanned with the wings of genius a wellnigh expiring
flame, and the fire kindled and became a beacon for
succeeding ages.

To sum up, it may be said of Schubert that his
music is full of deep true sentiment, full of warmth and
dramatic life. By his versatility and original power,
he has advanced the cause of art and given a stimulus
to the highest order of musical intelligence, and to him,
as a great inventive genius, was the task assigned of
presenting to the generation that succeeded him the
firstlings of his great intellect, as the fruit-bearing
germs of a new existence.

A LIST OF SCHUBERT'S PUBLISHED SONGS

(arranged in the sequence and order observed in the catalogue).

Erlkönig, Ballad by Göthe, composed in 1815 or 1816, published as Op. 1 by Cappi & Diabelli, at Vienna, in the year 1821, and dedicated by the composer to Count Moriz v. Dietrichstein. Herr Randhartinger, Hofcapellmeister at Vienna, possessed the original manuscript, which he presented to Madame Clara Schumann. Herr F. Flatz tells us that Herr Landsberg had a copy of this song in Schubert's handwriting.[1] The same gentleman was also the owner of the original sketch of the *Erlkönig*, which differed in some respects from the published copy. The accompaniment in triplets for the right hand is there marked for octaves throughout, and in several passages whole bars are inserted by Schubert. This manuscript is now at the Royal Library at Berlin.

Gretchen am Spinnrade, from Göthe's 'Faust.' Op. 2, published also by Diabelli in the year 1821, and dedicated by Schubert to the Reichsgraf Moriz v. Friess. The manuscript is in the Royal Library at Berlin. The sixteen first bars are incomplete.

Schäfers Klagelied, *Jägers Abendlied* (1816), *Heidenröslein* (1815), *Meeresstille* (1815). Poems by Göthe, published as Op. 3 in the year 1821, and dedicated to the Deputy-Director of the Hoftheater, Hofrath Ignaz v. Mosel. These are all in the Royal Library at Berlin, but Gustav Petter, of Vienna, has a second copy of the *Meeresstille* in Schubert's handwriting. The songs were published by Cappi & Diabelli.

---

[1] Landsberg, a well-known musical amateur, who died a few years since at Rome, had a considerable number of Schubert's MSS. which he had bought in the year 1844 of Ferdinand Schubert. After his death the entire collection was incorporated with the musical manuscripts of the Royal Library at Berlin. The librarian, Herr Espagne, was kind enough to give me a catalogue with some minute and valuable information respecting these manuscripts.

Der Wanderer, composed in the year 1816 by Georg Philipp Schmidt, of Lubeck. The original, on which Schubert has erroneously stated Zacharias Werner to have been the writer of the poem, is now in the possession of Dr. Carl v. Enderes, of Vienna. The pianoforte accompaniment in the original varies slightly from the printed copy. *Wanderers Nachtlied*, by Göthe (I.), *Der du von dem Himmel bist*, the original in the Royal Library at Berlin. *Morgenlied*, by Werner, published in the year 1821, as Op. 4, by Cappi & Diabelli, and dedicated by Schubert, in the year 1822, to the Patriarch Ladislaus Pyrker.

Rastlose Liebe, Nähe des Geliebten (February 27, 1815), *Erster Verlust* (July 5, 1815), *Der Fischer*, ballad, *König in Thule*, ballad (1816), words by Göthe, published by Cappi & Diabelli, as Op. 5, in the year 1821, and dedicated by the composers to Hofcapellmeister Anton Salieri. The manuscript of these works is in the Royal Library at Berlin. Gustav Petter has a second copy of *Erster Verlust*.

Memnon, by Mayrhofer, composed in March 1817. The original (in eight pages) in the possession of G. Petter. *Antigone und Oedip*, by Mayrhofer, composed in March 1817. *Am Grabe Anselmos*, by Claudius. Published by Cappi & Diabelli in 1821, and dedicated by the composer to the Manager and Member of the Court Opera Company, Johann Vogl.

Die abgeblühte Linde, Der Flug der Zeit, by Count v. Szechenyi. *Der Tod und das Mädchen*, published as Op. 7, in 1821, by Cappi & Diabelli, and dedicated to Count Louis Szechenyi v. Sarvári-Felsö Videk, by Schubert.

Der Jüngling auf dem Hügel, by Heinrich Hüttenbrenner, composed in the month of November, 1820. *Sehnsucht* (1824), *Erlafsee* (September 1817), *Am Strome* (March 1817), by Mayrhofer. Published as Op. 8 in the year 1822 by Cappi & Diabelli, and dedicated by the composer to Count Carl Esterhazy-Galantha.

Drei Gesänge des Harfner, from Göthe's 'Wilhelm Meister' (September 1816), dedicated by the composer to the Bishop of St. Pölten, Hofrath v. Dankesreither. Published as Op. 12 in the year 1822, by Cappi & Diabelli.

Der Schäfer und der Reiter, by De la Motte Fouqué (1817). *Lob der Thränen*, by Schlegel (1821). *Der Alpenjäger*, by Mayrhofer (January 1817), dedicated to Josef v. Spaun. Published in 1822, as Op. 13, by Cappi & Diabelli.

Suleika (I.), *Geheimes*, by Göthe. Composed in March 1821, and dedicated to his friend Franz v. Schober. Published as Op. 14 in the year 1822, by Cappi & Diabelli.

An Schwager Kronos (March 1827), *Ganymed* (March 1817), *An Mignon* (February 27, 1815), by Göthe. Published as Op. 19 in the year 1824 by Cappi & Diabelli, and dedicated to 'Geheimrath v. Göthe' in Weimar, to whom these works were sent in 1819. The original of *An Mignon* is in the Royal Library at Berlin.

Sei mir gegrüsst, by Rückert (1821). (Published also as a subject of the second movement of the *Fantasie* for pianoforte and violin, Op. 159). *Frühlingsglaube*, by Uhland. The original sketch (1820) is in the Royal Library at Berlin. The second arrangement bears date November 1822. *Hänflings Liebeswerbung*, by Kind (April 1817). Published as Op. 20, in the year 1823, by Sauer & Leidesdorf, at Vienna, and dedicated by Schubert to Madame Justine Bruchmann.

Auf der Donau, Der Schiffer, Wie Ulfru fischt, by Mayrhofer (January 1817). Three bass songs, dedicated to the poet, Op. 21. Published in 1823, by Sauer & Leidesdorf.

Der Zwerg, a fragment (1823). *Wehmuth*, by Matthäus v. Collin. Published as Op. 122, in the year 1823, by Sauer & Leidesdorf, and dedicated to the poet.

Die Liebe hat gelogen, by Count v. Platen. *Selige Welt, Schwanengesang*, by Senn. Manuscripts of both in the Royal Library at Berlin. *Schatzgräbers Begehr*, by Schober (1822). Published as Op. 23, in the year 1823, by Sauer & Leidesdorf.

Gruppe aus dem Tartarus, by Schiller (1817), sung in public for the first time at Vienna in the year 1821, by Preisinger. *Schlummerlied*, by Mayrhofer, 1817. Published in the year 1823, as Op. 24, by Sauer & Leidesdorf.

Twenty Songs from the cycle of Lieder : *Die schöne Müllerin*, by Wilhelm Müller (composed in 1823), in five series, containing : 1. Das Wandern ; 2. Wohin ; 3. Halt ; 4. Danksagung an den Bach ; 5. Am Feierabend ; 6. Der Neugierige ; 7. Ungeduld ; 8. Morgengruss ; 9. Des Müllers Blumen ; 10. Thränenregen ; 11. Mein ; 12. Pause ; 13. Mit dem grünen Lautenband ; 14. Der Jäger ; 15. Eifersucht und Stolz ; 16. Die liebe Farbe ; 17. Die böse Farbe ; 18. Trockene Blumen ; 19. Der Müller und der Bach ; 20. Des Baches Wiegenlied. Where the originals are is unknown. The manuscript of Lied No. 15, according to Herr Derffel, is in the hands of the Countess Wimpffen, of Vienna. The Lieder were published as Op. 25, in the year 1824, by Sauer & Leidesdorf, and dedicated by the composers to Freiherr v. Schönstein. Quite recently an edition, revised after a careful comparison with the original Liederkreis, by Herr B. Randhartinger, has been published by Spina.

Suleika's Gesang (II.), by Göthe, 1821. Published in the year 1825, as Op. 31, by Penauer, at Vienna, and dedicated to Anna Milder-Hauptmann, prima donna at the Royal Prussian Opera House, by Schubert. She first introduced the song to the public at a concert in the year 1825.

Die Forelle, by Schubert (1818), published as Op. 32, in the year 1825, by Diabelli. This song was written at midnight, in Anselm Hüttenbrenner's lodgings in Vienna.

Die zürnende (more correctly *Der zürnenden*) *Diana*, words by Mayrhofer (composed December 1823). *Nachtstück*, by Mayrhofer (October 1819). Published as Op. 36, by Cappi & Company, in the year 1825, and dedicated by Schubert to Madame Katharina Lascny, née Buchwieser.

Der Pilgrim, Der Alpenjäger, by Schiller (1817). Published as Op. 37 in the year 1825, by Cappi & Company, and dedicated by Schubert to the painter Ludwig Schnorr v. Karolsfeld.

Der Liedler, ballad by Kenner (1815), published as Op. 38, by Cappi & Company, in the year 1825, and dedicated to the poet. Moriz Schwind finished an illustration for this work.

Die Sehnsucht, by Schiller, re-arranged in the year 1821; sung for the first time in public at Vienna by Goetz, on February 8, 1821. Published as Op. 39 in the year 1826, by Pennauer. The first arrangement (April 15 to April 17, 1813), in eight sheets, the manuscript of which is in the Royal Library at Berlin, differs from the later. The finale alone is retained, 'Frisch hinein,' but even this part is altered.

Der Einsame, by Lappe, said by several of Schubert's friends to have been written in the year 1825, whilst the author was in the hospital. Published as Op. 41, in the year 1827, by Diabelli.

Die junge Nonne, by Craigher. *Nacht und Träume*, by Schiller. Published as Op. 43, in the year 1825, by Pennauer.

An die untergehende Sonne, by Kosegarten. Published as Op. 44, in the year 1827, by Diabelli.

Fünf einstimmige Gesänge from W. Scott's 'Lady of the Lake':—Ellens Gesang (I. and II.), Normann's Gesang, Hymne an die Jungfrau, and Lied des gefangenen Jägers, composed in 1825. Published as Op. 52, in the year 1826, by Artaria, and dedicated to the Countess Sofie Weissenwolf, *née* Countess v. Breuner.

Willkommen und Abschied, by Göthe (composed in 1822); manuscript in the Royal Library, at Berlin. *An die Leyer, Im Haine*, by Bruchmann. Published as Op. 56, in the year 1826, by Weigl, and dedicated to Herr Karl Pinterics.

Der Schmetterling, Die Berge, by Fr. Schlegel. *An den Mond*, by Hölty, Op. 57. Landsberg had the originals.

Hektor's Abschied (1815), *Emma* (April 1814), *Des Mädchens Klage* (March 1816), by Schiller, Op. 58.

Du liebst mich nicht, words by Count Platen. *Dass sie hier gewesen, Du bist die Ruh* (1823), *Lachen und Weinen*, words by Rückert. Published by Sauer & Leidesdorf, as Op. 59, in the year 1826.

Greisengesang, words by Rückert. *Dithirambe*, by Schiller. Published as Op. 60, in the year 1826, by Cappi & Czerny.

Three Lieder of Mignon, from Göthe's 'Wilhelm Meister':—1. *Nur wer die S hnsucht kennt* (1815 and 1816), three times set as a song, and once as a duett for soprano and tenor (Op. 62), once also as a quintett (unpublished). Albert Stadler, of Vienna, has the original of the last arrangement. 2. *Heiss mich nicht reden. So lass mich scheinen.* Published as Op. 62, in the year 1827, by Diabelli, and dedicated to the Princess Mathilde of Schwarzenberg.

Lied eines Schiffers an die Dioskuren (more properly *Schiffers Nachtlied*), by Mayrhofer (1816). *Der Wanderer*, by A. W. Schlegel (February 1819). *Aus Heliopolis*, by Mayrhofer. Published as Op. 65, in the year 1826, by Cappi & Czerny.

Der Wachtelschlag, by Metastasio (1822), published as Op. 68, in the year 1827, by Diabelli.

Drang in die Ferne, by Leitner (1823), published as Op. 71, in the year 1827, by Diabelli. Appeared also as a musical contribution to the 'Wiener Zeitschrift.'

Auf dem Wasser zu singen, by Stollberg (1823), published as Op. 72 in the year 1827, by Diabelli. This also appeared in the 'Wiener Zeitschrift.'

Die Rose, by Fr. Schlegel (1822), published as Op. 73, in the year 1827, by Diabelli. Appeared also in the 'Wiener Zeitschrift.'

Das Heimweh, by L. Pyrker, written at Gastein, in August 1825, and dedicated by the musician to the poet. Appeared as Op. 79, in the year 1827, published by Haslinger. The original is in the Royal Library at Berlin. The concluding part (some sixty bars in duration) differs from the printed copy; the printed part, however, does exist in manuscript also, and, marked as No. 4 of the ' Vier deutsche Gedichte,' is also at the Library of Berlin.

Die Allmacht, by L. Pyrker (Op. 79), has been twice set to music. Johann Herbeck, Deputy Hofcapellmeister at Vienna, has the original of an unfinished four-part song, for male voices, set to these words.

Der Wanderer an den Mond, by G. Seidl (1826). The original, written on four pages, is at the Royal Library of Berlin. *Das Zügenglöcklein* (1826), *Im Freien* (1826), by G. Seidl, at Berlin. These were published as Op. 80, in the year 1827, by Haslinger, and are dedicated to Herr Josef Witteczek.

Alinde, An die Laute, Zur guten Nacht (with chorus), by Friedrich Rochlitz, were published as Op. 81, in the year 1827, by Haslinger & Company, and dedicated by the publishers to the poet.

Drei italienische Gesänge (for a bass voice), by Metastasio:—1. L' Incanto degli Occhj; 2. Il Tradito deluso; 3. Il Modo di prendere Moglie, composed in 1827, published as Op. 83, by Haslinger, in the year 1827, and dedicated by Schubert to the singer Luigi Lablache.

Lied der Anna Lyle (1827), *Gesang der Norna* (1826), from W. Scott's ' Pirate.' Published as Op. 85, by Diabelli, in the year 1828.

Romanze des Richard Löwenherz, from Walter Scott's 'Ivanhoe,' (composed in 1826). Published as Op. 86, in the year 1828, by Diabelli.

Der Unglückliche, by Caroline Pichler (1821). *Die Hoffnung*, by Schiller, I. and II. (composed 1815); the first sketch of this song is in Landsberg's collection. *Der Jüngling am Bache*, by Schiller, three arrangements (1815), Op. 87.

Abendlied an die Entfernte, by A. W. Schlegel (1825). *Thekla*, by Schiller (I. 1813, II. 1817). The manuscript of the first arrangement is in the Royal Library at Berlin; Herr Joachim has an original copy of the same song written in 1817 (in C-sharp minor). *Um Mitternacht*, by C. Schulze (1826). *An die Musik*, by Schober (1817); published by Weigl as Op. 88, in the year 1827. The first setting of ' Thekla ' has not been printed.

Die Winterreise, by Wilhelm Müller (composed in 1826 and 1827), containing a cycle of 24 Lieder:—1. Gute Nacht ; 2. Die Wetterfahne ; 3. Gefrorne Thränen ; 4. Erstarrung; 5. Der Lindenbaum; 6. Wasserfluth ; 7. Auf dem Flusse ; 8. Rückblick ; 9. Irrlicht ; 10. Rast ; 11. Frühlingstraum ; 12. Einsamkeit ; 13. Die Post ; 14. Der greise Kopf ; 15. Die Krähe ; 16. Letzte Hoffnung ; 17. Im Dorfe ; 18. Der stürmische Morgen ; 19. Die Täuschung ; 20. Der Wegweiser ; 21. Das Wirthshaus ; 22. Muth ; 23. Die Nebensonnen ; 24. Der Leiermann. Published as Op. 89, in the year 1828, by Haslinger.

Der Musensohn (December 1822). Original in the Berlin Library. *Auf dem See* (1817); second arrangement. *Geistesgruss*, by Göthe (1816); twice set by Schubert. Published as Op. 92, in the year 1828, by Leidesdorf, and dedicated by Schubert to Madame Josefine Frank. The first arrangement differs from that contained in Op. 92. The original is in the Berlin Library.

Im Walde, Auf der Bruck, by Schulze, composed in 1825. Published first of all in the year 1828, by the firm of Kienreich, at Gratz, and afterwards as Op. 93, by Haslinger, in the year 1828.

Die Unterscheidung, Bei Dir, Die Männer sind mechant, Irdisches Glück, Refrainlieder, by G. Seidl, which were to have been followed by others of a similar kind. They are dedicated to the poet, and were published by Weigl, in the year 1828, as Op. 95.

Die Sterne, by Leitner (January 1828). *Jägers Liebeslied*, by Schober (February 1827). *Wanderers Nachtlied*, by Göthe (II.). *Fischerweise*, by Schlechta (March 1826), dedicated as Op. 96, by Schubert, to the Princess Caroline Kinsky, *née* Freiin von Kerpen, from whom Schubert received the following written acknowledgment, dated July 7, 1828 (now in my possession):—'Pray accept, dear Herr Schubert, my best thanks for the interest you take in the success of my concert, as also for the dedication of the Lieder lately received. I look forward to en-

joying them and admiring them next winter, if you and Baron Schönstein will graciously confer such a pleasure upon me. Accept the
enclosed as a feeble expression of my gratitude, and you will deeply
oblige yours obediently,   CHARLOTTE, PRINCESS KINSKY.'

Glaube, Hoffnung und Liebe, by Kuffner. Published as Op. 97, in
the year 1828, by Diabelli.

An die Nachtigall (November 1816), *Wiegenlied* (November 1816), by
Claudius; *Ifigenia*, by Mayrhofer (July 1817), Op. 98.

Der blinde Knabe, by Craigher (composed in the year 1825), Op. 101.
Appeared as a contribution to the ' Wiener Zeitschrift.'

Wiegenlied, Am Fenster (1826), *Sehnsucht* (1826), by G. Seidl, Op.
105. These three Lieder and the quartett for male voices, *Widerspruch*,
were first published by Czerny on November 21, 1828, the day of Schubert's funeral.[1]

Heimliches Lieben (1827), *Das Weinen, Vor meiner Wiege*, the last
three poems by Leitner, composed in 1827. *An Silvia*, from Shakspeare's ' Two Gentlemen of Verona ' (1826) ; dedicated, as Op. 106, to
Madame Maria Pachler, in Gratz.

Ueber Wildemann (in the Hartz Mountains), by E. Schulze, 1827.
Todesmusik, by Schober (1822). *Erinnerung* (more strictly ' Erscheinung '), by Kosegarten (April 1814), Op. 108.

Am Bach im Frühling (1816), *Genügsamkeit, An eine Quelle* (1816),
by Claudius, Op. 109.

Der Kampf (Freigeisterei der Leidenschaft), by Schiller (1815). Some
strophes set to music, Op. 110.

An die Freude, by Schiller (1815). *Lebensmelodien*, by Schlegel
(March 1816). *Die vier Weltalter*, by Schiller (1816), Op. 111.

Das Lied im Grünen, by Reil (June 1827); *Wonne der Wehmuth*, by
Göthe (February 1815). The original is in the Berlin Library.
Sprache der Liebe, by Fr. Schlegel (April 1816).

Die Erwartung, by Schiller (February 27, 1815), Op. 116. Dedicated
' to his friend ' Josef Hüttenbrenner.

---

[1] All the following Lieder, as well as Op. 134–146 (concerted vocal
pieces, pianoforte and chamber music) were not published until after
Schubert's death.

Der Sänger, ballad by Göthe (February 1816), Op. 117.

Geist der Liebe, by Kosegarten ; *Der Abend*, by Hölty ; *Tischlied*, by Göthe ; *Lob des Tokayers*, by Baumberg, composed in 1815 ; *An die Sonne*, by Th. Körner ; *Die Spinnerin*, ballad by Göthe. The manuscript in the Royal Library at Berlin.

Auf dem Strom, by Rellstab, with pianoforte accompaniment, and obligato for horn or violoncello. The horn part written for Herr Eduard Lewy, member of the Royal Opera band at Vienna (in the year 1828).

Viola, by Schober (March 1823), Op. 123.

Zwei Scenen, from the play 'Lacrimas,' by V. Schütz. Published by A. W. Schlegel (composed 1825), Op. 124.

Ballade, by Kenner (1814), Op. 126.

Der Hirt auf dem Felsen, by Wilhelmine Chezy, with pianoforte accompaniment, and clarionet obligato ; composed in the year 1828, for the operatic singer Anna Milder-Hauptmann, Op. 129.

Das Echo, by Castelli, Op. 130. Schubert intended to write, as supplementary to this, a series of cheerful Lieder.

Der Mondabend, by Erwin ; *Trinklied*, with chorus, by Herder (1813); *Klagelied*, by Rochlitz (1812), Op. 131.

Fourteen Lieder, published by Haslinger & Company, under the title *Schwanengesang* :—1. Liebesbotschaft. 2. Krieger's Ahnung. 3. Frühlingssehnsucht. 4. Ständchen. 5. Aufenthalt. 6. In der Ferne. 7. Abschied, by Rellstab. 8. Der Atlas. 9. Ihr Bild. 10. Das Fischermädchen. 11. Die Stadt. 12. Am Meere. 13. Der Doppelgänger, by Heine (supposed to have been written in August 1828). 14. Die Taubenpost, by Seidl, said to be Schubert's last *Lied* (October 1828).

Quite recently the following collection of Lieder, discovered after Schubert's death, has been published by Spina as Op. 165 :—*Die Liebende schreibt*, by Göthe (October 1819). *Die Sternennächte*, by Mayrhofer (October 1819), the original in the possession of Landsberg. *Das Bild* (1815). *Die Täuschung*, by Kosegarten (1815). *Altschottische Ballade*, by Herder, 1827, composed at Dr. Pachler's house in Gratz, and published there by the firm of Kienreich.

LIEDER (POSTHUMOUS).

Gesänge Ossians, in five numbers (Series 1–5) :—1. Die Nacht (February 1817). 2. Cronaan, Colmas Klage (June 22, 1815), Gustav Petter of Vienna has the original. 3. Lodas Gespenst (February 1815). 4. Shilrik und Vinvela. Ossians Lied nach dem Fall Nathos. Das Mädchen von Inistore (September 1815). 5. Der Tod Oskars (February 1816).

Elisium, by Schiller (April 15, 1813). The MS. of the sixth number is in the hands of J. Hüttenbrenner. *Des Sängers Habe*, by Franz v. Schlechta (1825). 7th Number. *Hyppolit's Lied*, from 'Gabriele,' a poem of Johanna Schoppenhauer (July 1826). *Abendröthe*, by Schlegel (March 1820). *Morgenständchen*, from Shakspeare's 'Cymbeline' (composed at Währing in July 1826). *Die Bürgschaft*, ballad from Schiller (August 1815). 8th Number. *Der zürnende Barde*, by Franz Bruchmann Junior (February 1823), two arrangements ; the 9th number is in Petter's collection of Schubert's autographs.

Am See, by Bruchmann (March 1817). *Abendbilder*, by Claudius (February 1819). *Acht geistliche Lieder* :—1. Dem Unendlichen, ode by Klopstock (July 15, 1815), the MS. in the library at Berlin. 2. Die Gestirne von Klopstock (1816). In Petter's collection. 3. Das Marienbild, by Schreiber (August 1818). 4. Vom Mitleiden Mariä, by Schlegel (December 1818). 5. Litany on the Feast of All Souls, the words by Jakobi (1816). 6. Pax vobiscum, by Schober (April 1817). The original is at Vienna, in Bermann's possession. 7. Gebet während der Schlacht, by Körner. 8. Himmelsfunken, by Silbert (February 1819).

Orest auf Tauris (more correctly *Der landende Orest*), 1820 ; *Der entsühnte Orest* (1820) ; *Philoktet* (March 1817) ; *Freiwilliges Versinken* (1820), by Mayrhofer. 11th Number.

Der Taucher, ballad by Schiller (begun September 1813, finished August 1814). *An mein Herz* (December 1825), *Der liebliche Stern* (December 1825), by Ernst Schulze. *Gränzen der Menschheit*, by Göthe (March 1821, twice set to music). *Fragment aus dem Aeschylus*, by Mayrhofer (June 1816). The MS. in Petter's collection. *Widerschein* (May 1828). *Liebeslauschen* (September 1820) ; *Todtengräberweise*, by Frh. v. Schlechta (1826).

Waldesnacht, by Schlegel (December 1826), the original MS. belonged to Witteczek.

Lebensmuth, by Schulze (1826). *Der Vater mit dem Kind*, by Bauernfeld (January 1817). The original in Petter's collection. *An den Tod*,
by Schubart. *Verklärung*, by Pope (May 4, 1813).

Pilgerweise, by Schober (April 1823). *An den Mond in einer Herbst-
nacht* (April 1818). *Fahrt zum Hades*, by Mayrhofer (January 1817).
The original in the possession of Jünger.

Orfeus, by Jakobi (1816). *Ritter Toggenburg*, ballad by Schiller
(March 13, 1816).

Im Abendroth, by Lappe. *Scene im Dom*, from Göthe's 'Faust,' with
chorus and organ accompaniment. Two settings of this piece, dated
December 12, 1813, and 1814. *Mignon's Gesang*, from Göthe. *Der
Blumenbrief*, by Schreiber (August 1818). The original in the possession of Gahy. *Vergissmeinnicht*, by Schober (May 1823).

Der Sieg (March 1814); *Atys; Beim Wind* (October 1819), the MSS.
in the Berlin Library; *Abendstern* (March 1824), by Mayrhofer.

Schwesterngruss, by Franz Bruchmann, composed in November 1822,
after the death of Madame Bruchmann. *Liebesend*, ballad by Mayrhofer
(September 1816). Ritter v. Frank has the original of the music.

Schiffers Scheidelied, by Schober (February 1827). *Todtengräbers
Heimweh*, by Kraigher (April 1828).

Fülle der Liebe, by Friedrich Schlegel (1825). The MS., in five sheets,
is in the Berlin Library. *Im Frühling*, by E. Schulze (1826). *Trost in
Thränen*, by Göthe (1815), published, also unnumbered, by Kistner, of
Leipsic.

Der Winterabend, by Leitner (January 1828). *Der Wallensteiner
Lanzknecht beim Trunk ; Der Kreuzzug; Fischers Liebesglück.* The
first three poems by Leitner were set to music by Schubert at the suggestion of Madame Pachler, in Gratz.

Hermann und Thusnelda (1815) ; *Selma und Selmar* (September 1815) ;
Das Rosenband (1815) ; *Edone* (1814) ; *Die frühen Gräber*, by Klopstock.

Stimme der Liebe (April 1816) ; *Die Mutter Erde* (August 1815), by
Stollberg. *Gretchens Bitte*, from Göthe's 'Faust,' a fragment (May 1817).
Abschied in das Stammbuch eines Freundes, by Franz Schubert (August
24, 1817). The original in the possession of Landsberg.

Tiefes Leid, by Schulze (January 27, 1817). *Clärchens Lied*, by Göthe (June 3, 1815). *Grablied für die Mutter; Die Betende; Der Geistertanz* (October 14, 1814); *An Laura, als sie Klopstock's Auferstehungslied sang* (October 7, 1814), by Mathisson.

Der Einsame (properly *Einsamkeit*), by Mayrhofer (1822).

Der Schiffer, by Fr. Schlegel. *Die gefangenen Sänger*, by A. W. Schlegel, composed January 1821. Original in the Petter collection.

Auflösung, by Mayrhofer (March 1824). *Blondel zu Marien*, by Grillparzer.

Die erste Liebe, by Fellinger (1825). *Lied eines Kriegers* (December 31, 1824). Original in the Petter collection.

Der Jüngling an der Quelle; Lambertine, by Mayrhofer (October 12, 1815). *Ihr Grab.*

Heliopolis (properly *Im Hochgebirg*, and in the new edition, *An Franz*), by Mayrhofer. The original, in four sheets, at the Royal Library, Berlin. *Sehnsucht*, from Göthe.

Die Einsiedelei, by Salis (May 3, 1817); a second setting is in the Petter collection. *Lebenslied*, by Mathisson. *Versunken*, from Göthe (February 1820). *Als ich sie erröthen sah*, by Ehrlich (February 10, 1815). *Das war ich*, by Körner (March 26, 1815). *In's stille Land*, by Salis.

Das Mädchen, by Kenner (1819). *Bertha's Lied in der Nacht*, by Grillparzer (February 1819), the MSS. in the possession of Gahy. *An die Freunde*, by Mayrhofer, March 1819.

Die Götter Griechenlands, by Schiller (fragment). *Das Finden*, by Kosegarten (June 25, 1815). *Cora an die Sonne*, by Baumberg (August 22, 1815). *Grablied*, by Kenner. *Adelaide*, by Mathisson, 1815.

Trost, by Mayrhofer (1819), the original in the Petter collection, ten sheets. *Zum Punsch*, by Mayrhofer (1816). *Die Nacht*, by Utz.

Frohsinn (January 1817), fragment. In Petter collection. *Trinklied*, with chorus by Herder (August 29, 1813). *Der Morgenkuss*, by Baumberg (August 28, 1815). *Epistel* to Josef Spaun, by Collin (January 1822). The original is in the possession of Josef v. Spaun.

Prometheus (1819), in the Petter collection; *Wer kauft Liebesgötter?* *Der Rattenfänger* (1815), *Nachtgesang* (1815); *An den Mond* (I. and II.,

1815). The latter is in the Berlin Library, with the *Vier deutsche Gedichte*, by Göthe.

Die Sterne, by Schlegel (1820). *Erntelied*, by Hölty (August 1816). *Klage*, by Hölty (I. and II., January and May 1816). Drinking song from Shakspeare's 'Antony and Cleopatra' (written at Währing in July 1826). *Mignon*, by Göthe, resetting, in the Petter collection. *Der Goldschmiedgesell; Tischlerlied*, by Göthe, 1815.

Auf der Riesenkoppe, by Körner. *Auf einem Kirchhof*, by Klopstock (February 2, 1815).

An die Apfelbäume, wo ich Julien erblickte, by Hölty (May 22, 1815). *Der Leidende*, by Hölty (May 1816). *Augenlied*, by Mayrhofer.

———

A LIST OF UNPUBLISHED SONGS

(the greater part of which have been copied and preserved in the Witteczek collection).

Hagar's Klage, said to be Schubert's first song, composed on March 30, 1811, at the Convict. *Der Vatermörder*, also written at the Convict in 1811. *Das Lied vom Reifen* (a fragment, only 10 bars). *Täglich zu singen*, a short but exquisite fragment, much in Mendelssohn's manner. *Maria:* 'Ich sehe dich in tausend Bildern,' &c. (commonplace). *Der Entfernten*: Wohl denk' ich allenthalben (also set as a quartett for male voices). *Ammenlied*, by Marianne Luby (December 1814): 'Am hohen Thurm, Da weht ein kalter Sturm' (a melodious but commonplace ballad). *Die entfernte Geliebte. Es träumen die Wolken*, a lovely and very suggestive song in the manner of the Müllerlieder. *Drei Hymnen*, by Novalis (1819) (not of any great value). *Nachthymne*, by Novalis (1820). *Die Sterbende*, by Kosegarten (1816), a beautiful song. *Daphne am Bach* (1816). *Die Erde, Vollendung*, author unknown.

Klage der Ceres, by Schiller. *Minnelied*, by Hölty (May 1816). *Amalie*, by Schiller (1815), in the Petter collection. *Liane*, by Mayrhofer (1815). *Bundeslied*, by Göthe (August 1815). *Der Gott und die Bajadere*, by Göthe, fragment (1815). *An Chloe*, by Jakobi (1816). *Gruss an den Mai*, by Erwin (1815). *Scolie*, by Deinhartstein (1815). *Die Sternenwelten*, by Fellinger (1815). *Die Macht der Liebe*, by Kalchberg (1815). *Die Erscheinung*, by Kosegarten (1814). *Die Täuschung*

(July). *Das Sehnen* (August); *Die Sterne; Nachtgesang; An Rosa* (I. and II.); *Idens Nachtgesang,* the original in the Petter collection. *Von Ida; Schwanengesang; Louisens Antwort,* by Kosegarten, composed in the year 1815. All these are trifling and unimportant songs. *Lied eines Kindes,* Fragment (November 1817). *Trost* (1817).

Four Canzonets by Vincenzo Monti (1820):—1. Non t' accostar all' urna; 2. Guarda la bianca luna; 3. Da quel sembiante appresi; 4. Mio bene ricordati, written for Madame v. Ronner (afterwards Madame Spaun). Herr Spaun has the original of the music.

Sehnsucht, by Schiller, first setting (1813). *An Cidli,* the MS. in the possession of Dr. Schneider; *Vaterlandslied,* by Klopstock, 1815. *Das gestörte Glück,* by Körner (1815), the original in the possession of Herr Bauernschmidt, of Ried. *Der Gondelfahrer,* by Mayrhofer (also set in a quartett for male voices). *Morgenlied* (1815). *Abendlied,* by Claudius (1816). *La Pastorella,* air (January 1817), the original in the Berlin Library; at the end of the song are written the opening bars of nine waltzes. *Vedi quanto adoro,* air in the Italian style. *Das Mädchen aus der Fremde,* by Schiller (I. and II.). *Die Schlacht,* by Schiller, with chorus (a sketch). *An den Mond* (the pianoforte accompaniment a mere sketch). *Auf den Sieg der Deutschen,* song, with chorus and accompaniment of stringed instruments (1814). *Jagdlied,* by Zach. Werner (1817). *Rundgesang,* with chorus, by Zettler (1815). *Schwertlied,* by Körner, with chorus (1815). *Der Hirt,* by Mayrhofer (1816); the original belongs to Dr. Karl Enderes, in Vienna. *Geheimniss,* by Schiller (I. and II.), 1815 and 1816; the Countess Almasy has the original copy. *Der Knabe in der Wiege,* by Ottenwalt. *Mahomet's Gesang,* from Göthe; fragment (1821) in the Petter collection. *Julius von Theone,* by Mathisson (1816). *An die Nachtigall* (1815); *Der Liebende* (1815), in the Petter collection; *Seufzer* (1815), by Hölty. *Lied,* from Schiller's *Es ist so angenehm, so süss* (an air improvised in a musical vaudeville). *Die Schatten* (1813); *Andenken* (1814); *Geister-nähe* (1814), by Mathisson. *Todtengräberlied,* by Hölty (1813). *An den Frühling,* by Schiller (I. and II., 1815). *Erinnerungen, Der Abend, Lied der Liebe, Lied aus der Ferne, Trost* (an Elisen), by Mathisson, composed 1814. *Die Mondnacht, Abends unter der Linde,* by Kosegarten (1815). *Der Traum, Die Laube,* by Hölty (1815). *An die Natur,* by Stollberg (1816). *Abschied von der Harfe* (1816). *Die Weh-muth, An die Harmonieen* (1816), by Salis. *Stimme der Liebe,* by Mathisson (I. and II., 1816); Johann Bernhard has the original copy. *Naturgenuss,* by Mathisson (1816), and composed as a quartett for

male voices. *An den Schlaf* (June 1816), *Die Liebesgötter*, by Utz.
Die frühe Liebe, Blumenlied, Seligkeit (May 1816), *Erntelied* (August
1816), by Hölty. *Thekla*, by Schiller (first setting August 22, 1813) ;
the original in the Berlin Library, and entirely different to the Lied
subsequently published. *Amphiaraos*, by Körner (1815) ; original in the
possession of Spina. *Emma und Adelwold, Minona*, ballad by Bertrand
(1815); original in the Spina collection. *Die Nonne*, ballad by
Hölty (1815); original in the possession of Spina. *Scolie*, by Mathisson
(1815), in the Petter collection. *Abschied*, by Mayrhofer (1816).
From *Diego Manazares*, by Freih. v. Schlechta (1816). *An die Geliebte*,
by Stollberg (October 15, 1815). *Brüder, schrecklich brennt die Thräne*,
for soprano or tenor, with instrumental accompaniment (1817); Dr.
Heinrich v. Kreissle, of Vienna, has the original. *Hochzeitslied*, by
Jakobi (August 1816). *Blanka*, by Schlegel (December 1818). *Wiegenlied*, by Körner (October 15, 1815). *Phydite, Abendlied, Zufrieden-
heit*, by Claudius (November 1816). *Auf dem See*, by Göthe (I.).
Sehnsucht der Liebe, by Körner (July 1815). *Bei dem Grab meines
Vaters*, by Claudius (November 1816). *Klage*, by Hölty (January
1816). *Gott im Frühling*, by Utz (June 1816). *Die Liebe*, by G. Leon
(January 1817). *Das Heimweh*, by Hell (July 1816). *In der Mitter-
nacht, Die Perle, Trauer der Liebe*, by Jakobi (August 1816). *Liebes-
rausch*, by Körner (April 8, 1815). *Der Zufriedene* (October 23, 1815).
Leiden der Trennung, by Collin, after Metastasio (1815); in the Petter
collection. *Vergebliche Liebe*, by Bernhardt (April 6, 1815). *Der
Sänger am Felsen*, by Caroline Pichler (September 1816). *Entzückung*,
by Mathisson (April 1816). *Ferne von der grossen Stadt*, by Caroline
Pichler (September 1816). *Huldigung, Alles um Liebe*, by Kosegarten
(July 26, 1815). *Der Weiberfreund* (August 25, 1815). *Lila an die
Morgenröthe* (August 25, 1815). *Fröhlichkeit* (1815). *Abendständchen
an Lina* (August 23, 1815). *An sie*, by Klopstock (September 14, 1815).
Lieb Minna, romance, by Albert Stadler (1815). *Liebeständelei*, by
Körner (May 26, 1815); the MS. in the Petter collection. *Zum Punsch*,
by Mayrhofer (October 1816). *Freude der Kinderjahre* (July 1816).
Grablied auf einen Soldaten (July 1816). *Die erste Liebe*, by Fellinger
(April 12, 1815). *Fischerlied*, by Salis (May 1817); in the Petter
collection. *Sängers Morgenlied*, by Körner (1815). *Laura's Abschied*
(August 1817), an unfinished fragment, in the Library at Berlin. *Der
Blumen Schmerz*, by Count v. Maylath (1821); Alois Fuchs has the
original. *Der Flüchtling*, by Schiller (March 1816). *Rückweg*, by
Mayrhofer (October 1816). *Laura am Clavier*, by Schiller (March
1816). *Der Jüngling und der Tod*, by Anton Spaun (March 1817).

Der Fürstin Abendlied, by Mayrhofer (November 1816), in the Berlin Library. *Sehnsucht*, by Göthe (III., April 1813); the original with Landsberg. *Die Sterne*, by Fellinger (April 6, 1815). *An die Sonne* (1815). *Todtenkranz für ein Kind*, by Mathisson (August 25, 1815). *Die Gebüsche*, by Schlegel (January 1819). *Am See*, by Mayrhofer (December 7, 1814), the Lied which introduced Schubert and Mayrhofer to each other. *Rosa von Montanvert*, romance by Mathisson (1815). *Die Vögel, Der Knabe, Der Fluss*, by Schlegel, composed in 1820. *Am Fluss*, by Göthe; two settings of this in the Royal Library at Berlin. *An den Mond*, by Göthe. *Hoffnung*, from Göthe, *Schaffe das Tagwerk*, &c. The original at Berlin.

Three Sonnets from Petrarch (translated by Schlegel).

Nach einem Gewitter, by Mayrhofer (May 1817). *Nachtviolen*, by Mayrhofer (April 1822). *Alte Liebe rostet nie*, by Mayrhofer (September 1816). *Die verfehlte Stunde*, by Schlegel (April 1816). *Wer ist wohl gross?* song with chorus and orchestral accompaniment (1813). *Gott im Frühling*, by Utz (June 1816); J. Brahms has the original. *Mein Finden*, by C. Heine. *Italian Air* (written in 1813 for Salieri). *Ihr Grab*, by Richard Roos, in the possession of J. Hüttenbrenner. *Romance*: 'Ein Fräulein klagt' (September 1814); Landsberg has the original. *Melodram*; the words form the concluding part of the dramatic poem *Der Falke*, composed by Frh. Adolf v. Pratobevera in the year 1825. Fragment from the 'Mohrenkönig.' *Die Schiffende*, by Hölty. *An die Entfernte*: 'So hab' ich wirklich dich verloren,' by Göthe; this is at Berlin. *Romance*: 'Ein Fräulein klagt im finstern Thurm' (September 29, 1814). The original in the Berlin Library. The handwriting on the first page is very neat and careful; later on it is as rapid and hurried as usual. At the end of the Lied we read 'Mathisson,' and then follow the date and Schubert's signature. *Die Sternennächte*, made up of two fragments. *Das Abendroth*: 'Du heilig glühend Abendroth,' by Schreiber (written at Zelész in 1818); the MS. in the possession of the Countess v. Almasy, in Vienna.

PART-SONGS AND CONCERTED VOCAL PIECES.

Das Dörfchen, by Bürger. *Die Nachtigall*, by Unger. *Geist der Liebe*, by Mathisson (the MS. in the collection of the Musik-Verein at Vienna). These three quartetts for male voices (two tenors and two basses), with pianoforte accompaniment, were published in the year 1822 as Op. 11, by Cappi & Diabelli, and were dedicated by Schubert to Josef Barth, the Hofcapellensänger. In 1819–1828 they were first publicly performed at concerts.

Frühlingslied, by Schober. *Naturgenuss*, by Mathisson (May 1816), quartetts for male voices, with pianoforte accompaniments, Op. 16, published in the year 1823 by Cappi & Diabelli.

Frühlingswonne, Liebe, Zum Rundetanz, Die Nacht, by Mathisson, quartetts for male voices, published in 1823, as Op. 17, by Cappi & Diabelli.

Der Gondelfahrer, by Mayrhofer, quartett for male voices, with pianoforte accompaniment (composed 1824), Op. 28.

Bootgesang, from Sir W. Scott's 'Lady of the Lake,' for two tenor and two bass voices, with pianoforte accompaniment (composed 1825), published as Op. 52, by Artaria, and dedicated to the Countess Weissenwolf.

Coronach (Todtengesang), from the 'Lady of the Lake,' for two soprano voices and one alto, with pianoforte accompaniment (composed 1825), Op. 52, published by Artaria, and dedicated to the Countess Weissenwolf.

Duett des Harfners und der Mignon, from Göthe's 'Wilhelm Meister,' or a tenor and a soprano, with pianoforte accompaniment, Op. 62, published in 1827 by Diabelli. Schubert has set the words several times as song for a single voice.

Wehmuth, by Dr. Heinrich Hüttenbrenner. *Ewige Liebe*, by Schulze. *Flucht*, by Lappe, quartett for male voices, Op. 64.

Die Advocaten, by Rustenfeld, a comic terzett for two tenors and a bass, with pianoforte accompaniment by Fischer, the accompaniment and song remodelled by Schubert, Op. 74. Fischer's original music was published by Eber, in Vienna.

Mondenschein, by Franz Schober, quintett for two tenors and three basses, with pianoforte accompaniment, Op. 102.

Der Hochzeitsbraten, by Schober, comic trio for soprano, tenor, and bass, with pianoforte accompaniment (composed 1827), Op. 104. MS. belongs to Spina.

Wiederspruch, from Seidl's 'Jägerlieder,' quartett for male voices, with pianoforte accompaniment. Published November 21, 1828, the day of Schubert's funeral, by Czerny.

Gott im Ungewitter, Gott der Weltschöpfer, by Utz. *Hymne an den Unendlichen,* by Schiller (1815), quartett for mixed voices, with piano accompaniment, Op. 112.

Gott in der Natur, by Gleim, for a soprano chorus, with pianoforte accompaniment; composed August 1822, Op. 133. MS. in the possession of Frl. Anna Fröhlich, in Vienna.

Nachthelle, by G. Seidl, for tenor solo and chorus of male voices, with piano accompaniment (1826). Performed for the first time January 25, 1827, in the Musikvereinsaal, Op. 134.

Ständchen, by Grillparzer, originally composed for an alto, solo, and a choir of male voices; afterwards re-arranged for female voices. MS. of the first arrangement is in the possession of Frl. Anna Fröhlich. The second arrangement is said to be in Spaun's collection. *Das Ständchen,* composed in 1827, was sung for the first time August 11, 1827, at Döbling.

Schlachtgesang, by Klopstock. Double chorus for male voices, written originally without accompaniment (also with piano or accompaniment *ad libitum*), Op. 151.

Trinklied of the fourteenth century, from Rittgräff's 'Historical Antiquities.' Chorus for male voices (with piano accompaniment *ad libitum*), Op. 155.

Nachtmusik, by Sekendorf, for a four-part chorus of male voices, with pianoforte accompaniment *ad libitum,* Op. 156.

Licht und Liebe, a night song, by Math. v. Collin, for soprano and tenor (No. 41).

Im Gegenwärtigen Vergangenes, by Göthe, for four male voices, and pianoforte accompaniment (No. 43).

Das Leben, by Wannovius, for three voices, with piano accompaniment (No. 45).

Nachtgesang im Wald, by G. Seidl, a four-part song for male voices, with piano or horn accompaniment (composed 1827). Performed for the first time at Ed. Lewy's concert in the Opera-House at Vienna, in 1827.

Gesang der Geister über den Wassern, by Göthe, double chorus for male voices, with accompaniment of stringed instruments (violin, violoncello, and double-bass). Composed 1820. Performed in public for the first time March 7, 1821, at the Opera-House. In 1858 it was reproduced at a concert by the Männergesangsverein at Vienna. It was dedicated to Dr. Leopold v. Sonnleithner, at Vienna, by the publisher Spina, as Op. 167. A manuscript score of this work (seven sheets, but not perfect) belongs to the Royal Library at Berlin. The instrumental parts are finished only on the first two sheets, from page 9 onwards, the rest is little better than a sketch. The vocal parts here and there have instrumental passages attached to them. Another MS. belongs to Spina.

Lob der Einsamkeit, by Salis, quartett for male voices, published by Spina.

Mond und Grab, by Seidl (September 1826); MS. (one sheet) in the Royal Library at Berlin. *Liebe und Wein*, by Haug, a quartett for male voices, in the collection of 'Minnesänger,' published by Haslinger at Vienna. This last piece was performed in 1862 in a Männergesangverein concert at Vienna.

UNPUBLISHED PART-SONGS.

Lied im Freien, An den Frühling, Fischerlied (the manuscript in the Petter collection). *Das Grab*, by Salis. *Räuberlied*, from Schubert's Opera 'Die Bürgschaft.' The original in the possession of Dr. Schneider, of Vienna. Quartetts for male voices without accompaniment.

Der Wintertag, quartett for male voices with pianoforte accompaniment, but the music has been lost, and replaced by an arrangement of Herr Gottdank's, of Vienna. The quartett was performed publicly for the first time at the Merchants' Gesangverein Festival at Vienna in the year 1863.

Das Abendroth (for three voices). *Bergknappenlied* (for three voices). *Im traulichen Kreise*, quartett for two sopranos, tenor, and bass. *Viel tausend Sterne prangen*, quartett for mixed voices. *Schlachtgesang*, by Klopstock, three-part chorus for male voices.

Gesang der Geister über den Wassern, by Göthe. First arranged as a four-part chorus for male voices (1817); second arrangement for four-part chorus with pianoforte accompaniment (1820). The latter differs from the original, and there is also a second arrangement. *Der Tanz*, by Schnitzer, quartett for mixed voices, with pianoforte accompaniment, composed in the year 1825 for the Kiesewetter family. *An die Sonne*, chorus for mixed voices, with pianoforte accompaniment (1816). *Nur wer die Sehnsucht kennt*, from Göthe's ' W. Meister,' vocal quintett for two tenors and three basses, the original in the possession of A. Stadler, of Vienna. *Der Geistertanz*, by Mathisson, quartett for male voices (November 1816), first given at a concert by the Vienna Männergesang-verein, on December 13, 1863, the manuscript in the Stadler collection. *Am Seegestad in lauen Vollmondsnächten*, vocal trio, in the Stadler collection. *Ruhe, schönstes Glück der Erde*, vocal quartett for two tenors and two basses, also in Stadler's collection. Trio for soprano, tenor, and bass, composed at the suggestion of Frl. Anna Fröhlich for the Baroness Geymüller, of Vienna (about 1826), who paid Schubert fifty florins for it.

Punschlied, im Norden zu singen, by Schiller (for two and three voices), composed August 18, 1815.

Trinklied vor der Schlacht, two alternate choruses for men's voices.

Leise, leise lasst uns singen, composed for Frl. Fanny Hügel. The manuscript in possession of J. Hüttenbrenner. *Das stille Lied*, quartett for male voices. Probably in Haslinger's collection. *Mailied*, by Hölty (I. and II.). *Der Morgenstern, Jägerlied, Lützow's wilde Jagd*, by Körner, in the Petter collection, for two voices, or two French horns. *Chor der Engel*, from Göthe's ' Faust' (quartett). *Todtengräberlied*, by Hölty (three voices). *Trinklied im Mai*, by Hölty (two sopranos and bass). *Acht Gesänge*, in canon form, set to strophes of Schiller's poem ' Elisium,' written at the Convict in the year 1813.

CANTATAS, PSALMS, HYMNS, ORATORIOS.

Mirjam's Siegesgesang (Miriam's Battle Song), by Grillparzer, for solo and mixed choir, with pianoforte accompaniment (1828), performed at a concert of Schubert's music, March 1828. The accompaniment was arranged later for an orchestra by Franz Lachner, in which form the cantata was performed in Vienna in 1858, Op. 136.

Gebet vor der Schlacht (a prayer before battle), by De la Motte Fouqué, for solo and mixed chorus, composed 1824, for the family of Count Carl Esterhazy in Széléz, Op. 139.

Der Frühlingsmorgen, for a mixed chorus, Op. 158.

Prometheus, by Filipp Dräxler v. Carin, for solo, chorus, and orchestra (1816); was lost in the year 1828.

Italian Cantata (in honour of Frl. Irene Kiesewetter), for a chorus of male voices (the finale for mixed voices), with accompaniment for two pianofortes (1827, unpublished).

Cantata in honour of the Jubilee Festival of the Hofcapellmeister Salieri (1816), for solo and chorus, with pianoforte accompaniment (unpublished).

Sänger, der vom Herzen singet, by A. Stadler, for soprano, tenor, and bass, with pianoforte accompaniment, composed in 1819, in honour of M. Vogl (manuscript).

Terzett zum Namenstag des Vaters, with guitar accompaniment, 1813 (manuscript).

Gratulationscantate (1811), mentioned by Ferd. Schubert.

Volkslied, by Deinhardstein, for chorus and orchestra, composed for the pupils of the Theresianum, at Vienna, and performed there Feb. 11, 1822, for the birthday fête of the Emperor Franz. In 1848, with different words, as ' Constitutionslied ' (also with pianoforte accompaniment), published by Diabelli as Op. 157.

Glaube, Hoffnung und Liebe, by Reil, for male voices and mixed chorus, with accompaniment of wind instruments, composed for the dedication of the bell of the church of the Holy Trinity, in the Alservorstadt, at Vienna (September 1828, at present unpublished).

The 23rd Psalm, for chorus of female voices, with piano accompaniment, composed 1828 for the four sisters Fröhlich. Manuscript in the possession of Frl. Anna Fröhlich, at Vienna, Op. 132. It has been rearranged for male voices.

The 92nd Psalm in the Hebrew tongue, for two baritones, soprano, alto, and bass, published without the knowledge of the composer in the ' Schir Zion,' of the Cantor Sulzer, at Vienna (composed 1828).

Hymn to the Holy Ghost, by Schmiedel, an eight-part chorus for male voices, with orchestral or pianoforte accompaniment, Op. 154. Composed March 1828. Manuscript, eight sheets, in the Royal Library at Berlin.

Grosses Hallelujah, by Klopstock (trio with pianoforte accompaniment), No 41.

Lazarus, or the Festival of the Resurrection. An oratorio from the religious writings of August Hermann Niemeyer, in three parts, composed for solos, chorus, and orchestra, 1820. Manuscript of Part I. in the possession of Spina. Part II. (the conclusion wanting) in the Vienna Musik-Verein. Part III. is the property of Herr J. Herbeck. Performed for the first time in Vienna in 1863.

PIANOFORTE MUSIC FOR A SINGLE PERFORMER.

Erste Walzer, two series, Op. 9 (Der Trauer-, or Sehnsuchtswalzer, also as duetts), published 1822, by Cappi & Diabelli. *Fantasie* in C major, composed about 1820, dedicated by Schubert to the pianist Liebenberg de Zittin, Op. 15. Published 1823 by Cappi & Diabelli. *Walzer, Ländler und Ecossaisen*, two parts, Op. 18, composed in 1820–1823. Manuscripts of the *Ecossaisen* (May 1820), of the *Atzenbrucker Allemande* (July 1821), of the twelve *Allemandes* (May 1823), of the *Ecossaisen* (January 1823), are in the possession of J. Brahms. Most of this music was published in 1823 by Cappi & Diabelli. Afterwards Spina published the twelve Ländler as Op. 171, for two and four hands. The four-handed arrangement was made by Herr Julius Epstein. Overture to the Drama *Rosamunde* (or more correctly *Zauberharfe*, 1823), originally written for an orchestra, published by Diabelli in an arrangement for two and four hands for the piano as Op. 33. *First Sonata*, in A minor, Op. 42 (1825), dedicated by Schubert to the Duke Rudolph. *Galoppe und Ecossaisen*, Op. 49. *Valses sentimentales*, two parts, Op. 50. Second great Sonata in D major, Op. 53, dedicated to his friend Carl Maria Bocklet. *Trauer Marsch*, in C minor, on the occasion of the death of Alexander, Emperor of Russia (1825), (also as a duett, Op. 66). *Grande Marche héroïque*, composed for the coronation of Nicholas, Emperor of Russia (1825), Op. 66. *Wiener Damen-Ländler* (hommage aux belles Viennoises), Op. 67. *Overture to the Opera Alfonso und Estrella*, written originally for the orchestra, but arranged by Schubert and J. Hüttenbrenner for the pianoforte. Published by the firm of Diabelli & Cappi as a duett and single piece for the piano, Op. 69. This overture formed in 1823 the introductory movement to *Rosamunde*. Manuscript in the possession of Spina. *Overture to the Opera Fierrabras*, originally written for an orchestra (1823), published by Diabelli as Op. 76 for two or four hands. *Valses nobles*, Op. 77. *Fantasie, Andante, Menuetto and Allegretto*, Op. 78. A sonata of which the first movement is entitled *Fantasie*, Op. 78, dedicated by Schubert to Josef v. Spaun. *Impromptus.* Two pieces for the pianoforte thus entitled by the publisher

Haslinger, Op. 90. *Grazer Walzer*, Op. 91, composed in memory of a residence at Gratz (1827). *Moments musicals*, two pianoforte pieces, Op. 94. *The Third Sonata* in A major, Op. 120. *Fourth Sonata* in E-flat, Op. 122 (1817). *Letzte Walzer*, Op. 127. *Four Impromptus*, Op. 142, sonatas dedicated by the publisher Haslinger to Franz Liszt. Manuscript nominally belongs to Haslinger. *Grosse Sonate* in A major, Op. 143, dedicated by the publisher Diabelli to Felix Mendelssohn-Bartholdy. *Adagio and Rondo*, Op. 145 (apparently a fragment). *Grosse Sonate* in B major (1817), as Op. 147, dedicated by Diabelli to Sigmund Thalberg. Manuscript belongs to T. Brahms. *Sonata* in A minor, Op. 164 (1823). *Three grand Sonatas*, in C minor, A major, and B major, probably composed in the year 1828. Schubert desired to dedicate them to Hummel; the publisher Diabelli dedicated them to R. Schumann. *Reliquie*, an unfinished sonata (1825), published 1861–1862, by Whistling, at Leipsic, to whom the manuscript belongs.

UNPUBLISHED COMPOSITIONS.

Andante and Variations, in E-flat (1812), manuscript belonging to Ferdinand Schubert. *Twelve Minuetts* (1812). *Thirty Minuetts*, with trios, written for his brother Ignaz in 1813; lost. *Two Sonatas* for the piano in C and F major (1815). *Zwölf Deutsche mit Coda* (1815); manuscript belongs to Ferd. Schubert. *Ten Variations* (Ferdinand Schubert). *Sonata* in E minor (first movement and Scherzo); manuscript, with date June 1817, four large sheets, in the Royal Library, Berlin.

Ecossaisen (1816), apparently those which Schubert wrote for Frln. Marie Spaun, as 'prisoner of Herr Witteczek in Erdberg.'

Two Scherzi with Trio. Thirteen Variations upon a theme from Anselm Hüttenbrenner's 'Streichquartett.' *Variation* on a theme upon which all the composers of Vienna have tried their hands. *Sonata* in F (1816); manuscript in the possession of Ferd. Schubert. *Walzer* (1824). *Walzer* for Josef Hüttenbrenner. *Allegretto* 'in memory of my dear friend Walcher,' composed 1827, when Walcher left Vienna.' Manuscript in the possession of the Archduke Hofrath Ferd. Walcher, at Vienna. *A Sketch in the Album* of Frau Anna Mayrhofer v. Grünbüchel, *née* Hönig, daughter of Dr. Karl Hönig, at Vienna. *Adagio*, a piece for the pianoforte (G major ⁴⁄₄), composed April 8, 1815; manuscript in the possession of Dr. Heinrich v. Kreissle. *Sechs Deutsche. Signs of the future Musician Franz Schubert* (1814), written by Johann Senn, an officer 'bei Kaiserjäger,' 1830 (supposed to be by Schubert).

DUETTS FOR THE PIANOFORTE.

Variations upon a French Song, Op. 10 (composed about 1822), dedicated to Ludwig van Beethoven 'by his devoted admirer.' Published 1822, by Cappi & Diabelli.

Six Marches and Trios (Op. 40), dedicated to his friend Bernhardt (who died in the year 1844, at Constantinople).

Trois Marches héroïques, Op. 27. *First grand Sonata*, Op. 30, dedicated to Count Palffy. *Overture in A*, Op. 34. *Variations upon an original Theme*, Op. 35. *Three Military Marches*, Op. 51. *Divertissement à la Hongroise*, Op. 54, dedicated to Frau Lascny, *née* Buchwieser. *Sechs Polonaisen*, two parts, Op. 61. *Divertissement en forme d'une Marche brillante et raisonnée*, Op. 63. *Vier Polonaisen mit Trios*, Op. 75. *Variations upon an Air from the Opera ' Marie,'* by Herold, Op. 82, Part I., dedicated to the Professor Cajetan Neuhaus. MS. with the date February 1827, in 12 sheets, the score forming a part of the collection of autographs made by Wagener, now in the Royal Library at Berlin. *Variations upon the same*, Op. 82, two parts, published by Schuberth, at Hamburg, a firm which had acquired the copyright from Haslinger, the publisher. This part contained an Introduction and Variations. *Fantasie in F minor*, Op. 103, dedicated by the publisher (and not by Schubert, as the title-page implies) to the Countess Caroline Esterhazy. *Grand Rondeau*, Op. 107, composed July 1828, for Domenico Artaria ; MS., with date, in the possession of Artaria, at Vienna. *Marches charactéristiques*, Op. 121, arranged for orchestra, by Liszt, and in this form performed at Vienna. *Notre amitié est invariable*, Rondeau, Op. 138. *Grand Duo in C major*, Op. 140 (composed 1824) ; MS. belongs to Clara Schumann ; arranged for an orchestra by J. Joachim. The score is in the possession of Herr Spina ; it appeared in this form at Leipsic in 1864. *Lebensstürme*, a characteristic Allegro (composed 1828), Op. 144.

UNPUBLISHED.

Three Fantasias, written in the years 1810, 1811, 1813 ; MS. belongs to Ferd. Schubert. *Two Overtures in C and D* (1817) ; MSS. Diabelli. *Sonata* in C minor (1814) ; MS. A. Stadler. *Fugue* in E minor (1828) ; MS. J. Hüttenbrenner. *Sonata* in E minor (1828) ; MS. Diabelli. *Sonata* in E minor (1817) ; MS. Landsberg.

CHAMBER MUSIC.

First stringed Quartett in A minor, Op. 29. Published very recently by Spina.

Rondeau brillant for the violin and piano in B minor, Op. 70 (1826), published by Artaria. MS. in the possession of a Russian nobleman, Hr. Balsch.

Trio in B (1826), Op. 99.

Trio in E-flat (November 1827), published 1828 by Probst, Leipsic ; MS. in the possession of Frau Gräfin Rosa v. Almasy, at Vienna. MS. of a sketch for the same belongs to J. Brahms.

Quintett (for the piano, violin, violoncello, and double-bass), Op. 114 ; composed 1819 for Herr Paumgartner, in Steyr. *Two stringed Quartetts* in E-flat and E major, Op. 125. *Three little Sonatas* for piano and violin (1816), Op. 137. *Nocturne*, for piano, violin, and violoncello, Op. 148. *Fantasie* for piano and a violin, Op. 159, said to have been composed for the violinist Swatié (Prague), and performed by him on February 5, 1827, at Vienna. On January 3, 1864, it was performed by Laub and Epstein at Vienna. *Introduction*, upon an original air, for piano and flute, Op. 160; probably composed in 1824, for the flute-player Ferd. Bogner.

Stringed Quartett in G major, composed between June 20 and 30, 1826.

Duett for piano and violin in A major, Op. 162 (this was played at the concert given for the Schubert memorial).

Stringed Quartett in C major (1828) ; appeared in parts, published by Spina, Op. 163.

Stringed Quartett in D minor (1826), arranged as a pianoforte duett by R. Franz.

Octett for stringed and wind instruments, composed 1824 for Count F. Troyer, at Vienna. MS. in the possession of Spina, Op. 166. Piano arrangement for four hands, by S. Leitner (Dr. Leopold v. Sonnleithner) ; likewise belongs to Spina.

Stringed Quartett in B major (1814), published by Spina in parts as Op. 168; MS. Spina. Schubert began this as a trio, then struck out the first ten lines, and made it into a quartett. Performed at a quartett concert given by Hellmesberger, February 23, 1862.

String Quartett in G minor (composed 1815, between March 25 and April 1); MS. in the library of the Musikverein at Vienna. Published in November 1863, in Hellmesberger's collection of quartetts.

Quartett-Overture in B-flat (1812); MS. belonged to Ferd. Schubert. *Sonata* for piano, violin, and violoncello (1812); Diabelli. *Franz Schubert's funeral music*, octett for two clarinets, two oboes, two bassoons, and two horns; MS. Ferd. Schubert. *Fünf Minuette und sechs Deutsche* with trio for a string quartett and two horns (1813); MS. Ferd. Schubert. *Six string Quartetts* in B-flat and C (1812), in C, B-flat, E-flat, and D (1813); MSS. Diabelli. *A string Quartett* (1811); MS. Diabelli. *Quintett-Overture*, composed 1811 for Ferd. Schubert, to whom the MS. belongs. *Two Quartetts for stringed instruments* in D major and C minor (1814); MSS. Diabelli. *Trio* for violin, viola, and violoncello (1816–17); MS. Diabelli. *String Quartett* in F (1816); MS. Diabelli. *Sonata* for piano and violin (1817); MS. Diabelli, Op. 159 or 162. *String Quartett* in C minor, first movement (1820). *Violin-Concerto* in D (1816); MS. Ferd. Schubert. *Polonaises* for violin (1817); MS. Ferd. Schubert. *Sonata* for piano and a small harp (arpeggione), in A minor (composed in November 1824). *Skizzirte Variationen* for the violin in A (December 1817); MS. Ferd. Schubert. *Concerto* for violin, with orchestral accompaniment, composed for his brother Ferdinand; MS. (probably the same as that mentioned above) in the possession of Diabelli.

COMPOSITIONS FOR ORCHESTRA.

Overtures in C and D (composed in May and November 1817); MSS. in possession of Spina. *Overtures* in B-flat; (MS. in the possession of Dr. Schneider), in E minor and C minor. *Three Minuetts and three Trios* for orchestra, 1813.

Sinfonie in D, composed 1813 at the Convict; Dr. Schneider has the original score.

Two Symphonies in B-flat (1815 and 1816); one of these 'without trumpets and drums.' Dr. Schneider has the score.

Symphony in D (1815). The finale was performed at Vienna in 1860.

Symphony in C minor (the tragic, written in 1816); the MS. with Dr. Schneider. The first two movements performed at Vienna in 1860.

Symphony in C (the sixth), composed 1818. The MS. in Dr. Schneider's collection. The Scherzo was performed at Vienna in 1860. The symphony, in its entirety, was first heard in December 1828, and the beginning of the ensuing year.

Symphony in C (the seventh), March 1828 ; the MS. in the library of the Musikverein at Vienna. Performed for the first time at Leipsic in the year 1839. The score, parts, and pianoforte edition of this work have been published by Breitkopf & Härtel.

Symphony in B minor (composed 1822). Josef Hüttenbrenner states that his brother Anselm, in Gratz, has the original score of this work ; further, that two movements are complete, and the Scherzo unfinished. Josef Hüttenbrenner has a copy arranged for the pianoforte. There are no other copies in existence.

Symphony in E. According to Ferdinand Schubert, there is a sketch of this, which in 1846 came into the hands of Felix Mendelssohn. The original of this sketch is in Dr. Schneider's collection.

OPERAS, OPERETTAS, MELODRAMAS.

Des Teufels Lustschloss, musical extravaganza in three acts, by August v. Kotzebue, begun in 1813, and finished in 1814. The original of this work in Dr. Schneider's collection, and a copy of a new arrangement (the second act lost) in that of J. Hüttenbrenner. At a concert performance of the Operetta ' Der häusliche Krieg,' the overture to ' Des Teufels Lustschloss ' was played as an introduction.

Fernando, an operetta in one act, by Albert Stadler (1815). The MS. in Dr. Schneider's collection.

Die beiden Freunde von Salamanka, operetta in two acts, by Mayrhofer (1815). The original score in Dr. Schneider's collection.

Claudine von Villabella, opera in three acts, by Göthe (1815), the original score of the first act in the possession of J. Hüttenbrenner. He has lost the other two acts.

Die Bürgschaft (after Schiller), author unknown. Opera in three acts, the first of which is complete, and the second nearly so, the third is not in existence (1816). The MS. in Dr. Schneider's collection.

Die Zwillinge, musical vaudeville in one act, after the French, the music in the library of the Musikverein at Vienna. Ferdinand Schubert's pianoforte arrangement is in the possession of Josef Freiherr v. Spaun. It was first performed at Vienna on June 14, 1820.

Alfonso und Estrella, grand opera in three acts, by Franz von Schober (1820–1822). The original score, without an overture, is in the library of the Musikverein, at Vienna. Spina has the original of the overture, which bears date December 1823. It was first performed at Weimar, in 1855. The overture, a bass and tenor air, have been published (the latter in the 'Auserlesene Sammlung') by Diabelli, with pianoforte accompaniment. The MSS. of the two songs are in Petter's collection.

Fierrabras, grand opera in three acts, by Josef Kupelwieser (1823). MS. (without overture) in Dr. Schneider's collection. The overture has been published by Diabelli, arranged for pianoforte. Parts of the opera were given at concerts in Vienna.

Der häusliche Krieg (Die Verschwornen), operetta in one act, by J. Castelli (composed probably in 1823). The original score is missing. Dr. Schneider has a copy, and Petter the MS. of a duett from this work. A pianoforte edition with words and other arrangements of this opera by Dr. Schneider were published by Spina in 1862. The music was first performed in 1861 at a concert by the Musikverein, at Vienna, and was given as an operetta for the first time in Frankfort on the Maine.

Die Zauberharfe (1818–1819), melodrama, with songs and choruses, in three acts, by Hofmann. The original score of the entr'acte, after the first and second act of the play, an overture to the third act, and a finale, are in Spina's collection. Josef Hüttenbrenner has a romance, and the finale of the second act as a sketch. The overture was published in the pianoforte edition by Diabelli as the overture to *Rosamunde*. The melodrama was performed for the first time on August 19, 1820, at the theatre 'an der Wien.'

Sakontala, opera in three acts, by Josef Filipp Neumann (1820), sketches of two acts. In the Schneider collection.

Rosamunde, drama in four acts, by Helmine Chezy, with airs, choruses, and dance music (1823). Original score unknown. The *huntsman's* chorus, one for *shepherds*, and another for *spirits*, the romance, and the overture (more correctly speaking *Zauberharfen* overture) were published by Diabelli as Op. 26. The drama played for the first time in 1823 in the theatre 'an der Wien.'

Zwei Einlagen, a tenor air, and a duett for bass and tenor in Herold's Opera *La Clochette*. Josef Freiherr v. Spaun possesses a copy of it, and the pianoforte accompaniment.

Der Spiegelritter, opera in three acts, by Kotzebue. The original of a fragment of the first act is in the collection of the Musikverein at Vienna ; composed probably in 1815.

Der Minnesänger, musical vaudeville; lost.

Adrast, opera by Mayrhofer (1815); the words have been lost. J. Hüttenbrenner states that Schubert set a fragment of this poem to music. Alois Fuchs confirms the statement.

Der Graf von Gleichen (1827–28). Bauernfeld and Lachner mention a musical sketch of this opera, for which (according to Lachner) Bauernfeld composed a libretto.

CHURCH MUSIC.

Tantum ergo, in C, for chorus and orchestra, Op. 45. *Erstes Offertorium*, for soprano or tenor solo and violin or clarinet obligato (Op. 46), dedicated to his friend Tieze. *Zweites Offertorium*, for soprano solo, with orchestra (1815), Op. 47. *Mass in C*, for four voices and orchestra (1816), dedicated to his friend Michael Holzer, Op. 48. *A second Benedictus* for this Mass (October 1828). *Antifonen zur Palmenweihe* (1820), for four voices, written with black chalk upon packing-paper. Ferdinand Schubert had the original copy, which was published as Op. 113 by Diabelli. *Mass in B-flat*, for four voices and orchestra (1815) ; published by Haslinger as Op. 141. *Salve Regina*, for four male voices, with organ accompaniment *ad libitum* (1824), Op. 149; the MS. in the Vienna Musikverein collection. *Graduale*, for four voices, with orchestra and organ accompaniment, Op. 150. *Third Offertorium*, for soprano or tenor solo, with quartett or pianoforte accompaniment (January 28, 1823), Op. 153. *Mass in F*, for four parts and orchestra (1814); Schubert's first Mass, produced in 1814 at the parish church of Lichtenthal. Dr. Schneider has the original score.

A second Dona Nobis for the F Mass (1815).

Mass in G, for four voices and orchestra (1815), composed for the Lichtenthaler choir. Published in Prague by Marco Berra as the work of Robert Führer (died 1861), and dedicated by him to the Archduchess Maria Caroline, Abbess of the Theres. Damenstift at Hradschin.

Mass in A-flat for four parts and orchestra (1822) ; the original score in the library of the Vienna Musikverein.

Grand Mass in E-flat (June 1828). The score, consisting of eighty sheets, in Schubert's handwriting, is in the Royal Library at Berlin. J. Hüttenbrenner has a copy of this work.

Di utsche Messe in A-flat, words by Johann Filipp Neumann, for mixed voices with organ or band accompaniment (also arranged for male voices), with a supplementary piece, *The Lord's Prayer*, composed in 1827 for the audience at the Polytechnic School in Vienna. First *Stabat Mater* (1815); a copy of this is in Spina's collection. Second *Stabat Mater* (1816), for solo voices, chorus, and orchestra. Pianoforte edition by Ferdinand Schubert. Both Spaun and Spina have copies. *Salve Regina* (1812) and *Fourth Kyrie* (1812 and 1813). The MS. of both were in F. Schubert's possession. *Salve Regina*, for tenor solo, with orchestral accompaniment (July 1814). *Magnificat* (1815). *Grosses Magnificat* in C (September 25, 1816), for chorus and orchestra; the original score in Spina's collection. Duett, *Auguste jam cœlestium* (1816); Spina. *Offertorium* (1814). *Salve Regina* in A (1818). *Sacred Air* for tenor solo and chorus (1828). *Requiem*, only finished as far as the fugue in the Kyrie (July 1816). *Messgesänge*, for four voices, attributed to Franz Schubert; set for three voices by his brother Ferdinand. *Deutsche Trauermesse*, attributed to Franz, but without doubt a requiem written by Ferdinand Schubert.

TO SCHUBERT'S COFFIN

(sung to the melody of Schubert's ' Pax vobiscum,' and performed at his funeral).

Der Friede sei mit Dir, Du engelreine Seele !—
Im frischen Blüh'n der vollen Jugendkraft
Hat Dich der Strahl des Todes hingerafft,
Dass er dem reinen Lichte Dich vermähle,
Dem Licht, von dem hienieden schon durchdrungen
Dein Geist in heil'gen Tönen uns gesungen,
Das Dich geweckt, geleitet und entflammt,
Dem Lichte, das von Gott nur stammt.

O sieh, verklärter Freund, herab auf uns're Zähren,
Vergib dem Schmerz der schwachen Menschenbrust,
Wir sind beraubt, wir litten den Verlust,
Du schwebst befreit in heimathlichen Sphären.
Für viele Rosen hat dies Erdenleben
Dir scharfe Dornen nur zum Lohn gegeben,
Ein langes Leiden und ein frühes Grab,
Dort fallen alle Ketten ab.—

Und was als Erbtheil Du uns hast zurückgelassen,
Das Wirken heisser Liebe, reiner Kraft,
Die heil'ge Wahrheit gross und unerschlafft,
Wir wollen's tief in uns're Seelen fassen.
Was Du der Kunst, den Deinen Du geworden,
Ist offenbart in himmlischen Accorden.
Und wenn wir nach den süssen Klängen gehen,
Dann werden wir Dich wieder sehen.

FRANZ SCHOBER.

November 21, 1828.

APPENDIX[1]

BY GEORGE GROVE, ESQ.

ON the 5th October, 1867, I had the happiness to find myself
for the first time in the city of Vienna. It was a place which
I had looked forward to, almost hopelessly, as a kind of El
Dorado, for years. I was with one of my best friends, and
the object of my visit was as dear and congenial to me as
possible. Could I have been more happily situated?

My immediate object was to endeavour to obtain some of
the great orchestral works of Franz Schubert, which I had
reason to believe were lying neglected, or at least unper-
formed, there; and of these especially his Symphonies, and the
completion of the incidental music to the Drama of 'Rosamunde.'

My readers must know that I am Secretary to the Crystal
Palace Company, that I take a lively personal (as well as
official and commercial) interest in the success of the 'Saturday
Concerts,' and that it was mainly in relation to these that my
enthusiasm for Franz Schubert had arisen, and had led me to
Vienna.

My acquaintance with the music of this truly remarkable
composer began in the year 1846 or 1847, and was then confined to his songs, of which, however, I knew not only those
commonly known, but others, then more rarely tried; not

only the 'Müllerlieder,'the 'Erlkönig,' and the 'Wanderer,' but the series of the 'Winterreise ' and the 'Schwanengesang,' as well as such detached songs as 'Todesmusik,' the 'Lied der Anna Lyle,' 'An eine Quelle,' and a few other less known songs. Thus it remained till 1856 or 1857, in which year, with very inadequate means, Mr. Manns, the admirable conductor of the Crystal Palace orchestra, and my very kind and excellent friend, played the C major Symphony of Schubert, the only one of his orchestral works then known in England; at that time, too, believed to be his only Symphony, and, if I am right, never before played in England, though since performed by the Musical Society of London, and by the 'New Philhar-monic Society' of Dr. Wylde. Mr. Manns's band had also Schu-bert's ' Overture to Rosamunde ' (Op. 26) in their repertoire. The C major Symphony was performed at the Crystal Palace more than once during the following years; but the band was then so small, and the locality so unfavourable, and the Sym-phony itself so long for ordinary ears, that it is not wonderful it should have achieved no success, and awakened no enthusiasm.

This went on till the year 1865, when the 'Life of Schubert,' by Dr. Kreissle von Hellborn, of which the present work is a translation, was published. It at once attracted my attention ; I was delighted with the catalogue at the end, and espe-cially interested with the entr'actes to the drama of ' Rosa-munde,' which were therein described. I at once corresponded with Mr. Spina, the well-known music-publisher of Vienna, successor to the ancient firm of Diabelli & Co., with whom the Crystal Palace Company had already had communications on matters of business. Mr. Spina met my advances in the most gratifying way. He informed me that the parts of several num-. bers of the ' Rosamunde ' music were in his possession, and that two of them were then in the press. These were the entr'actes between the first and second, and third and fourth acts, in

B minor and B-flat respectively. The printed score and parts
of these arrived at the end of October, 1866; they were immediately tried, and great was our delight to find how original
and beautiful they were. They were first played on this side
the water on the 10th November, 1866, with the lovely Romance in F minor, sung by Mdlle. Enequist, and scored for
this occasion by Mr. Manns from the pianoforte arrangement
in which it was published by Schubert. They were most
favourably received, and have become stock-pieces in the re-
pertory of the Crystal Palace music. This success naturally
increased our appetite for more of the same treasures, and after
some correspondence, we obtained two more numbers of the
same composition—this time in MS. The first of these, 'No 2,
Ballo,' is a piece in the fashion of an *entr'acte*, in the key of
B minor, like No. 1, and to a certain extent formed on the
same themes, though with different treatment, and ending in
a most naïve and charming curtain-tune in G major. The
other, No. 9, is a Ballet Air, also in G, and in Schubert's
best and liveliest style. This was first played on the 16th
March, 1867.

But the 'Rosamunde' music was not, even as far as we
then knew it, complete. The three Choruses had, like the
Romance, been printed during Schubert's lifetime with pianoforte accompaniment; the trombone parts to the 'Geister-Chor'
were also printed. But all enquiries for the orchestral accompaniments to the other two, or to the Romance, failed to
produce any result. Mr. Spina had not got them, and could
not tell who had.

In the course of the autumn we received from Mr. Spina
MS. copies of the Overtures to 'Alfonso and Estrella' and
'Fierrabras,' which were performed at the concerts of No-
vember 3rd, 1866, and February 2nd, 1867, respectively.
The latter of these was not entirely new to England, having

been brought over by Mendelssohn with the MS. of the great C major Symphony, No. 9, and played at the Philharmonic under his direction on June 10, 1864; but it does not appear to have been repeated, and the Overture to ' Alfonso and Estrella' had certainly never been played in this country. A little later we received from our good correspondent in Vienna the score and parts of the ' Overture in the Italian Style in C,' since published as Op. 170, which was also an entire novelty, and was first played on December 1, 1866. These works are all characteristic and interesting, but they were thrown into the shade by the unfinished Symphony in B minor, No. 8, which was published early in 1867, and which we received on April 2, and first performed at the concert of the following Saturday, April 6, 1867.

This most original and beautiful composition stimulated our desire to obtain more of the same kind of music in the very highest degree. I eagerly asked everyone whom I met—Mr. Joachim, Madame Schumann, and others—for information as to the rest of the Symphonies, but without success ; no one had seen them or knew anything about them. At length, in the autumn of '68, a succession of fortunate circumstances, for which I can never be too grateful, put it into my power to visit Vienna, in company with a gentleman who is at once one of my best friends, and—in the absence of Mr. Manns, then unable to leave his duties—better able, perhaps, than any-one else to advise and assist me in my search, namely, Mr. Arthur Sullivan.

At Vienna, then, we arrived on October the 5th, and our first care was to make the acquaintance of Dr. Schneider. This we were enabled to do through the kindness and tact of Mr. Spina, who proved himself in every way a valuable friend. Dr. Schneider's office, or chambers (for he is a barrister in full practice) is in the Tuchlauben. First, there is the spacious outer room, or clerks' office; then, behind it, Dr. Schneider's own sanctum, and in a roomy cupboard in this are contained the treasures which we had come to seek. We had sent our letters of introduction before us, and on calling found the doctor ready to receive us, with the books on the table before him. A quarter of an hour's conversation was sufficient to put us perfectly *en rapport*, and I soon had the scores of the first, second, third, fourth, and sixth of Schubert's Symphonies in my hands.

Two things strike one in a Schubert manuscript—its remarkable neatness and freedom from erasures or corrections, and the careful manner in which it is dated and signed. The signature always has *mpia.*, i.e. ' *manu propriâ*,' after it. Often the separate movements are dated; and we shall find one instance of the hour and minute of the beginning and ending of a movement having been recorded.

I took my treasures to a table by the window in the clerks' office, and worked quietly at them till I had got all that I was able. What that was, my readers shall now know.

THE FIRST SYMPHONY: IN D.

The FIRST SYMPHONY—possibly not the actual first, but the earliest yet known—is in D. It is in an oblong volume of full-sized music-paper, half bound, and occupies 183 pages. The writing is very careful and precise, almost like that of a copyist, or rather perhaps of a lad writing with a deep sense of the importance of his occupation. There is no title-page, as is usually the case: it has possibly been abstracted by the same zealous autograph collector who has carefully cut out the signature from the right-hand top corner of the first page. Over the top of the music is written ' Synfonia' : that and the gap aforesaid are the only heading. The Symphony begins, like seven out of the nine, with an Introduction, Adagio,.of twenty bars. Then follow Allegro vivace in D ; Andante in G; Minuet and Trio in D ; and Finale in D. In the Allegro vivace twenty-four bars have been struck out in pencil; and including these, but not counting repeats, the movement contains 533 bars. Pretty well for a beginner : for the first movement of Beethoven's ' Pastoral Symphony ' contains only 512. At the bottom of the last page of the Finale is written—' Der 28te Oct. 813. Finis et Fine.' Schubert was at this time, therefore, far on in his seventeenth year. He was still in the Konvict establishment, and Herr Kreissle states, though without quoting his authority, that the Symphony was written for the birthday or baptismal day of Lang, the then Director of the Konvict.

N.B.—In the theme of the Finale the two first crotchets were originally written a minim.

SYMPHONY No. 1. (MS.)

[For 2 Violins; Viola; Flute; 2 Oboes; 2 Clarinets; 2 Bassoons; 2 Horns; 2 Trumpets; Drum; Cello; and Bass.]

'Synfonia.' ['Franz Schubert.]

SYMPHONY 1—*continued.*

THE SECOND SYMPHONY: IN B-FLAT.

This is also the autograph MS.—oblong as before, and bound. The handwriting, however, is much freer than in No. 1. The title-page is intact, and bears the words ' Synfonie in B, von Franz Schubert, mpia.'

Over the first page of the music is written ' Synfonia. Franz Schubert,' and at the left-hand bottom corner, ' der 10 Dez. 814.' At the end of the Allegro vivace is written—and partly cut off by the wretched bookbinder—' der 26 Dezember 814.' At the beginning of the Finale we find ' der 25 Fe-bruar 1815 ;' and at the end, ' der 24 März 815.   Fine.'

SYMPHONY No. 2. (MS.)

[For 2 Violins; Viola; 2 Flutes; 2 Oboes; 2 Clarinets; 2 Bassoons; 2 Horns;
2 Trumpets; Drums; Cello; and Bass.]

"Synfonie in B, von Franz Schubert. mpia."

"Synfonia. Franz Schubert. der 10 Dez. 814."

SYMPHONY 2—*continued.*

THE THIRD SYMPHONY: IN D.

The autograph manuscript of the Third Symphony is oblong, like the two former. It is not, however, bound, but is
in seven loose quires or portions. The handwriting is much
more free than before. There is no title-page, but on the
first page, above the music, is written 'Synphonie. Der 24
May 1815. Franz Schubert. Mpia.' At bar 47 of the first
Allegro we find '11 July,' and at the end of the same movement—161 bars farther on—'der 12 July 1815.' The Allegretto was begun three days afterwards, being dated at the
beginning 'der 15 July 1815.' At the end of the Finale
we find 'Fine, der 19 July 1815.' The writing is very neat
throughout, and contains very few corrections : only, close to
the end of the Finale, six bars are inserted.

SYMPHONY No. 3. (MS.)

[For 2 Violins; Viola; 2 Flutes; 2 Oboes; 2 Clarinets; 2 Bassoons; 2 Horns; 2 Trumpets; Drum; Cello; and Bass.]

'Synphonie. Der 24 May 1815. Franz Schubert. Mpia.'

SYMPHONY 3—*continued.*

THE FOURTH SYMPHONY: IN C MINOR.

Dr. Schneider's manuscript of this is not the autograph, but
a copy by Ferdinand Schubert. The original appears to be
lost; at any rate, neither Schneider, Spina, nor Kreissle, knew
anything of it.

The MS. bears the title 'Tragische Sinfonie in C minor,
von Franz Schubert. Componirt im Aprill 1816.'

Dr. Schneider permitted me to have a copy made of the
scores of this and No. 6; and this Symphony was played for
the first time in England (probably anywhere at all) at the
Crystal Palace, at a rehearsal on Thursday, February 27, 1868,
and first performed in public at the concert of the following
Saturday, February 29.

SYMPHONY No. 4, (MS.)

[For 2 Violins; Viola; 2 Flutes; 2 Oboes; 2 Clarinets; 2 Bassoons; 4 Horns;
2 Trumpets; Drums; Cello; and Bass.]

·'Tragische Sinfonie in C minor, von Franz Schubert. Componirt im Aprill
1816.' [Copy by Ferdinand Schubert.]

SYMPHONY 4—*continued.*

THE FIFTH SYMPHONY: IN B-FLAT.

The autograph of this Symphony appears also not to be forthcoming at present. I, at any rate, have only approached within two removes of it. A copy of the score and parts is in possession of the Musik-Verein of Vienna, and during my visit they were in the keeping of Mr. Herbeck, the Court Capellmeister and conductor of the concerts of the Verein. Mr. Herbeck was good enough to show me the parts, and from them I extracted the themes given on the opposite page. They are in the handwriting of Ferdinand Schubert, and bear the following title: 'Symphonie in B, von Franz Schubert. Aus der Original Partitur, die Orchester-Stimmen copirt von Ferd. Schubert.' It was probably composed for some amateur or provincial orchestra, for there are no parts for either clarinets, trumpets, or drums. It will be observed that it wants the Introduction, which is *de rigueur* in the others. I omitted to take the length of the various movements, but my impression is that it is shorter than either of its predecessors. However, Mr. Herbeck has since given me permission to have it copied, and I hope that before long it will be produced at the Crystal Palace.

I have placed this Symphony as No. 5, on the warrant of Dr. Kreissle, but in the absence of any date this is uncertain. The date is probably on the copy of the score.

SYMPHONY No. 5. (MS.)

[For 2 Violins; Viola; Flute; 2 Oboes; 2 Bassoons; 2 Horns; Cello and Bass.]

'Symphonie in B, von Franz Schubert. Aus der Original Partitur, die Orchester-Stimmen copirt von Ferd. Schubert.'

SYMPHONY 5—*continued.*

THE SIXTH SYMPHONY·: IN ·C MAJOR.

This was the last of the five in Dr. Schneider's possession. The autograph is an oblong MS. like the others, not bound, written in a very neat, but free and rapid hand. It is entitled 'Grosse Sinfonie in C. Franz Schubert.' No date appears at the commencement, but at the end we find 'Februar 1818. Fine.'

I am sorry to say, that having obtained Dr. Schneider's permission to have this copied, I did not pay that minute attention to the state of the autograph that I did in the other cases. But our copy was made under the immediate super-intendence of Mr. Pohl (most accurate of men), and I have no reason to think that it contains any other dates or notes than those given on our copy and quoted above. The Symphony was first performed at the Crystal Palace on Nov. 21, 1868.

And here we ought perhaps properly to leave the Symphonies, and speak of the other MSS. in Dr. Schneider's possession ; but I think it better to proceed with the three remaining ones, and return afterwards to the good doctor.

SYMPHONY No. 6. (MS.)

[For 2 Violins; Viola; 2 Flutes; 2 Oboes; 2 Clarinets; 2 Bassoons; 2 Horns; 2 Trumpets; Drums; Cello; and Bass.]

"Grosse Sinfonie in C. Franz Schubert."

SYMPHONY 6—*continued.*

564 bars

THE SEVENTH SYMPHONY: IN E.

This, like the Eighth, is incomplete, though its incompleteness is entirely of a different nature. Dr. Kreissle refers more than once to the sketch of a Symphony in E which had been made in 1821, and was presented by Ferdinand Schubert to Mendelssohn in 1845. As this was necessary to make up the magic number of nine, I was naturally anxious to discover what condition of completeness it was in, and how far it answered to the usual meaning of the word 'sketch.' I made enquiries of various members of Mendelssohn's family, but without success, and was led to believe that it was lost, or had probably been taken by some discerning friend or collector of autographs. However, I persevered, and was at length rewarded by receiving in August last, from Mr. Paul Mendelssohn of Berlin, the brother of the composer, the original MS. sketch which I had so anxiously desired. I had imagined a sketch of the nature of Beethoven's —two or three leaves of paper covered with disjointed memoranda. Judge of my astonishment and delight when on undoing the parcel I found a whole Symphony in forty-four sheets ! It is one of the most singular and interesting works to be found in all the musical art. The Introduction and a portion of the Allegro are fully scored and completed; but at the 110th bar (the end of a page) Schubert appears to have grown impatient of this regular proceeding, and from that point to the end of the Symphony he has made merely memoranda. But these memoranda are perfectly orderly and intelligible. . Every bar is drawn-in through the entire work ; the *tempi* and names of the instruments are fully written at the beginning of each movement; the very double bars and flourishes are gravely added at the end of each, and ' Fine ' at the conclusion of the whole ; and Schubert evidently regarded the work as completed. And so it practically is ; for each subject is given at full length, with a bit of bass, or accompaniment, or figure, or fugato passage. There is not one bar, from beginning to end, that does not contain the part of one or more instruments ; so that I am assured, by the most competent authority, that it would be quite possible to write in the missing parts and complete the work as Schubert would have done it.

Mr. Sullivan has played it through to me on the piano, and I am allowed by him to say that in quality it appears to be inferior to none of its predecessors, and to abound in beauties ; which I do, earnestly trusting that some means may before long be found of restoring this lost treasure to the world. I have heard that Mendelssohn had at one time the intention of filling it up, but of this I know nothing certain.

SYMPHONY No. 7. (MS. Sketch.)

[For 2 Violins ; Viola ; 2 Flutes ; 2 Oboes ; 2 Clarinets ; 2 Bassoons ; 2 Horns ;
3 Trombones ; 2 Trumpets ; Drums ; Cello and Bass.]

' Sinfonia.   August 1821.   Frz. Schubert. Mpia.'

34 bars

SYMPHONY 7—*continued.*

[Second subject.]

Andante.

Scherzo.

[Trio.]

The Eighth Symphony: in B minor.

This, like the preceding, is unfinished, but in a different manner. The two first movements are complete, and nine bars of the third; but there the composition absolutely stops: no hint remains to guide us to the remainder. At the time of our visit to Vienna, the MS. was in the hands of Mr. Herbeck, who was kind enough to show it to us. It is on oblong paper, very freely but very neatly written, with great grace in the writing, and with very rare corrections. On the first page is the date, ' Wien, d. 30te Oct. 1822.'

The score and parts are published, and the Symphony is performed so frequently at the Crystal Palace[1] and elsewhere, and has been so often commented upon, that it is unnecessary for me to say anything of its many and remarkable beauties, except that (speaking as a mere amateur) every time I hear it I am confirmed in the belief that it stands quite apart from all other compositions of Schubert or any other master. It must be the record of some period of unusual *attendrissement* and depression, unusual even for the susceptible and passionate nature of Schubert.

What a commentary do these two movements form on the following sentence from his Journal !—' My compositions are the result of my abilities and my distress ; and those which

[1] The score was published early in 1867, and the Symphony was first performed at the Crystal Palace on the 6th April. It was also played by the Philharmonic Society on the 20th May in the same year.

distress alone has engendered appear to give the world most pleasure.'

This and No. 5 are the only ones out of the nine which have no Introduction to the first movement.

SYMPHONY No. 8.

Vienna, C. A. Spina, [March] 1867.

[For 2 Violins ; Viola ; 2 Flutes ; 2 Oboes ; 2 Clarinets ; 2 Bassoons ; 2 Horns ;
3 Trombones ; 2 Trumpets ; Drums ; Cello and Bass.]

'Wien.   d. 30te Oct. 1822.'

THE NINTH SYMPHONY: IN C MAJOR.

This, which is the last, is also—as a Ninth Symphony should be—the longest of the nine. It is in five movements—for the opening Andante, like the Introduction to Beethoven's No. 7, is quite long enough to be counted as a separate movement—and, if played with the repeats indicated, it occupies very nearly an hour. With an ordinary English audience this will always be a drawback to the work, though to anyone who is acquainted with it, and who listens to music for the purpose of hearing beautiful thoughts and experiencing delightful emotions, the Symphony will never be one moment too long.

It was composed, or commenced, in March 1828, eight months before Schubert's death, and after an interval, therefore, of five years and a half since his last work of the same nature.[1] How pleasant the return to this great region of his art must have been to him, is evident from the remark which he is said to have made on presenting the score to the Musik-Verein (see vol. ii. p. 133)—'that he wished henceforth to hear nothing more of Lieder, but meant to live now entirely in Operas and Symphonies.' The story of the discovery of this Symphony by Robert Schumann, in 1838, and of its performance at the Gewandhaus concert, on March 22, 1839, under the direction of Mendelssohn, has been told by Schumann himself in one of his most genial and characteristic papers, and may be read at length in Dr. Kreissle's pages. (Vol. ii. pp. 221-229.) I may say *en passant* that the first *great* performance of it at Sydenham was on Saturday, April 21, 1866 ; and it was played by the Crystal Palace Band at St. James's Hall on March 28th, 1867.

The score and parts were published by Breitkopf & Härtel in January 1850; and as the work is performed at least once a year in or near London, it is unnecessary to say any-

---

[1] Unless, indeed, the allusions in Schubert's letter to Kupelwieser, and Schwind's to Schubert, of March 31, 1824, and August 14, 1825 (see vol. ii. pp. 5 and 43), refer to a Symphony written in the interval, and not yet discovered. I think also that Dr. Kreissle (ii. 231 *note*) has dismissed too lightly Ferdinand Schubert's mention of a Symphony in C, dating 1817. Ferdinand appears to have been usually very accurate.

thing of its nature or contents. A few particulars of the original manuscript may, however, be interesting, especially as it differs from the MSS. of all Schubert's other Symphonies that I have had the privilege of examining, in containing very many and very important alterations and afterthoughts. These were noted by Mr. Sullivan, when we looked through the manuscript together in the library of the Musik-Verein, on the 8th October, 1867, and they may therefore be received with perfect confidence.

The MS. is a volume of 218 pages, and, as usual, on oblong paper; the page containing sixteen staves, of which fourteen are filled. There is no autograph title-page, but as a heading to the first page of the music is 'Symfonie, März 1828. Frz. Schubert Mp.' The alterations commence at the very beginning. Thus the opening theme (page 1 of the printed score) in the two horns stood at first thus :—

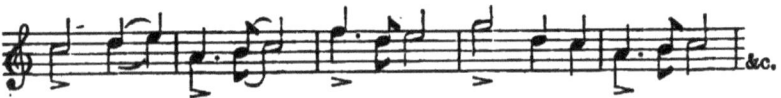

and has then been altered, both in melody and expression, to the form in which it now stands in the printed score :—

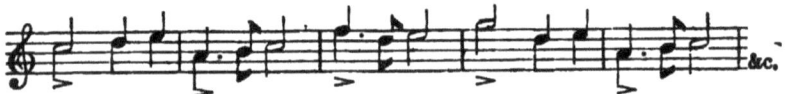

The first theme of the Allegro (page 13 of the printed score) stood originally thus :—

instead of

as it now stands, and was evidently altered much later, since it appears in its original form all through the first movement, and has been at every recurrence scratched through with the pen.

On page 25 of the printed score, bars 2 to 6 stood originally thus :—

instead of

On repetition, later in the movement, it appears in the altered form.

On page 101 of the printed score, bars four to seven originally stood thus :—

instead of

In the Andante, the opening melody (page 105 of the printed score) was originally given to the A-clarinet instead of the oboe, and is erased with the pen accordingly for three bars.

Page 160 of the printed score originally stood as follows :—

In the Scherzo, at page 166 of the printed score, bars one
to six stand originally thus :—

instead of

The delicious melody in the flute, with its repetition half a
note higher, which now forms such an ornament to the Scherzo

(commencing at page 173, bar five, in the printed score) proves
to have been entirely an after-thought. The passage originally
stood as follows (page 172, last bar), and the new bars are
crammed in between the old ones.

The two last bars of the Scherzo before the Trio (page 189
of the printed score) were added afterwards.

In the Finale there are but few alterations, and those of no importance. It has evidently been written straight off, and towards the end the pen seems to have rushed on at an impetuous speed, almost equalling that of the glorious music itself. The first four movements, on the other hand, are literally crowded with alterations; so much so that the work looks as if it were made up of after-thoughts. The handwriting is neat and perfectly distinct, though it has lost the peculiar charm which it has in the MSS. of the Seventh and Eighth Symphonies.

SYMPHONY No. 9.

[For 2 Violins; Viola; 2 Flutes; 2 Oboes; 2 Clarinets; 2 Bassoons; 2 Horns; 2 Trumpets; 3 Trombones; Drums; Cello; and Bass.]

Leipzig: Breitkopf & Härtel. [Jan. 1850.]

'Symfonie März 1828. Frz. Schubert Mp.'

324

SYMPHONY 9—*continued.*

Such is an account, as far as I am able to give it, of the original MSS. of Schubert's nine Symphonies. I fear they are likely to remain in manuscript for some time to come, for even in Vienna he is not the object of that general enthusiasm which is felt for him by the best musicians and amateurs of England, or, as we should imagine, would naturally be felt by the countrymen of one of the most remarkable musical geniuses that ever was born or resided in Vienna. An exception must be made in favour of Herr Herbeck, the Imperial Capell-meister, and leader of the Vienna Concert Orchestra, who is unwearied in the service of Schubert, and has given his time, abilities, and best exertions in the cause. Kreissle von Hell-born, Dumba, Speidl, Pohl, and a few others may be mentioned; and Herr Spina, notwithstanding the charges brought against him, has merited the thanks of musicians and lovers of music for his many recent publications, the style of which is all that could be wished. But in general the Viennese are cold towards their great brother; and so, I regret to say, we found the chief musicians in the large towns of more northern Germany.

It is, however, hard to sit down in the belief that some effort will not be made to procure the publication of all the six earlier Symphonies; for the seventh is too incomplete to justify its being printed. The experiment made with the 'Tragic Symphony,' No. 4, at the Crystal Palace in February last, was amply justified by the result. Young as Schubert was when he wrote it (nineteen years old), the music showed no sign of immaturity, but, on the contrary, was allowed by all competent judges to be of first-rate excellence and interest. And as much may be said of the No. 6, produced in November. But what is wanted is not performance only: the works should be printed, and accessible to all orchestras and all audiences, instead of being fettered with the restriction which Dr. Schneider and Mr. Spina (very justifiably) laid on their possession by the Crystal Palace.[1]

Schubert's First Symphony ought to be as interesting and valuable as Mendelssohn's first—a work which is constantly played, and enjoyed every time it is heard. And if his First, then surely his Second, Third, Fourth, Fifth, and Sixth also. Is it too much to hope that some means may shortly be found of accomplishing this most desirable end?

To return, however, to Dr. Schneider. After I had completed my examination of the six MSS. in his possession, and

---

[1] In the case of the 'Rosamunde' ballet music, and the Fourth and Sixth Symphonies—all in MS.—we are prohibited from allowing copies to be taken, or performances made from our copies, without express permission.   Y 2

my memoranda from them, and he had with great kindness given us permission to have the scores of Nos. 4 and 6
copied, we explored the other treasures contained in the cupboard. There we saw the original MSS. of the 'Teufels Lustschloss,' 'Fernando,' 'Der vierjährige Posten,' 'Die Freunde
von Salamanka,' the Mass in F, and several other works, which
will all be found enumerated by Dr. Kreissle. The Overture
to the last-named Opera he was good enough to permit me to
have copied. It is scored for 2 Violins; Viola; 2 Flutes;
2 Oboes; 2 Clarinets; 2 Bassoons; 2 Horns; 2 Trumpets;
Drum; Cello; and Bass; and is of similar character to
Mozart's 'Impresario.' It begins as follows:—

So far success—brilliant success. But I had failed in one
chief object of my journey. The 'Rosamunde' music was
almost dearer to me than the Symphonies. Besides the
entr'actes in B minor and B-flat, the 'Ballo, No. 2,' and
the 'Ballet Air, No. 9,' which we had already acquired
in 1866, we had found at Mr. Spina's an entr'acte after the
second act, and a 'Hirten-Melodie' for clarinets, bassoons,
and horns; but we still required the accompaniments to
the Romance and the two Choruses, as well as the total
number of pieces and their sequence in the drama. To
quit Vienna without these would have been too cruel, and
yet neither from Dr. Schneider, nor Mr. Spina, nor in the
library of the Musik-Verein—where the admirable librarian,
Mr. C. F. Pohl, was entirely at our service—had we succeeded
in finding a trace of them.

It was Thursday afternoon, and we proposed to leave on Saturday for Prague. We made a final call on Dr. Schneider, to take leave and repeat our thanks, and also, as I now firmly believe, guided by a special instinct. The doctor was civility itself; he again had recourse to the cupboard, and showed us some treasures which had escaped us before. I again turned the conversation to the ' Rosamunde ' music ; he believed that he had at one time possessed a copy or sketch of it all. Might I go into the cupboard and look for myself ? Certainly, if I had no objection to being smothered with dust. In I went ; and after some search, during which my companion kept the doctor engaged in conversation, I found, at the bottom of the cupboard, and in its farthest corner, a bundle of music-books two feet high, carefully tied round, and black with the undisturbed dust of nearly half a century. It was like the famous scene at the monastery of Souriani on the Natron lakes, so well described by Mr. Curzon :—' "Here is a box ! " exclaimed the two monks, who were nearly choked with the dust; "we have found a box, and a heavy one too." " A box ! " shouted the blind abbot, who was standing in the outer darkness of the oil-cellar—"a box ! where is it ?" " Bring it out ! bring out the box ! Heaven be praised ! we have found a treasure ! Lift up the box ! Pull out the box ! " shouted the monks in various tones of voice.' We were hardly less vociferous than the monks, when we had dragged out the bundle into the light, and found that it was actually neither more nor less than what we were in search of. Not Dr. Cureton, when he made his truly romantic discovery of the missing leaves of the Syriac Eusebius[1], could have been more glad or more grateful than I was at this moment. For

---

[1] One of the greatest romances in discovery that ever occurred. See his interesting account in the ' Edinburgh Review,' No. ccxiv. pp. 449-453.

these were the part-books of the whole of the music in 'Rosa-munde,' tied up after the second performance, in December, 1823, and probably never disturbed since. Dr. Schneider must have been amused at our excitement; but let us hope that he recollected his own days of rapture; at any rate he kindly overlooked it, and gave us permission to take away with us and copy what we wanted, and I now felt that my mission to Vienna had not been fruitless.

On reaching the hotel with our precious discovery, we found the order of the music to be as follows:—

> Overture ('Alfonso and Estrella').
> Entr'acte after Act I. (B minor).
> Ballo (B minor) and Curtain-tune (G).
> Entr'acte after Act II. (D).
> Romanze.
> Geister-Chor.
> Entr'acte after Act III. (B-flat).
> Hirten-Melodie.
> Hirten-Chor.
> Jäger-Chor.
> Ballet Air (G).

It was now late in the day, but we summoned our kind and faithful friend Pohl to our aid, and by dint of dividing our work into three, and writing our hardest, we contrived, before two in the morning, to get all the missing accompaniments copied, as well as every note and stage direction that could throw light on the connection between the drama and the music.[1] For I ought to have said that I had entirely failed to find the libretto of 'Rosamunde.' Dr. Sonnleithner was kind enough to search his vast collection of opera-books for us, but without effect. Dr. Kreissle had never seen it, and had

---

[1] These were in red pencil. That prefixed to the wind-parts of th 'Geister-Chor' was 'Unter dem Bodium' (Podium).

taken his analysis (i. 288, &c.) from a periodical of the period. It is therefore probable that it was never printed, and that if it exists at all, it is in the archives of the Theater an der Wien, where I hope to find it, or at least to search for it, another day.

Our visits to Herr Spina were also both interesting and fruitful. We saw the autograph of the first part of ' Lazarus; ' a Duett with orchestra—' Auguste jam cœlestium'—an exact imitation of Mozart; a Magnificat (1815), also very Mozartish; two pieces for the violin, with orchestral accompaniments, of little-interest; a string Trio, in B-flat, very good; an Entr'acte and Hirtenmelodie to ' Rosamunde,' already mentioned; a March and Chorus from ' Fierrabras; ' a large number of songs, some of them of great beauty, including three Sonnets from Petrarch by Schlegel. We also saw the autograph of the B-flat Quartett (Op. 168), a MS. of remarkable interest. Schubert commenced it as a string Trio, and wrote ten lines in that form, but he has crossed them out and begun the composition afresh as a quartett. The movements are all dated: the first, at the beginning, ' 5te Sept. 1814,' and at the end, ' der 6te Sept., in 4½ Stunden angefertigt,' so that it must have been dashed off in the dead of the night. At end of slow movement, ' 10te Sept. 814,' and of Finale ' 13te Sept. 1814.' Also a ' Stabat Mater' to Klopstock's German version, a long work, much of it of great beauty. This and several other things Mr. Spina was kind enough to undertake to have copied for us, and they are now in the library of the Crystal Palace. I cannot be too grateful both to Mr. Spina and Dr. Schneider for their generous kindness to a stranger—in the latter case an entire stranger. Mr. Spina in particular was most kind and hospitable: we had a piano to ourselves, and were allowed to do as we liked for several hours.

At Mr. Herbeck's we saw the parts (Ferdinand Schubert's copying) of the Symphony No. 5 (in B-flat),—the score he could not at that moment lay his hands on ; also the original MS. of No. 8, and the original MS. of the Opera of 'Fierrabras,' which I understood Mr. H. to say he was then preparing for the stage, and which contains most curious evidence of Schubert's rapidity in composition. The first act, containing 304 pages of large oblong paper, fully scored, was dated at beginning and end, 25th and 31st May, 1823—six days only apart ! The second act, 300 pages, 31st May and 5th June—five days !

At the Library of the Musik-Verein, besides the autograph of the Great Symphony in C, No. 9, I saw the copy of a Sonata by Schubert for piano and arpeggione (whatever that may have been), which, being dated as late as November 1824, ought to possess some value. The themes of the movements are as follow :—

Here I found also the score of ‘Miriam’s Siegesgesang,’ as instrumented by Franz Lachner from the Pianoforte arrangement in which alone it was published by Schubert.

Of the other wonderful treasures in this library I do not speak, as my only object at present is Schubert.

I have nothing more to say, except to reiterate my thankfulness for the enjoyment thus afforded me, and for the kindness of all whom I met at Vienna.

As for Schubert, his place in the world is certain. Whether his Symphonies and Operas are published and performed now, or twenty years later, is not of much importance to his fame. He can afford to wait. They will assuredly be done some day or other, and then the world will find out what it has lost by waiting so long, and wonder that it did not recognise its jewel sooner. Certainly what poor Schubert said was right, that

the music that was the fruit of his distress had given the world
most pleasure; and the world seems to have known it, for it
kept him in his poverty and harass and disappointment, till
he died of it. Good God! it makes one's blood boil to think
of so fine and rare a genius, one of the ten or twelve topmost
men in the world, in want of even the common necessaries
of life. Failure, disappointment, depreciation, and suchlike
shocks and wounds of the heart and soul, these are the necessary accompaniments of a fine intellect and a sensitive
heart; but to want the ordinary comforts and amenities of life,
to want bread! it is too dreadful to think of. And yet such
troubles have been the lot of all the great men from David
downwards: only Schubert's was peculiarly hard, for he had
all the struggles of youth and none of the repose of age.
He died on the rapids, before he came to the broad, smooth,
sunny water—before it was even in sight. He, too, like
David, 'ate ashes for bread, and mingled his drink with weep-
ing;' but, unlike David, God took him away 'in the midst of
his days,' and he never came into the 'large room,' and 'the
goodly heritage,' that would have made up for his early
troubles. Made up?—a rash word! No doubt there is compensation in all things: some there must be, or such trials
could not be survived. And as the Three Holy Children, even
in the very crisis of their fate, when they fell down bound
and helpless in the fire, had the angel at their side, and found
the 'midst of the furnace as it had been a moist whistling
wind,' and thence intoned their glorious hymn, so there are
doubtless some alleviations even in the fiery trials which Schubert and Beethoven underwent—alleviations of which those
who have not their genius can never taste the sweets. At any
rate we profit by the struggles of the heroes, and drink at our
leisure and our ease the rich wine that they trod out with so
much toil and so many tears. Honour and love to them all!
and honour and love in a special degree to our last and our
dearest—FRANZ SCHUBERT!

INDEX.

———+———

SPOTTISWOODE AND CO., PRINTERS, NEW-STREET SQUARE AND PARLIAMENT STREET

ERRATA. Vol. II.

Page 20, line 2, and note 1, line 2, *for* Scheumann *read* Schellmann.

,, 133, line 14, *add the following note to the word* death :—It was given for the first
time on the 12th December, 1828, in the great Redouten-Saal, at the second
Gesellschafts-Concert, and repeated on the 12th March, 1829, in the Landständischen Saal, with better effect.

,, 192, note, line 10, *for* allmächtig *read* allnächtlich.

,, 288, line 7 from bottom, *for* Archduke *read* archducal.

,, 290, line 1, *read* Published also in score very recently, &c.

WORKS BY JOHN HULLAH,

PROFESSOR OF VOCAL MUSIC IN KING'S COLLEGE AND QUEEN'S COLLEGE,

LONDON, AND ORGANIST OF CHARTERHOUSE.

RE-ISSUE OF HULLAH'S PART MUSIC,

SACRED AND SECULAR, FOR SOPRANO, ALTO, TENOR, OR BASS,

WITH PIANOFORTE ACCOMPANIMENTS.

The SECULAR SERIES, complete in TWO VOLUMES, imperial 8vo. price 14s. The SACRED SERIES, complete in TWO VOLUMES, imperial 8vo. price 14s.

This Edition includes everything in the original Work which experience has proved to be most interesting in performance, and most useful for the practice of Choirs and Classes, together with much additional matter. Each Number is printed in Score, with the addition of a Pianoforte Accompaniment; and also in Parts (Soprano, Alto, Tenor, or Bass), uniform with the Score in size, but in larger type. The Scores have been carefully revised throughout: many Pieces have been re-arranged; and besides the ordinary indications of Time, Metronome marks have been added to each movement. The Alto, as well as the Soprano parts, are printed in the Treble Clef. Those of the Tenor and Bass in their proper Clefs respectively as before; thus the notation of each Part represents literally the pitch of the sounds composing it.

SACRED MUSIC FOR FAMILY USE:

A SELECTION OF PIECES FOR ONE, TWO, OR MORE

VOICES, BY THE BEST COMPOSERS, FOREIGN

AND ENGLISH.

EDITED BY JOHN HULLAH.

One Volume, large music folio, price 21s. half-bound, with gilt top.

VOL. II.   z´

New Editions, Revised and Reconstructed in 1849, of

WILHEM'S METHOD OF TEACHING SINGING,

Adapted by JOHN HULLAH to English use.

Under the Superintendence of the Committee of Council on Education.

FOR THE USE OF TEACHERS AND PUPILS.

THE MANUAL.—Parts I. and II. 2*s.* 6*d.* each ; or together, in cloth, 5*s.*

FOR THE USE OF PUPILS ONLY.

THE EXERCISES and FIGURES contained in Parts I. and II. of the Manual. Books I. and II. 8*d.* each.

LARGE SHEETS, containing the Figures in Part I. of the Manual. Nos. 1 to 8, in a Parcel, 6*s.*

LARGE SHEETS, containing the Exercises in Part I. of the Manual. Nos. 9 to 40, in Four Parcels of Eight Nos. each, 6*s.* per Parcel.

LARGE SHEETS, containing the Figures in Part II. of the Manual. Nos. 41 to 52, in a Parcel, 9*s.*

☞ The above New Editions, ' Revised and Reconstructed in 1849,' are strictly uniform with one another, and include such additions and alterations as seven years' experience (the Second Edition having been published in 1842) has shown to be desirable.

The Editions of Wilhem's Method by Hullah, published in 1842, are now out of print

---

A GRAMMAR OF COUNTERPOINT.

PART I. super-royal 8vo. price 2*s.* 6*d.*

The object which the Author has kept before him in this work, has been to reduce a vast number of *rules* into a few general *principles*, and to show that the numberless facts of which the theory of music is composed are not isolated, dissimilar, and irreconcileable, but inseparably connected together, continually acting and reacting on one another, and resulting from like causes and amenable to like treatment.

The SECOND PART, treating of Double Counterpoint, Imitation, and Fugue, and completing the work, will follow shortly.

PSALMODY.

TUNES for PSALMS and HYMNS. 2s.

This collection includes sixty-eight Tunes, among which will be found the best of those in common use, with others less extensively known, or now published for the first time.

CHANTING.

CHANTS, chiefly by English Masters of the Seventeenth and Eighteenth Centuries; with the Gregorian Tones harmonised by Thomas Morley. Second Edition. 6d.

This collection contains forty-eight single and fifteen double Chants, among which will be found the whole of those in *Boyce's Cathedral Music.*

A SHORT TREATISE on the STAVE; to serve as an Introduction to the Practice of Reading or Playing from Score. 2s.

The RUDIMENTS of MUSICAL GRAMMAR. 3s.

A GRAMMAR of MUSICAL HARMONY: being the substance of Lectures delivered in St. Martin's Hall and the Training Schools of the National Society. New Edition (the Fifth). Royal 8vo. 3s.

EXERCISES to GRAMMAR of MUSICAL HARMONY. 1s.

A GRAMMAR of COUNTERPOINT, Part I. Super-royal 8vo. 2s. 6d.

EXERCISES for the CULTIVATION of the VOICE.

For Soprano or Tenor. Third Edition. 2s. 6d.
For Contralto or Bass. Third Edition. 2s. 6d.

INFANT SCHOOL SONGS. 6d.

SCHOOL SONGS for TWO and THREE VOICES. Two Books, 6*d*. each.

GOD SAVE the QUEEN, arranged in Three, Four, and Five Parts. On a Card, 1*d*.

MUSIC in the PARISH CHURCH: a Lecture. 6*d*.

MATERIALS FOR SINGING CLASSES.

A STANDARD TUNING FORK, accurately adjusted by a scientific process, to 512 vibrations per second. Reduced to 2*s*.

STANDS for Hullah's Large Sheets. 7*s*. 6*d*.

A MUSIC COPY-BOOK, for Manuscript Music. 1*s*.

MUSIC PAPER, same size as Hullah's Large Sheets. Twelve Staves on a Sheet, in Parcels of Six Sheets. 3*s*.

Ditto ditto, Eight Staves on a Sheet. 3*s*.

A FIRST COURSE of LECTURES on the HISTORY of MODERN MUSIC, delivered at the Royal Institution of Great Britain. Post 8vo. with Chronological Tables. 6*s*. 6*d*.

SECOND COURSE of LECTURES on the THIRD or TRANSITION PERIOD of MUSICAL HISTORY, from the beginning of the 17th to the middle of the 18th Century, delivered at the Royal Institution. Including FORTY SPECIMENS of the Works of Twenty-six Eminent Composers, with English Words adapted to the German Vocal Pieces, and a Pianoforte Accompaniment to nearly every Specimen. 8vo. price 16*s*.

London; LONGMANS and CO. Paternoster Row.